DATE DUE			

ALSO BY TOREY HAYDEN

ONE CHILD

SOMEBODY ELSE'S KIDS

MURPHY'S BOY

THE SUNFLOWER FOREST

JUST ANOTHER KID

GHOST GIRL

the tiger's child

TOREY HAYDEN

A LISA DREW BOOK

SCRIBNER

NEW YORK LONDON TORONTO SYDNEY TOKYO SINGAPORE

Scribner
1230 Avenue of the Americas
New York, NY 10020

Excerpts from *The Little Prince* by Antoine de Saint-Exupèry, copyright 1943 and renewed
1971 by Harcourt Brace & Company, reprinted by permission of the publisher.
Lines from "The Stolen Child" by W. B. Yeats are from *The Poems of W. B. Yeats:
A New Editing,* edited by Richard J. Finneran (New York: Macmillan, 1983).

SCRIBNER and design are trademarks of Simon & Schuster Inc.
Designed by Songhee Kim

Manufactured in the United States of America

1 3 5 7 9 10 8 6 4 2

Library of Congress Cataloging-in-Publication Data
Hayden, Torey L.
The tiger's child/Torey Hayden
p.   cm.
"A Lisa Drew Book."
1. Abused children—Rehabilitation—Case studies. I. Title.
RJ507.A29H39 1995   94-36740
618.92'858223—dc20
CIP

ISBN 0-02-549150-4

the tiger's
child

Prologue

IT WAS A MOMENT OF DÉJÀ VU.

Home in Montana visiting my mother, I had nipped out alone on a Sunday morning while she and my young daughter went swimming. It was just after eleven and I was walking through the shopping mall. Most of the stores weren't open yet, and as a consequence, the broad concourse was shadowy, illuminated only by security lighting.

Suddenly I saw her. Some distance ahead of me down the mall, she was standing in the shadows of a large planter. Long, unkempt hair tumbled down over her shoulders; bangs hung into her eyes; thick, sensual lips were pushed out in a dramatic pout. She stood with arms crossed tightly over her chest, her shoulders pulled up, her face set in an expression of fierce defiance; and yet there was a poignancy about all that fierceness. I suspect she already knew she wasn't going to win. I was well down the mall when I first saw her, but I recognized her so instantly that adrenaline shot through my veins. *Sheila.*

A second or two later my intellect caught up. It wasn't Sheila, of course. More than twenty years have passed since I watched Sheila depart from my classroom on that warm June afternoon. I am no longer the angry young teacher I was. My teaching days are, at least for the time being, behind me and I have exchanged youth—with some reluctance—for middle age. Yet, for those brief few minutes in the shopping mall, the years disappeared. I was pulled back into the seventies, into my workaholic twenties, to feel once again, however fleetingly, the person I had been and the world as it was then.

Then reality began to impose, layering itself down over the incident rather the way one lays a transparency down over a page. I approached the girl with curiosity, drew up even with her and paused, feigning interest in a nearby shop window so that I could unobtrusively study her. She was older than Sheila had been. She was perhaps seven or even eight. Her hair was darker, more mouse-brown than blond.

My nearness didn't put off her anger any. I was a stranger, so she ignored me and concentrated all her attention on the open doorway of the huge department store behind me. I couldn't discern who had upset her so. They had disappeared into the store, but she stood on, her small fists clenched, her tousled hair falling forward, her hopeless, helpless anger emanating from her. Anonymous and silent, I remained where I was, half a dozen feet away, and marveled at how such a small encounter could wipe away so many years, how Sheila could still set my heart beating fast.

*   *   *

Sheila and I, as student and teacher, were only together for five months. Our relationship over that short time evoked dramatic changes in Sheila's behavior and vastly altered the course of her life. Although less obvious at the time, our relationship also dramatically changed me and vastly altered the course of my life too. This little girl had a profound effect on me. Her courage, her resilience and her inadvertent ability to express that great, gaping need to be loved that we all feel—in short, her humanness—brought me into contact with my own.

The five months Sheila was in my class I chronicled in *One Child*. It was a private book, never initially written with the intention of publication, but only as my own effort to understand more fully this deeply felt relationship. I was teaching a university graduate class in special education at the time and it is to a student in that class that I owe my thanks. The last day of class she gave me a copy of Ron Jones's *The Acorn People*, and inscribed it in the front: To Torey, in hopes that someday you might write about Sheila, Leslie and all the others.

One Child now spans the world in twenty-two languages and has brought me into contact with individuals from Sweden to South Africa, from New York to Singapore. One reader wrote from a base in Antarctica; a handful of letters came from behind the Iron Curtain before it fell; and I have just recently received my first correspondence over *One Child* from mainland China. The universal appeal of watching Sheila grow and change has only been matched by one thing, a question: What happened next?

One Child is a true story, based on real people and real people's experiences. I hesitated to write a sequel simply because six-year-old Sheila was so appealing and the period we spent together was so positive. Indeed, my *One Child* editor went so far as to suggest I not include in the epilogue of the book what had actually been happening to Sheila in the time since we had parted. Real lives are seldom as satisfying as fiction, or even as satisfying as judiciously edited nonfiction, and it was felt the interim period between my class and the time I wrote *One Child* would make too grim an ending for such an upbeat story. Thus, the book concluded with Sheila's beautiful poem, but no details.

I've now changed my mind, not only in response to the countless queries from my readers, but also in response to Sheila, who, against remarkable odds, has grown into an engaging, articulate young woman. Those five months we spent together did have a profound effect on her, but *One Child*, although I hadn't meant it to, tells my story. The experience for Sheila was quite a different one and here, to quote Paul Harvey, is the rest of the story.

part
one

one

The article in the newspaper was tiny, considering the crime. It told of a six-year-old girl who had lured a local toddler from his yard, taken him to a nearby woodland, tied him to a tree and set fire to him. The boy, badly burned, was in hospital. All that was said in what amounted to no more than a space filler below the comic strips on page six. I read it and, repulsed, I turned the page and went on.

Six weeks later, Ed, the special education director, phoned me. It was early January, the day we were returning from our Christmas break. "There's going to be a new girl in your class. Remember that little girl who set fire to the kid in November . . . ?"

*   *   *

I taught what was affectionately referred to in our district as the "garbage class." It was the last year before congressional law would introduce "mainstreaming," the requirement that all special needs children be educated in the least restrictive environment; and thus, our district still had the myriad of small special education class-rooms, each catering to a different disability. There were classes for physically handicapped, for mentally handicapped, for behaviorally disordered, for visually impaired . . . you name it, we had it. My eight were the kids left over, the ones who defied classification. All of them suffered emotional disorders, but most also had mental or physical disabilities as well. Out of the three girls and five boys in the group, three could not talk, one could but refused and another spoke only in echoes of other people's words. Three of them were still in diapers and two more had regular accidents. As I had the full number of children allowed by state law for a class of severely hand-icapped children, I was given an aide at the start of the year; but mine hadn't turned out to be one of the bright, hardworking aides already employed by the school, as I had expected. Mine was a Mex-ican-American migrant worker named Anton, who had been trawled from the local welfare list. He'd never graduated from high school, never even stayed north all winter before, and certainly had never changed diapers on a seven-year-old. My only other help came from Whitney, a fourteen-year-old junior high student, who gave up her study halls to volunteer in our class.

By all accounts we didn't appear a very promising group, and in the beginning, chaos was the byword; however, as the months passed, we metamorphosed. Anton proved to be sensitive and hard-working, his dedication to the children becoming apparent within the first weeks. The kids, in return, responded well to having a man in the classroom and they built on one another's strengths. Whit-ney's youth occasionally made her more like one of the children than one of the staff, but her enthusiasm was contagious, making it easier for all of us to view events as adventures rather than the dis-asters they often were. The kids grew and changed, and by Christ-mas we had become a cohesive little group. Now Ed was sending me a six-year-old stick of dynamite.

* * *

Her name was Sheila. The next Monday she arrived, being dragged into my classroom by Ed, as my principal worriedly brought up the rear, his hands flapping behind her as if to fan her into the class-room. She was absolutely tiny, with fierce eyes, long, matted blond hair and a very bad smell. I was shocked to find she was so small. Given her notoriety, I had expected something considerably more Herculean. As it was, she couldn't have been much bigger than the three-year-old she had abducted.

Abducted? I regarded her carefully.

Bureaucracy being what it is in school districts, Sheila's school files didn't arrive before she did; so when she went off to lunch on that first day, Anton and I took the opportunity to go down to the office for a quick look. The file made bleak reading, even by the standards of my class.

Our town, Marysville, was in proximity to a large mental hospital and a state penitentiary, and this, in addition to the migrants, had created a disproportionate underclass, many of whom lived in appalling poverty. The buildings in the migrant camp had been built as temporary summer housing and many were literally nothing but wood and tar paper that lacked even the most basic amenities, but they became crowded in the winter by those who could afford nothing better. It was here that Sheila lived with her father.

A drug addict with alcohol problems, her father had spent most of Sheila's early years in and out of prison. He had no job. Currently on parole, he was attending an alcohol abuse program, but doing little else.

Sheila's mother had been only fourteen when, as a runaway, she took up with Sheila's father and became pregnant. Sheila was born two days before her mother's fifteenth birthday. A second child, a son, was born nineteen months later. There wasn't much else relating to the mother in the file, although it was not hard to read drugs, alcohol and domestic violence between the lines. Whatever, she must have finally had enough, because when Sheila was four, she left the family. From the brief notes, it appeared that she had intended to take both children with her, but Sheila was later found abandoned on an open stretch of freeway about thirty miles south of town. Sheila's mother and her brother, Jimmie, were never heard from again.

The bulk of the file detailed Sheila's behavior. At home the father appeared to have no control over her at all. She had been repeatedly found wandering around the migrant camp late at night. She had a history of fire setting and had been cited for criminal damage three times by the local police, quite an accomplishment for a six-year-old. At school, Sheila often refused to speak, and as a consequence, virtually nothing was contained in the file to tell me what or how much she might have learned. She had been in kindergarten and then first grade in an elementary school near the migrant camp until the incident with the little boy had occurred, but there were no assessment notes. In place of the usual test results and learning summaries was a catalog of horror stories detailing Sheila's destructive, often violent, behavior.

At the end of the file was a brief summary of the incident with the toddler. The judge concluded that Sheila was out of parental control and would be best placed in a secure unit, where her needs could be better met. In this instance, he meant the children's unit at the state mental hospital. Unfortunately, the unit was at capacity at the time of the hearing, and thus, Sheila would need to await an opening. A recently dated memo was appended detailing the need to provide some form of education, given her age and the law, but no one bothered to mince words. Her placement was custodial. This meant she had to be kept in school for the time being, because of the specifics of the law, but I need not feel under any obligation to teach her. With Sheila's arrival, my room had become a holding pen.

Youth was my greatest asset at that point in my career. Still fired with idealism, I felt strongly that there were no problem kids, only a problem society. Although initially reluctant to take Sheila, it had been because my room was crowded and my resources overstretched already, not because of the child herself. Thus, once I had her, I regarded her as mine and *my* class was no holding pen! My belief in human integrity and the inalienable right of each and every one of my children to possess it was trenchant.

Well, almost. Before she was done, Sheila had given all my beliefs a good shaking and she started that very first day. As Anton and I were sitting in the front office that lunch hour, reading Sheila's file, Sheila was in our classroom scooping the goldfish out of the aquarium and, one by one, poking their eyes out.

*   *   *

Sheila proved to be chaos dressed in outgrown overalls and a faded T-shirt. Everything she said was shrieked. Everything she touched was broken, hit, squashed or mangled. And everyone, myself included, was The Enemy. She operated in what Anton christened her "animal mode." There was not much "child mode" present in the early days. The slightest unexpected movement she always interpreted as attack. Her eyes would go dark, her face would flush, her body would take on alert rigidity, and from that point it was a finely balanced matter as to whether she would fight, or panic and run away. When she was in her animal mode, our methods were a whole lot more akin to taming than teaching.

Yet . . .

Sheila was different. There was something electric about her, about her eyes, about the sharpness of her movements that super-imposed itself over even her most feral moments. I couldn't articu-late what it was, but I could sense it.

*   *   *

I loved my children dearly, but the truth was, they were not a very bright lot. Most children with emotional difficulties use so much mental energy coping that there simply isn't much left for learning. Additionally, other syndromes often occur in conjunction with psy-chological problems, either contributing to them or resulting from them. For example, two of my children suffered from fetal alcohol syndrome and another had a neurological condition that was caus-ing a slow deterioration of his central nervous system. As a conse-quence, none of the children was functioning at an average level for his or her age, although undoubtedly several were of normal intelli-gence. Thus, it came as a surprise to me to discover during Sheila's early days with us that she could add and subtract well, because she had managed only three months of first grade.

A bigger surprise came days later, when I discovered she could give the meanings of unusual words. One such word was "chattel."

"Wherever did you learn a word like this?" I asked when my cu-riosity finally overwhelmed me.

Sheila, little and dirty and very smelly, sat hunched up on her chair across the table from me. She peered up through matted hair to regard me. "*Chattel of Love,*" she replied and added in her pecu-liar dialect, "it be the name of a book I find."

"Book? Where? What book?"

"I don't steal it," she retorted defensively. "It be in the garbage can. I *find* it."

"Where?"

"I do find it," she repeated, obviously believing this was the issue I was trying to explore.

"Yes, okay," I replied, "but where?"

"In the ladies' toilets at the bus station. But I *don't* steal it."

I smiled. "No, I'm sure you didn't. I'm just interested in hearing about it."

She regarded me suspiciously.

"What did you do with the book?" I asked.

Sheila clearly couldn't puzzle out why I wanted to know these things. "Well, I read it," she said, her voice full of disbelief, as if I'd asked a very silly question. There was a worried edge to it, however. She still sensed it was an accusation.

"You read it? It sounds like a rather grown-up book."

"Well, I don't read all of it. But on the cover it say *Chattel of Love* and so I do be curious about it, 'cause of the picture, 'cause of what the man be doing to the lady on the cover."

"I see," I replied uncertainly.

She shrugged. "But I couldn't find nothing good in it, so I throw it away again."

With an IQ we soon discovered to be in excess of 180, Sheila was electric all right. Indeed, she was more like nuclear.

*   *   *

Discovering Sheila was a highly gifted child intellectually did nothing to change the facts of her grinding poverty, her abusive background or her continuing and continually outrageous behavior. Uncertain where to start when there was so much that needed improving, I began with the very smallest things, those I knew were within my power to change.

Sheila's hygiene was appalling. She literally had only one set of clothes: a faded brown-striped T-shirt and a pair of worn denim overalls, a size too small. With these went a pair of red-and-white canvas sneakers with holes in the toes. She had underwear, but no socks. If any of these were ever washed, there was little evidence of it.

Certainly Sheila wasn't washed. The dirt was worn in on her

hands and her elbows and around her ankles, so that dark lines had formed over the skin in these areas. Worse, she was a bed wetter. The smell of stale urine permeated whatever part of the classroom Sheila occupied. When I quizzed Sheila about washing facilities, I discovered they had no running water.

This seemed the best place to start. She was so unpleasant to be near that it distracted all of us from the child herself; so I came armed with towels, soap and shampoo and began to bathe Sheila in the large sink at the back of the classroom.

I was washing her when I first noticed the scars. They were small, round and numerous, especially along her upper arms and the insides of her lower arms. The scars were old and had long since healed, but I recognized them for what they were—the marks left when a lit cigarette is pressed against the skin.

"Does your dad do things that cause these?" I asked, trying to keep my voice as casual and conversational as possible.

"My pa, he wouldn't do that! He wouldn't hurt me bad," she replied, her tone prickly. "He loves me." I realized she knew what I was asking.

I nodded and lifted her out of the water to dry her. For several moments Sheila said nothing, but then she twisted around to look me in the eye. "You know what my mama done, though?"

"No, what?"

She lifted up one leg and turned it for me to see. There, on the outer side just above the ankle, was a wide white scar about two inches long. "My mama, she push me out of the car and I fall down so's a rock cutted up my leg right here. See?"

I bent forward and examined it.

"My pa, he loves me. He don't go leaving me on no roads. You ain't supposed to do that with little kids."

"No, you're not."

There was a moment's silence while I finished drying her and began to comb out her newly washed hair. Sheila grew pensive. "My mama, she don't love me so good," she said. Her voice was thoughtful, but calm and matter-of-fact. She could have been discussing one of the other children in the class or a piece of schoolwork or, for that matter, the weather. "My mama, she take Jimmie and go to California. Jimmie, he be my brother and he be four, 'cept he only be two when my mama, she leave." A moment or two elapsed and Sheila examined her scar again. "In the beginning, my mama taked Jimmie *and* me, 'cept she got sick of me. So, she open up the door and push me out and a rock cutted up my leg right here."

*   *   *

Those early weeks with Sheila were a roller-coaster ride. Some days were up. Delighted awe at this new world she found herself in made Sheila a sunny little character. She was eager to be accepted into the group and in her own odd way tried desperately to please Anton and me. Other days, however, we went down, sometimes precipitously. Despite her brilliant progress right from the beginning, Sheila remained capable of truly hair-raising behavior.

The world was a vicious place in Sheila's mind. She lived by the creed of doing unto others before they do unto you. Revenge, in particular, was trenchant. If someone wronged Sheila or even simply treated her a bit arbitrarily, Sheila exacted precise, painful retribution. On one occasion, she caused hundreds of dollars' worth of damage in another teacher's room in retaliation for that teacher's having reprimanded her in the lunchroom.

What saved us was a complicated bus schedule. In the months prior to coming into my room, Sheila's behavior had gotten her removed from two previous school buses and the only one available to her now was the high school bus. Unfortunately, this did not leave for the migrant camp until two hours after our class got out. Thus Sheila had to remain after school with Anton and me until that time.

I was horrified when I first found out, because those two hours after school were my planning and preparation time and I couldn't imagine how I would get on with things while simultaneously having to baby-sit as unpredictable a child as Sheila. There was, however, no choice in the matter.

Initially, I let her play with the classroom toys while I sat at the table and tried to get on with my work, but after fifteen minutes or so on her own, she'd inevitably pull away and come to stand over me while I worked. She was always full of questions. What's that? What's this for? Why are you doing that? How come this is like this? What do you do with that thing? *Constantly.* Until I realized we were talking much of the time. Until I realized how much I enjoyed it.

She liked to read and she could, I think, read virtually anything I placed in her hands. What stopped her was not her ability to turn the letters on the page into words, but rather to turn them into something meaningful. Sheila's life was so deprived that much of what she read simply made no sense to her. As a consequence, I began reading with her.

There was something compelling about sharing a book with Sheila. We would snuggle up together in the reading corner as I prepared to read aloud to her and Sheila would be so ravenous for the experiences the book held that her entire body'd grow taut with excitement. Winnie the Pooh, Long John Silver and Peter Pan proved sturdier magic than *Chattel of Love.* However, of all the books, it was Saint-Exupéry's *The Little Prince* that won Sheila's heart. She adored this bemused, perplexing little character. His otherness she understood perfectly. Mature one moment, immature the next, profound, then petty, and always, always the outsider, the little prince spoke deeply to Sheila. We read the book so many times that she could quote long passages by heart.

When not reading, we simply talked. Sheila would lean on the table and watch me work, or we would pause at some point in a book for me to explain a concept and the conversation would go from there, never quite returning to the story at hand.

Progressively, I learned more about Sheila's life in the migrant camp, about her father and his lady friends who often came back to the house with him late at night. Sheila told me how she hid his bottles of beer behind the sofa to keep him from drinking too much, and how she got up to put out his cigarettes after he had fallen asleep. I came to hear more about her mother, her brother and the abandonment. And I heard about Sheila's other school and her other teachers, about what she did to fill her days and her nights, when she wasn't with us. In return, I gave her my world and the hope that it could be hers as well.

Those two hours were a godsend. All her short life Sheila had

two

The real issue for Sheila was what had happened between her and her mother on that dark highway two years earlier. Given her extraordinary giftedness, the matter did not remain inarticulate. With exquisite clarity, she gave a voice to her agony.

The relationship between the abandonment and Sheila's difficult behavior became most obvious over schoolwork. Despite her brilliance, Sheila simply refused to do any written papers. I hadn't made the connection initially. I saw the aggressive misbehavior as waywardness and only afterward realized it was a ploy to keep her from having to sit down at the table and take a pencil in hand. Coercing her to the table proved a major battle and even then she held out, refusing to work. When she did eventually start accepting paperwork, she would still crumple two or three imperfect efforts before finally finishing one.

On one occasion, she wasn't even in class but alone after school with me. She had found a ditto master of a fifth-grade math test in the office trash can, when she had come down with me while I ran off some papers. Sheila loved math. It was her best subject and she fell upon this with great glee. It was on the multiplication and division of fractions, subjects I had never taught Sheila, but as she scanned the paper, she felt certain she could do them. Back in the classroom, she settled across the table from me and began to write the answers on the paper—a very unusual response for Sheila. When she finished, she proudly showed it to me and asked if she had done them right. The multiplication problems were done correctly, but unfortunately she had not inverted the fractions for the division, so those were all wrong. Turning the paper over, I drew a circle and divided it into parts to illustrate why it was necessary to invert. Before I had even spoken, Sheila perceived that her answers weren't right. She whipped up the paper from under my pencil, smashed it into a tiny ball and pounded on the table before flopping down, head in her arms.

"You didn't know, sweetheart. No one's taught you this."

"I wanted to show you I could do them without help."

"Sheil, it's nothing to get upset about. You did nicely. You *tried*. That's the important part. Next time you'll get them right."

Nothing I said comforted her and she sat for a few moments with her hands over her face. Then slowly her hands slid away and she uncrumpled the paper, pressing it smooth on the tabletop. "I bet if I could have done math problems good, my mama, she wouldn't leave me on no highway, like she done. If I could have done fifth-grade math problems, she'd be proud of me."

"I don't think math problems have anything to do with it, Sheila."

"She left because she don't love me no more. You don't go leaving kids you love on the highway, like she done me. And I cut my leg, see?" For the hundredth time the small white scar was displayed. "If I'd been a gooder girl, she wouldn't have done that."

"Sheil, we just don't know what happened, but I suspect your mama had her own problems to straighten out."

"But she copeded with Jimmie. How come she copeded with Jimmie and left me?"

"I don't know, love."

Sheila looked across the table to me, that haunted, hurt expression in her eyes. "Why did it happen, Torey? Why did she tooked him and leaved me behind? What made me such a bad girl?" Her eyes filled with tears, but as always, they never fell.

"Oh, lovey, it wasn't you. Believe me. It wasn't your fault. She didn't leave you because you were bad. She just had too many of her own problems. It wasn't *your* fault."

"My pa, he says so. He says if I be a gooder girl she'd a never done that."

My heart sank. There was so much to fight, so little to fight with.

*   *   *

The issue colored everything: her work, her behavior, her attitude toward other children and toward adults. As the weeks passed and particularly as we spent so much of the after-school hours in close contact, I knew very well what was being encouraged to happen. I was the first stable, nurturing adult female Sheila had occasion to spend much time with and she grasped at the relationship with greedy desperation.

Was it right to let her? This question was never far from my mind. My training, both in education and in psychology, cautioned rigorously against getting too personally involved with children, and I strove to keep the proper balance. On the other hand, I had always rebelled against the idea of not becoming involved at all. The cornerstone of my personal philosophy was commitment. I felt it was the unequivocal commitment of one individual to another, of me to the child I was working with, that evoked positive change. How could there be genuine commitment without involvement? That was a contradiction in terms.

On a gut level I felt Sheila *had* to have this relationship and without it she could never go forward. She needed the esteem that comes only from knowing others care for you, others value you sufficiently to commit themselves to you. She needed to know that while her mother might not have been able to provide this kind of commitment, this did not mean that Sheila was unworthy of it. Yet on an intellectual level I knew I was treading a dangerous path.

Just how dangerous came home to me in February, after Sheila had been with us about seven weeks. I had to attend an out-of-state conference, which meant I would be gone from class for two days. Having ample warning, I endeavored to prepare my class for my absence and the anticipated substitute teacher. Sheila reacted with rage.

"I ain't never, *never* gonna like you again! I ain't *never* gonna do anything you ask. It ain't fair you go leave me! You ain't supposed to do that, don't you know? That be what my mama done and that ain't a good thing to do to little kids. They put you in jail for leaving little kids. My pa, he says."

Tirade after tirade and nothing I said, no effort I made to explain

I would be gone only for two days abated Sheila's anger. In my absence she reverted to all the worst of her old behaviors. She fought with the other children, bloodying noses and cracking shins. The record player was destroyed and the small window in the door was cracked. Despite Anton's efforts to keep her in check, Sheila devastated the classroom and the substitute ended her days in tears.

I had expected better from Sheila and my anger, when she proved so uncooperative, was not a whole lot less than her's. She was a bright girl. She knew how long two days were. And I had gone to strenuous efforts to explain where I'd be, what I'd be doing and when *precisely* I would be back. She *knew*. Why could I not trust her to keep herself together for two lousy days?

To be more exact about the matter, I felt betrayed. Having known I was following such a dangerous course in allowing her growing dependence on me, I had wanted straightforward evidence that I was doing the right thing, that her dependence was natural and healthy and not *too* serious. I was, after all, going to have to walk out of her life in, at most, three and a half months' time, when the school year ended, and in even less time, if the opening in the children's unit at the state hospital occurred. For my own peace of mind, I needed reassurance I was helping more than hurting and— I suppose if I'm honest—I expected it from her. I had given her so much that, in my heart of hearts, I had trusted her to give this bit back to me. When she hadn't, I reacted with an anger I didn't control at all well.

We had, to put it mildly, a bad day, and even after school, when we were alone, the strained silence remained between us. I offered to do the things we'd come to enjoy so much: to read aloud to her, to let her help me correct my papers, to come down with me to the teachers' lounge and share a soft drink, but she simply shook her head and busied herself in the far corner of the room with some toy cars. The first after-school hour passed. She rose and went to look out the window. When I next glanced up, she was still there but had turned to watch me.

"How come you come back?" she asked softly.

"I just went away to give a speech. I never intended to stay away. This is my job, here with you kids."

"But how come you come back?"

"Because I said I would. I like it here. I belong here."

Slowly, she approached the table where I was working. Her guard had dropped. The hurt was so clear in her eyes.

"You didn't believe I was coming back, did you?"

She shook her head. "No."

three

Our falling-out over my absence did not appear to have any lasting effects. Indeed, just the opposite. Sheila developed an intense desire to discuss the incident: I had left her; I had come back. She had gotten angry and destructive; I had gotten angry and, in my own way, destructive. Each small segment she wanted to discuss again and again until it slowly slotted into place for her. The fact that I *had* come back was, of course, very important to her, but so too was the degree of my anger. Perhaps she felt that now that she had seen me at my worst, she could more fully trust me. I don't know. Intriguingly, Sheila's destructiveness virtually disappeared after this incident. She still became angry with great regularity, but never again did she fly into one of her rampaging rages.

Sheila bloomed, like the daffodils, in spite of the harsh winter. Within the limits of her situation, she was now quite clean and, better, she recognized what clean was and endeavored to correct unacceptable levels of dirtiness herself. Increasingly, she interacted with the other children in the class in a friendly and appropriate manner. She had gone home to play with one of the other little girls in the class on a few occasions and they indulged in the usual rituals of little girls' friendships at school. Academically, Sheila sailed ahead, excited by almost anything I put in front of her. We were still coping with her fear of committing her work to paper, but that too improved through March. It seldom took more than two or three tries before she felt secure enough with what she had written down to let me look at it. She was still extremely sensitive to correction, going off into great sulks, no matter how gently I pointed out a mistake; and on moody days, she could spend much of the time with her head buried in her arms in dismal despair, but we were coping.

*   *   *

It was after school and Sheila and I had returned to *The Little Prince* yet again. Snuggled down in the pillows of the reading corner together, we had just begun the book. I had come to the part where the little prince demands that the author draw him a sheep.

> "A sheep—if it eats bushes, does it eat flowers too?"
> "A sheep," I answered, "eats anything in its reach."
> "Even flowers that have thorns?"
> "Yes, even flowers that have thorns."
> The thorns—what use are they . . . ?"
> The prince never let go of a question, once he had asked it. As for me, I was upset over the bolt. And I answered with the first thing that came into my head:
> "The thorns are of no use at all. Flowers have thorns just for spite!"
> "Oh!"
> There was a moment of complete silence. Then the little prince flashed back at me with a kind of resentfulness:
> "I don't believe you! Flowers are weak creatures. They are naive—"

Sheila laid her hand across the page. "I want to ask you something. What's 'naive' mean?"

"It means someone whose ways are simple. They haven't much experience with the world," I replied.

"Do I be naive?" she asked, looking up.

"No, I wouldn't say so. Not for your age."

She looked back down at the book. "The flower thinks she has experience."

I nodded.

"But the prince knows she doesn't." She smiled. "I do love this part. I love the flower."

We read on:

> So, too, she began very quickly to torment him with her vanity—which was, if truth be known, a little difficult to deal with. One day, for instance, when she was speaking of her four thorns, she said to the little prince:

"Let the tigers come with their claws!"

"There are no tigers on my planet," the little prince objected. "And anyway, tigers do not eat weeds."

"I am not a weed," the flower replied sweetly.

"Please excuse me . . ."

"I am not at all afraid of tigers—"

The door to the classroom opened and the secretary stuck her head around the door. "Sorry to interrupt, Torey, but there's a telephone call for you in the office."

Handing Sheila the book, I rose and went down to take it.

It was the call I was dreading. The director of special education was on the other end of the line: a vacancy had come up in the children's unit at the state hospital. Sheila's time in my classroom was over.

To say I was devastated diminishes the enormity of the emotions I felt at that news. Whatever her difficulties, Sheila in no way belonged in a mental hospital. Intelligent, creative, sensitive, perceptive, she belonged here with us and, eventually, back in a normal class in a regular school.

I moaned, I pleaded, eventually I raged. The director listened. We got on well, he and I. I had always counted him among my allies in the district, the sort of man I relied on as a mentor, and this, if anything, made his call harder to take.

"It was settled long before any of us got into it, Torey," he said. "You know that. There's nothing we can do."

Pathetic little flower, I thought, so proud of her fierce thorns, and when the tigers really came, the thorns gave no protection at all.

*　　　*　　　*

I simply couldn't let it happen without a fight. When she had arrived in January, she had presented as bleak a case as I had ever encountered, and if they'd come for her then, I might have accepted it. But now . . . ? The very thought of a child of Sheila's caliber ending up institutionalized at six froze me to my soul.

That evening when I was home, ostensibly watching television

with my boyfriend, Chad, a plan formed in my mind. I had so much
evidence of both Sheila's intelligence and her progress that I wondered if there might be a chance of changing things. It would have
to be approached in a formal, unequivocal manner to be taken seriously and it would have to be undertaken rapidly. I glanced over at
Chad. He was a very new junior partner in a law firm downtown
and was spending much of his time as a court-appointed lawyer to
those who couldn't afford their own legal advice. So he knew the
ropes.

"Is there a legal way to contest what they want to do with
Sheila?" I asked cautiously.

"*You* fight it?" he replied, sensing the meaning under my words.

"Someone has to. I'm quite sure the school district would support
me. The school psychologist has been in to administer IQ tests. He
had evidence of her giftedness. And Ed knows."

A pause. A few mutterings. I was the sort of person inclined, as
Chad described it, "to get the bit between my teeth and run," so I
think he could guess the obsessive nature of what was going to happen.

"Would you take it on for me?" I asked.

"*Me?*"

Yeah, him.

And so it was. With admirable solidarity, the school district did
back me fully. They even paid for Chad's services. I marshaled together the videotapes I'd made of Sheila in class, her schoolwork,
the psychologist's evaluations and whatever other examples I could
find to support Sheila's steady improvement. The weakest link in
the chain was Sheila's father, who had been in and out of so many
institutions himself that he didn't seem to believe there was any
point to pursuing a different life for his daughter. He was deeply suspicious of us because we did. Beneath his boorish behavior, I felt he
did genuinely love Sheila, but it took several rather beery evenings
between us to convince him we were right.

The hearing was held on the very last day of March, a dark, windy
day that promised to bend the daffodils down yet again with snow.
Sheila had had to come along, still dressed in her T-shirt and now
badly outgrown overalls. They were clean and I had managed to get

her father to accept socks and mittens for her from our church dona-
tion box, but that was the best I could do. She sat outside the courtroom with an attendant, in case we needed to call her in.

Inside, I saw the parents of the little boy whom Sheila had abducted and set alight. It was the first time I'd encountered them. Up
to that moment, the incident that had placed her in my class had
seemed distant to me. In truth, I suppose I had kept it distant in my
mind in an effort to make such an act of calculated cruelty unreal.
Sheila certainly *had* done some outrageous things and she had done
plenty of them in my presence, so I'd always felt I had a realistic picture of her, but for the first time I had to confront the veracity of another point of view. This upset me, if for no other reason than that I
had so desperately wanted to feel a hundred percent right in what I
was doing just then. In a way I still did. Revenge would not undo
the harm done to their son and it would cripple Sheila for life. This
was the only right route for this girl. Yet the hearing brought home
to me the enormity of what she had done.

The judge ruled in Sheila's favor. She was to remain under Social
Services supervision, but the order for detainment in the children's
unit was rescinded. Joy broke out in the halls of the courthouse, and
afterward, Chad and I took Sheila out to celebrate.

It was a magical evening, one of those times when the experience
is greater than the sum of its parts. Still high from our success, we
went for pizza in a place Chad and I haunted frequently, full of
smoke and jazz music and people speaking Italian. Sheila had never
had pizza and took to the new experience with animated delight.
Indeed, she took to Chad, and he, likewise, to her. He was soon as
much under her spell as I was.

They got into a silly contest, the two of them. What would you
like best? To eat a worm sundae or brush your teeth with a spider
toothbrush? That sort of thing. Until Chad went serious and asked
what was the thing she would like best in all the world—for real. A
dress, as it turned out. Something pretty to wear. Unable to resist
this opportunity to play Santa Claus, Chad soon had us out to the
shopping center. Despite all Sheila's fears that her father wouldn't
let her accept a dress, Chad reassured her and helped her find the
one she liked best.

Sheila fell asleep on the way back to her house in the migrant camp.

"Well, Cinderella," Chad said, coming around to my side of the car and opening the door. He reached down and lifted her up. "The ball's over."

She smiled sleepily at him.

"Come on. I'll carry you in and tell your daddy what we've been up to."

She buried her face in my hair. "I don't wanna go," she whispered.

"It's been a nice night, hasn't it?" I said.

She nodded and she pressed tighter against me. "Can I kiss you?"

"Yes, I think so," I said and enveloped her in a tight hug and kissed her first.

four

My class would cease to exist at the end of that school year. The mainstreaming law with its edict that every handicapped child should be placed in the least restrictive alternative was the primary cause. Most of the special education classes were being closed and teachers like myself were being redeployed as "resource people" to provide support to the regular classroom teachers, who would now have special education children among their students.

I wasn't terribly comfortable with this change. While I would have liked to accept the law on the ideological grounds it was being put forth on— that it would promote greater equality and opportunity for handicapped children—I was too much of a natural cynic. The far more obvious factor to me was that it was a cheaper way to educate handicapped children.

On a personal level, my style of teaching was best suited to the closed environment of a self-contained classroom. It was in this setting I was at my best. I could create the tight-knit, supportive milieu that became my trademark and it was under these circumstances I could encourage the most positive growth among my students. Consequently, I was loath to become a floating resource person with my children reduced to a catalog of educational problems I was given twenty minutes a week to sort out. Most difficult, however, was being boxed in theoretically. I was an eclectic, picking and choosing my methods of operation from a wide variety of sources, some of them entirely outside education. This seemed the only sensible approach when dealing with such varied difficulties as one comes across in human behavior. However, with the new law we were going to be restricted, generally to some form of behavior modification. I was competent enough with this approach but felt it vastly overrated as a method and rather dangerous as a theory. Thus, not feeling that I was ready to commit myself to all of this, I applied and was accepted at an out-of-state university to do further graduate work.

It was May and school would end the first week in June. In the four and a half months Sheila had been with us, she had metamorphosed into a lively, sunny-natured girl. We had had no serious breaches of behavior since that week in February when I had gone to the conference, and while she was still capable of a hearty tantrum when provoked, normal methods of discipline brought her back into line. She could now express anger without destructiveness; she could be reasoned with; and she could even accept a small amount of gentle criticism without falling to pieces. In short, I didn't feel Sheila would need a special class any longer. She was still fragile and the placement would need to be well thought out, but I was convinced she had the capacity to get on in a normal classroom.

I had a good friend, Sandy McGuire, a third-grade teacher in another school who I felt would be an ideal next teacher for Sheila. She was young, innovative and had a reputation for sensitivity toward her students, many of whom came from minority backgrounds or extreme poverty. And while we had quite different styles of teaching, we shared similar philosophies. I felt confident that if Sheila went with her, she would receive the support and encouragement she would need to make the transition back into the mainstream.

In the beginning, Ed, the director of special education, was not in favor of this, as it would mean not only releasing Sheila back into regular education, but also advancing her a grade, a practice he frowned upon; however, after much discussion we mutually concluded this was the best choice. Academically, Sheila was at least two grades above her chronological peers and she had no current peer friendships to disrupt anyway. Moreover, I feared that if Sheila did not receive a certain amount of academic challenge, she would get herself into trouble just to stay occupied. The most important factor, however, remained the teacher. Sheila *had* to have a flexible, supportive teacher to cope with the transition from me and my room to a new setting and I held tight to my belief that Sandy best fulfilled this capacity. In the end, Ed and the placement team agreed.

Sheila didn't.

I approached the whole issue cautiously, although not tentatively, as Sheila would home in on anything done with uncertainty. Moreover, there was nothing to be tentative about. June was coming and that was the end.

Tears, anger and great silences met my early efforts to broach the subject. We spent the better half of a week dancing nervously around the matter, once it had been raised.

"This here be my class," Sheila muttered to me after school. Her peculiar usage of the word "be" had almost disappeared over the months since she had been in our room, but now it came back. "I ain't going in no other class. This here be mine."

"Yes, it is, but the school year will be over in a few weeks' time. We need to think about next year."

"I'm gonna be in here next year."

My heart sank. "No, sweetie."

"I am too!" she shouted. "I'll be the baddest kid in the whole world. Then they won't *let* you make me go away!"

"Oh, Sheil. Oh, sweetheart, that's not what's happening. I'm not kicking you out. I'd *love* to have you with me."

She remained angry, her face flushed, her eyes hurt. She pressed her hands over her ears.

"This class isn't going to be here next year," I said softly.

She heard me, even through her hands. The color drained from her face. "What d'you mean? Where's it going?"

"It's a grown-up decision. The school district decided they don't need it and everyone can go into other classes."

Tears filled her eyes. Taking out the chair across the table from me, she slumped into it, folded her arms on the table and lay her head on it. The tears just fell. Her pain was palpable. I'm sure I could have touched it, had I reached out, and when I didn't, it pressed in against me.

All I could think of at just that moment was how much we expected from her in terms of tolerance, acceptance and understanding, and here she was, only six. *Six*, for God's sake, not even seven until July.

What had I gotten her into? There I was with all my ideologies on commitment and how it was better to have loved and lost than never to have loved at all. But did *she* think that? Had I ever given her a choice?

On the other hand, what choice was there? To have done what I did, or to have left her as she was and simply counted off the days until they would come for her? There hadn't been many alternatives. Watching her as she wept, I did not know if even with so few alternatives I had chosen the right one.

Sheila rose from the table and went to bury herself among the pillows in the reading corner. I remained at the table, listening to her as she cried. At last, I rose and went over.

"How come you ain't staying to make me good?" she asked me, her voice confused.

"Because it isn't me who makes you good. It's you. I'm here to let you know that someone cares if you're good or not. And in that way, I'll never leave you, because I'll always care."

"You're just like my mama," she said.

"No, I'm not, Sheil."

"You're gonna leave me, just like her."

"No, Sheila, this is different."

"She never loved me really," she said softly, matter-of-factly. "She loved my brother better than me. She left me on the highway like some dog, like I didn't even belong to her."

"I'm not her. I don't know what her reasons were for what she did, but this is different, Sheila. I'm a teacher. My ending comes in June. But I'll still love you. I won't be your teacher any longer, but I'll still be your friend."

"I don't wanna be friends. I wanna be in this class."

I reached over to her. "I know you do, sweetheart. I do too. I wish it could go on forever."

She pulled away. "You're bad as my mama."

"This is *different*."

"It don't feel any different to me."

*   *   *

They were an emotional few weeks, those last ones. Sheila was in tears as often as not. Not angry tears, though, just tears, popping up at the most unexpected moments: while we were baking cookies on Wednesday afternoon, while giving water to our cantankerous rabbit, while reading on her own in the book corner. I felt they were a natural part of the separation process, so I accepted them, giving her what comfort she sought and otherwise letting her come to terms at her own pace. And tears were by no means her only expression. There were plenty of boisterous, happy moments too.

I took her over to visit Sandy and her classroom and then we arranged for Sheila to go spend a trial day there. As I suspected would happen, Sheila was seduced by Sandy's warm, cheerful personality and by the more stimulating environment of the third-grade classroom. These children were actively learning, busy with intriguing projects and undertakings, many of them self-generated. All in all, quite a different atmosphere from our classroom, where going to the toilet was considered an achievement. Sheila came back vibrant from her visit, her conversation full of "Next year, when I'm in Miss McGuire's class . . ." I knew then I had been outgrown.

Then the last day.

We had a picnic in the park to celebrate our year together. All the parents were invited and we brought packed lunches and ice cream and all the trappings for a good day out. Ours was an extraordinarily beautiful municipal park with a long, winding lane lined with locust trees, a babbling brook that tumbled down through natural rock cascades to empty into a large duck pond ringed with weeping willows. In all directions there were large expanses of grass stretching out beneath ancient sycamores and oaks.

Sheila loved the park. She had never been there before coming to our room, as it was a long way from the migrant camp; but it was only a few blocks from the school, so I had taken my class over on several occasions. Her father did not come that day, but it was obvious he was making more of an effort with Sheila. She came dressed in a bright-orange cotton sunsuit and excitedly told us how her father had taken her down to the discount store the night before and bought it, especially for her to wear to the picnic. She was so ebullient that day, skipping, dancing, pirouetting in the sunshine, that I still call to mind that bobbing form of sunlit orange every time I smell locust blossoms or see duck ponds.

And then, finally, the end—the last good-bye at the door of the classroom to Anton, the last walk together over to the high school to meet her bus. I had given her the now dog-eared copy of *The Little Prince* to take with her, a tangible reminder of these last five months, and she clutched it to her as we walked.

Running up the bus steps, she went straight to the back and clambered up on the bench seat to wave to me from the back window. The bus rumbled to life and diesel fumes overpowered the scent of locust blossoms. "Bye," she was saying, although I couldn't hear her because of the glass and the noise of the engine. The bus began to pull away and she waved frantically.

"Bye-bye," I said and lifted my hand to wave too, as the bus turned the corner and disappeared from sight. Then I turned to walk back to my classroom.

five

When autumn came, I was a thousand miles away from the school, the migrant camp and the locust trees. Settled into graduate school, I was devoting most of my spare time to research. Some years earlier I had become intrigued by psychologically based language problems, elective mutism in particular, where an individual can speak but does not do so for emotional reasons; however, I had had to put this on the back burner while teaching full-time, because there just hadn't been time to pursue it. Now I was able to devote the kind of attention to the work I wanted. As a consequence, I was still in daily contact with children, but it was of a different kind and quality to what the classroom had given me. This was okay. I had been ready for the change, and thus was finding this new work rewarding.

Chad and I had parted ways over the summer. We'd been together for much of the previous three years and the last year, in particular, we'd grown close. Sheila, in her own way, had brought us closer still. Previously, Chad had only been part of my personal life, a world I tended to keep strictly separate from my life in the classroom, but with Sheila's hearing in March, he had been drawn into that too. The magic of that night when Chad had taken Sheila and me out for pizza had been powerful and all three of us, I think, got caught up in a dreamy moment of believing we were a family. It'd seemed so right just then—Chad, Sheila and I; however, in the cold, hard light of day, I knew it wasn't right. Chad was older than I was and had sown his wild oats, but I was still very young. I knew I was not yet ready for the commitments that a closer relationship with Chad would entail. Because commitments were so important to me, I wouldn't make them lightly. So, seductive as the vision of family life was at that point, I knew I would fail at it if I tried it now.

So this, too, lay behind my decision to change tracks and move away from the area. I loved Chad and I didn't want to break up our relationship, but I didn't want to intensify it either. Putting distance between us seemed a reasonable solution.

Chad, of course, figured out what I was doing and he wasn't particularly happy about it. For him the time was right to settle down and get married. If anything, those last eight weeks with Sheila had verified for him that this was what he wanted and he chafed at my uncertainty, angry with me one moment for my immaturity, poignantly vulnerable the next, when he bemoaned the unfairness of the fact that no matter how much a man might be ready to be a father, he couldn't be one without a woman. I felt awful, as one always does when relationships crumble, but I went ahead with my plans regardless, knowing in my heart even more certainly that this was the right thing to do.

*   *   *

Sheila went into Sandy McGuire's third-grade class, and for all intents and purposes, she did extremely well. Sandy kept me well informed with letters each month or so. I was gratified to hear that Sheila was settling in, making friends and achieving good academic results, and even more so to hear that she was coming to school cleaner and better fed, which made me hope the home situation was improving.

My only other source of information was Anton, who still lived in the migrant camp himself and occasionally saw Sheila there. Despite my misgivings when Anton had first come to my classroom the previous autumn, he had turned out to be a natural teacher. He had tremendous rapport, particularly with the slower children and with the Spanish-speakers, of whom there were many in our migrant population. As a consequence, he had decided to work on his teacher qualifications at the nearby community college while still continuing as an aide in the school district. He was well informed on how all my former students were doing, and thus, a letter from Anton was a real treat.

I wrote to Sheila, as I had promised her I would do, and Sheila occasionally wrote back. She was, however, only seven, and as with all seven-year-olds, no matter how gifted, letters were clearly a chore. They came erratically and if I had not had Sandy's letters in the interim, I really wouldn't have had any idea of what was going on. Indeed, the contents of Sheila's letters were even more erratic than their number. She was given to sending me her homework for some reason and that was all I sometimes received for months on end.

All went smoothly. Sheila finished her year with Sandy an enthusiastic, if somewhat quirky, student, and was promoted to the fourth grade. I received a school picture of her from Sandy, showing her in a bright-yellow dress, her smile sweet and toothless. She looked well, if not too clean.

Autumn came but Sheila didn't. I received a puzzled note from Sandy saying that Sheila had been withdrawn from the register. It was Anton who investigated the matter and wrote back to tell me that Sheila and her father had moved to a small city on the far side of the state, some two hundred miles away. They had left in June, just after school had let out, apparently because her father thought he had found a job.

I wrote to the only address I had, her old one, and received no answer. Distressed at the thought that I had actually lost contact with Sheila, I made a few phone calls in an effort to trace her. During the course of these, I discovered that she had apparently gone into foster care at the end of the summer, but it was only a rumor and I couldn't confirm it. I knew no one in this new city to which she and her father had moved and I was twelve hundred miles away. It proved impossible to find out where she was and how she was doing.

This upset me profoundly. Confiding in an older colleague one afternoon after an abortive effort to trace Sheila, I was reassured that this was better, that I shouldn't try to hold on to old students. She smiled gently and patted my shoulder. "Never look back. You've got to love them and leave them."

*   *   *

It was three years before I managed to go back to Marysville to visit my old friends. By then Anton was gone. He had completed his two-year course at the community college and won a scholarship to the state university to finish his bachelor's degree. I visited with Sandy, however, and Whitney, who was now a senior in high school; and I went back to walk through my old classroom, now converted into a resource center.

Chad and I had separated amicably and we'd stayed in touch. He was married now to a fellow lawyer named Lisa and she was expecting their first child in a month's time.

We decided to lunch together and I came up to his law office to meet him. He had been held up in a meeting, so I paced languidly about the reception desk waiting for him. It was then I noticed a paper lying in the outgoing basket. I just caught it with the corner of my eye, but the name pulled me back. It was Sheila's father's name. Glancing at the receptionist, I realized I couldn't really look, but I was desperate to hear what Chad had to say.

"Didn't you know he's back in prison?" Chad replied to my query.

"*No*. When did this happen? You never told me."

"Well, I couldn't really, could I?" he said apologetically. "I mean, confidentiality and all. Besides, I assumed you did know." What he didn't mention was that we had never exchanged much more than Christmas cards anyway since we'd parted. But still, I felt somehow cheated.

Chad smiled gently. "I'm not handling many legal aid cases these days, so I didn't know myself until I saw the folder."

"What's happened?"

"I can't really discuss it, Torey."

"I'm not just anybody, Chad. I was the one who brought him to you in the first place." I was feeling hurt and heartsick. I knew it was hardly Chad's fault and I fully understood his need to keep confidence with clients, but the shock made me irritable.

"Well, suffice it to say he's been wholly predictable. He's up for the same tricks as always."

"Where's Sheila then?"

"Don't know. He's been living over in Broadview for a couple of years now and he was arrested and booked over there. They sent over here just looking for files. I've never seen him or anything."

"But where's Sheila?" I murmured, lowering my head.

*   *   *

Heartbroken at this discovery, I endeavored to find out about Sheila's fate, but I had few resources at my fingertips. Broadview was still two hundred miles off and was a much bigger city. Finding one small girl was no easy matter. The most I could confirm was that she had been taken into foster care as a direct result of her father's arrest and imprisonment and was, apparently, still placed. Where, with whom and for how long I could not determine. Rumor had it that she had been repeatedly in and out of foster care from the time they had moved.

Foster care. Practically the whole time Sheila was in my class, all of us had viewed foster care as a panacea to her problems. If only Sheila were away from the poverty, if only she were in a stable home with loving parents, if only . . . We hadn't been able to get her into foster care then simply because the Social Services were so over-stretched in Marysville and she did have her natural father. Now she was in foster care and I should have felt glad. The fact was, I didn't.

Back home, I sat down and wrote a very long letter to Sheila. I told her about my visit to our old school and our old friends. I mentioned that I knew her life had been disrupted in the last eighteen months and that I knew she was now with foster parents. I said that I hoped all was well and that if there was any way I could help, I would be happy to try. Including my phone number, I said she could call me collect any time, if she wanted. Then I added a photograph from the visit of Sandy and me and an old one I had taken of Sheila on our last-day picnic. Folding everything together, I put them in a large envelope. But where would I send it? In the end, I sent it to her father, in care of the prison, and asked him to forward it to her.

*   *   *

I never heard whether Sheila received my letter or not, whether she ever knew that I was trying to find her again. There was no answer, and as the months went by, I began to accept there wasn't going to be one.

This was difficult for me to come to terms with. It seemed inconceivable to me that she had disappeared from my life. Yet the words of my colleague kept returning to me: you've got to love 'em and leave 'em.

Two years later, a small envelope arrived on my desk. It was addressed not to my home, but rather to the university where I now taught. I recognized Sheila's loose, scrawly handwriting immediately and tore the envelope open. There was only one sheet of paper inside, a crumpled piece of lined notebook paper. The writing was done in blue felt-tip marker with many of the words watermarked, as if the paper had gotten splattered by rain. Or was it tears?

To Torey with much
Love

All the rest came
They tried to make me laugh
They played their games with me
Some games for fun and some for keeps
And then they went away
Leaving me in the ruins of games
Not knowing which were for keeps and
Which were for fun and
Leaving me alone with the echoes of
Laughter that was not mine.

Then you came
With your funny way of being
Not quite human
And you made me cry
And you didn't seem to care if I did
You just said the games are over
And waited
Until all my tears turned into
Joy.

There was nothing else, no letter, not even a note. As with the days when she had sent me only her homework, Sheila seemed to feel no need for explanations. It was my turn to cry then and so I wept.

part
two

six

I can remember the moment precisely when the magic began. I was eight, a not-very-outstanding third grader in Mrs. Webb's class. I didn't care much for school. I never had. My world in those days was the broad, swampy creek that ran below our house; that and my beloved pets. School was something that got in the way of my enjoyment of these things.

On one particular morning, my reading group had been sent back to our desks to do our seatwork, while Mrs. Webb listened to the next group read. On my desk, under my workbook, I had hidden a piece of paper, and instead of doing what I should have been doing, I sneaked the opportunity to write. At home I had a dachshund, which had been a present to me from my mother on my seventh birthday, and I made him the hero of a rather lurid tale involving our old mother cat and a band of marauding, eye-plucking crows. So absorbed did I become in spinning this tale that I failed to notice Mrs. Webb on the move, and what inevitably happens to eight-year-old girls who do not do their reading workbooks happened. Mrs. Webb snatched the story away from me and I had to stay in from recess to do my work.

The incident itself was minor, the sort of thing to which I was unfortunately rather prone, and as a consequence, I forgot all about it. Then, a couple of weeks later, I was ill and kept out of school for a few days. When I returned, I had to stay after school that afternoon to make up some of the work I had missed. Mrs. Webb apparently took this opportunity to clean out the drawers of her desk. Anyway, when I had finished, she handed over a piece of paper to me. "Here, I think this is yours," she said. It was the story about my dog and the crows.

Collecting my coat and belongings to go home, I began to read it as I walked down the school corridor, dark and silent because all the other children had left so long before me. Once at the end of the hall, I pushed open the heavy double doors of the school and then sat down on the concrete steps at the entrance to finish reading.

That precise moment I remember with such exquisite clarity—the feel of the cold concrete through my skirt, the late-autumn sunshine transposed against the darkness of the school entranceway, the uncanny silence of the empty playground, even the faint anxiety of knowing that I should be on my way home because my grandmother would worry if I was too late. The paper, however, held me spellbound.

It was all there: my dog, his adventure, the excitement such melodramatic experiences always created in me. I felt just as excited by the story reading it as I had been writing it. Astonished when I realized this, I lowered the paper. I *remember* lowering the paper, looking over the top of it, seeing someone's hopscotch game chalked onto the playground asphalt, and being overwhelmed by a sense of insight. *Wow!* I had always written because I found writing like pretending: an opportunity to turn myself into someone else for the moment I was doing it and be that individual, feeling his or her feelings and experiencing his or her adventures; but once the act of creation was over, I had never really gone back to what I had written. Now here it was, two weeks later, and I was feeling exactly what I had experienced earlier when I was writing it. Exactly. Again. As if the two weeks hadn't happened. I had *stopped time.* There, on the school steps, I knew I had stumbled onto magic of the first order. *Real magic!*

For the rest of my childhood, through my adolescence and into adulthood, writing compelled me. It was an internal, almost autonomic, activity, like circulation or digestion, that happened simply as a natural part of me. I wrote in all forms: diaries, anecdotes, stories. I wrote to understand other people, to give myself the opportunity to be inside them a while and see what it felt to see the world from another point of view. I wrote to understand emotions and experiences I had not yet encountered. And I wrote to understand myself.

It proved a powerful, if somewhat unusual, education. In particular, it fostered my abilities to be objective and to empathize, which in turn allowed me a greater general acceptance of differences; and, of course, it made me a keen observer.

*　　*　　*

I was in the final year of a doctorate I hadn't meant to find myself doing. I had weathered the mainstreaming law that had so disconcerted me the year I'd had Sheila. Although still not happy with all aspects of its implementation, I'd returned to the classroom a couple of years later and taken up teaching again as a "centered" resource teacher, which meant I stayed in the same room but the children came and went. It wasn't quite as fulfilling as having my own class, but at least I saw the same boys and girls on a regular basis.

Then the administration in Washington changed and with it, the general attitude of the country. Issues I'd fought heart and soul to see achieved a decade earlier were swept away with a single signature. Lower taxes and cuts in public spending became the bywords of the day. Because treating handicapped children in the public schools is labor intensive, and thus expensive, ours were among the first programs to be targeted. Further emphasis was put on placing special education children in the regular classroom as the cheaper alternative. We were being forced to respond to children in ways that were not necessarily the most beneficial to the child—or the teacher, either, for that matter, as many regular education teachers had little grounding in dealing with handicapped children. These philosophies, however, were the only ones that allowed us to process children through the system at the cost demanded of us by the government. The market economy was now being applied to education.

Angry at this change and all too aware that if I continued in the classroom, I too would soon find myself unemployed, I'd decided to work on a doctorate in special education. This was a stupid decision. The degree would overqualify me for the only part of the special education hierarchy I genuinely loved: teaching. Worse, it threw me into the hotbed of those creating the theories that I was trying to escape. Consequently, my heart was never in it.

I coped by finding other outlets. In this case, it was the continuation of my long-standing research into psychological language prob-

lems. This work was of little interest to my colleagues in special education; however, I soon found a niche across campus in the university hospital complex. There, in the department of child and
adolescent psychiatry, among others, I discovered willing partners
among the psychiatrists and other professionals. Despite my hybrid
credentials, my ideas were accepted and encouraged and my research flourished.

As always, I continued to fill my spare time with writing. Indeed,
I was writing more then than at any previous time; in part, I suspect,
because I wasn't fully engaged in my work.

The desire to write about my experiences with Sheila had been
with me for some time. I had saved a lot of material from that class,
not with the intention of using it to back up writing at a later date,
but just because I was a bit of a hoarder and a sentimental one at
that. Although I hadn't kept a daily diary while working in the class,
I had kept copious anecdotal records; moreover, I had had liberal use
of a video camera, and as a consequence, had quite a lot of Sheila on
tape. I went through these things periodically, and all the while I
could hear Sheila in my head: the inflections in her voice, the
strange lilting grammatical constructions. I had to write it down. I
had to liberate those five months from the onward rush of time.

Then, driving home on the freeway from work one dark January
evening, the beginning came to me: *I should have known.* I went home
and started writing. Eight days and 225 pages later, I was finished.

It was only in the aftermath that I realized what had happened.
At 225 pages, this wasn't a little something done for my own amuse-
ment, it was a book. I knew then that I had to find Sheila and let
her read it before the matter went any further.

seven

The job advertisement that caught my eye was for a small private psychiatric clinic in a major city about four hours' drive west of Marysville. In all my years back east, I had missed the Midwest. Admittedly, Sheila also crossed my mind. Broadview, where she had last been living, was a satellite community of the city. Six months had elapsed since I had written the book and I was no closer to finding Sheila. The idea of living near her, of perhaps reestablishing contact and renewing our relationship was appealing.

I was accepted at the Sandry Clinic as a research psychologist to coordinate and oversee the various research projects among the staff, as well as to continue my own research work with elective mutism. There were seven staff. Five, including the director, Dr. Rosenthal, were established child psychiatrists. They had founded the clinic together several years before and overseen the conversion of the elegant old building into a series of quality offices and therapy rooms.

I liked the Sandry Clinic very much. My colleagues were creative people, all lively and articulate, who worked well together as a team. The pinnacle among us in more ways than one was our director. Dr. Rosenthal was a giant of a man physically, standing over six and a half feet tall, with a giant-sized intellect to match. He had about him that charisma powerful men seem to have, which make them handsome whatever their actual physical characteristics. I was in awe of him much of my first year there. Although born and bred in America, he had a European formality about him. For instance, he never called any of us by our first names. "Doctor" was his usual method of catching someone's attention, but as I didn't merit that, I remained steadfastly Miss Hayden. This gave him a certain aura of unapproachability, which, combined with his formidable intellectual reputation, kept me shy around him. Nonetheless, I came to know him as a gentle man, firm but kind with his staff in much the same way he was with the children he worked with, and always, always fair.

Life at the clinic was luxurious compared to what I had become accustomed to while teaching in the state school system. We had wonderful facilities, including a large, sunny therapy room full of things I would have killed for when in special education, such as a five-foot-tall doll's house, complete with extended doll family, a pony-sized wooden rocking horse, an indoor sandbox and a water tray.

Similar luxury applied to my workload. Children were parceled out to me for therapy mostly by virtue of their language or lack of it, but I was also allowed a generous amount of time to work on the research projects or to consult with colleagues. Not completely comfortable with the fifty-minute "psychiatric hour," I was given the freedom of seeing my own clients two or three times a week, if I preferred that to the more traditional one session or of seeing them in their own settings, rather than at the clinic.

The only fly in the ointment from my point of view was that the majority of my colleagues were committed Freudians, which boxed in their views as tightly as behaviorism had with my education colleagues. And there I was, the atheist admitted to the monastery. To me, there is no single framework upon which we can hang all interpretations of human behavior. We create theories as a way of ordering the chaos sufficiently to have a chance of effecting change, but it is *we*, the practitioners, who have created this order, because it is we who need it. Any given theory, to my way of thinking, simply provides one route to interpretation and, like climbing the proverbial mountain, there are many other paths one could take.

I could cope with this disparity most of the time, as the general ethos of the clinic did not demand I practice as my colleagues did, and given that I was not qualified in psychiatry, they didn't expect me to. Indeed, it was my varied point of view, I suspect, that had attracted Dr. Rosenthal. Nonetheless, I found myself having to do a lot of tongue-biting.

Not being a full-fledged psychiatrist, I didn't merit one of the offices up front. Instead, I shared an oversized closet in the back of the building with Jeff Tomlinson.

Jeff, already a doctor, was in his last year of training as a child psychologist. He was one of those individuals so intellectually gifted that it is taken for granted. No modesty with him. He was brilliant and he knew he was brilliant, and he knew everyone else knew. "Does Superman fly?" he would say casually whenever I evidenced amazement at some mental feat, but he was so ingenuous when he said it that one never minded. Too much.

Unfortunately, Jeff might as well have been Freud's grandson. Indeed, he might as well have been Freud himself, for all his ability to quote what the old master said. With a near photographic memory, Jeff could bludgeon me into silence with word-for-word regurgitation of endless cases the old boy had worked on. It became a game with us after a while, to see who could outdebate the other.

Truth was, I loved Jeff. We were the youngest members of staff by quite some years, if not decades, and ours was like a sibling relationship there among the grown-ups. The other psychiatrists all had magnificent offices up front with cornices and fireplaces, carpets and leather couches. In the back of the building Jeff and I shared a windowless closet of an office, which had once housed another psychologist's research animals and still smelled. Here we had festooned the walls with posters, cartoons and matching Pink Panther nameplates. And here we worked, fought and shared our problems.

What saved Jeff from certain annihilation for his Freudian idiocy was an extraordinary sense of humor. He had a particular gift for funny voices and mimicry, which he displayed with the aplomb of a stand-up comic. As a consequence, the inanimate objects in our office—the filing cabinet, the desks, the radiator—were all inclined to join unexpectedly into conversations, each with its own weird little Robin Williams–type voice. The kids, of course, adored this when they heard it, but it even worked on me. It was difficult to get angry with a guy who had the furniture on his side.

All in all, I was pleased with this career move away from special education. It still felt funny to dress for work in wool skirts and dangly jewelry, to know that I could leave my long hair unbound because no one was likely to try and pull it out of my head; and, indeed, I found I missed my jeans and track shoes too much and was back in them after the first few months. But I fully enjoyed the ample resources and stimulating colleagues and felt that for the moment, at least, this had been the right move.

eight

Sheila was three months short of her fourteenth birthday when I finally located her. I hadn't seen her in seven years—half her lifetime past—and other than the poem I'd received through the mail two years earlier, I hadn't heard from her in five. I found her back with her father, living in an outlying suburb of Broadview. After a telephone conversation with her father, I asked if I could visit.

They were living in a duplex, a brown-colored building with peeling paint, in a run-down area where the yards were littered with car bodies and rusting appliances; however, compared to Sheila's home in the migrant camp, this was luxurious.

I knocked at the door. A long moment passed with no sound beyond the door and I found to my surprise that my knees were shaky. All the ghosts of long ago came crowding in around me as I waited on the doorstep and I could hear them so clearly. A child's laughter echoed, shouting, squealing, the sounds of a classroom, and then the dark, blowy silence I remembered experiencing as I had stood on the doorstep of Sheila's tar-paper shack in the migrant camp. Then, back to the present. Footsteps came toward the door and it opened.

I don't think I would have recognized Sheila's father if I hadn't assumed it would be he opening the door. He had changed dramatically in seven years. The dumpy, overweight boozer I recollected was not there. Instead, the man opening the door was slim and athletic-looking and, most startling to me, *young*. I had been in my early twenties when I had last seen him and I had always regarded him as being in my parents' generation. Now, with shock, I realized he was, in fact, not much older than I was.

"Mr. Renstad?" I asked tentatively.

He nodded.

"I'm Torey Hayden."

He smiled in a genuinely welcoming fashion and held the door open. "Come in. Sheila's not here at the moment. She's just run over to the store for some milk, but she'll be back in a few minutes." He opened the door to let me into the living room. It was small, with a television, a well-worn brown sofa and two old-fashioned armchairs. Indeed, the whole room had a sort of brownish quality to it, but it was comfortable.

Sudden shyness struck us both. All these years I had pondered this moment and now that it was here, I didn't know quite what to say. He obviously felt just as uncertain.

After a moment, he snatched a photograph from the top of the television. "Here, you want to see this? These are my boys."

It was the photo of a baseball team, the boys appearing to be about ten or eleven. They were posed in two rows, the first kneeling, the others behind. Mr. Renstad was on the left of the back row.

"I been coaching a year now," he said, moving beside me to look at the picture. "See that kid? His name is Juma Washington and you listen out for that name, because he's going to be great someday. Like Hank Aaron, that kid. And it was me that taught him to hit. Wouldn't do nothing for us when he first came. Was a wild, jazzy kid. And now he's gonna make the major leagues. You watch and see. I know he's gonna make it big."

"That's super."

He looked at me. "I'm clean now, you know. Sheila tell you that? No more booze or stuff. I been clean eighteen months now and now it's me helping them."

"I'm pleased," I said.

"I mean it. I'm not having no trouble at all anymore, and now I got these boys. We won four games already this season. Didn't win no games at all before I took 'em over. Were wild kids, crazy as monkeys. But we're making it big now. Got Juma. Got a couple of other good ones too. Here, let me show you." He took the photograph. "Him, that's Salim. And him, Luis. You ought to see 'em play. Can you come down some Saturday?"

Just then the door banged and there stood Sheila.

Sheila?

Who stood there was a gangly adolescent with—honest to God—orange hair. Not strawberry blond, not red. Orange, like a road cone. It was longish, and permed into frizzy ringlets, a Cubs baseball cap pulled down over the top of it.

Would I have known this was Sheila if I had encountered her on the street? She'd grown taller than I'd expected. She'd been such a tiny, malnourished thing when I'd had her, that I had always kept her small in my mind, but here she was, a good five feet four or so and only thirteen. Adolescence hadn't worked its full magic with her yet, however. She was gangly and still had the undeveloped figure of a child.

No question about whether or not she recognized me. On seeing me, she stopped abruptly, as if seeing a most unexpected sight. Her cheeks colored. "Hi," she said and smiled shyly. That smile did it. Her features grew familiar instantaneously.

"Hi."

All three of us were uncomfortably self-conscious. After anticipating this reunion for so long, I hadn't expected to find myself at a loss for words, but that's what happened. Sheila, equally thunderstruck, clung on to her half gallon of milk and stared at me. Only Mr. Renstad seemed able to find his voice. He went back to talking about his baseball team; however, he never asked me to sit down, so we all continued standing there in the middle of the living room.

Sheila's father just kept chattering. Several times he reassured me that he had given up drugs and alcohol and put his past behind him. This embarrassed me, making me feel as if he were interpreting my visit as checking up on him. He appeared to think Sheila and I had had much more contact with each other over the years than we'd had and so alluded to events that I knew nothing of. I felt it would be indelicate of me to inquire further at this point and thus said nothing, but from what I could make out, Sheila had been in foster care between the ages of eight and ten and then again for a while when she was eleven. They had been living together since his last parole, about eighteen months earlier.

Sheila said absolutely nothing. Like her father and me, she still stood in the middle of the living room, but she made no effort to join in the conversation. I stole glances at her, particularly at her dyed hair, because it was such an unusual color. Then at her clothes. When in my classroom, she had had one single outfit—a brown-striped boy's T-shirt and a pair of denim overalls—which she had worn day in, day out until her father had finally accepted the dress Chad had bought for Sheila after the March hearing. Sheila didn't look as if she was faring much better these days. She wore an enormously oversized white T-shirt with a ragged jeans jacket minus the arms layered over the top. Underneath the T-shirt I assumed there was something besides underwear, as I could see what might be the fringed edge of cut-off jeans, but I wasn't sure. Contemplating the outfit, I assumed this was fashion and not poverty showing.

Finally, when her father paused, I turned to her. "I passed a Dairy Queen coming over. Would you like to go get a sundae with me?"

*   *   *

Alone in the car with me, Sheila remained silent. It was by no means a hostile silence, but it was uncomfortable enough. I found myself wandering back to the very first day I had met Sheila. She had been silent then too, fiercely silent, breaking it only to announce with tigerish vehemence that I couldn't make her talk. I kept calling back to mind that charismatic little girl I had known and trying to find her in this nervous adolescent. I was only too aware that I didn't know this strangely clad, deerlike thing at all.

Pulling into the parking lot of the Dairy Queen, I looked over. "Remember when I used to take everybody over to the Dairy Queen and buy those boxes of Dilly bars? And how Peter always wanted something different? Never mattered what it was, he never wanted what everyone else was having."

"Who's Peter?"

"You remember. In our class. He used to always tell those awful jokes. The real groaners. Remember him?"

A pause. "Yeah . . . I think. He was Mexican, wasn't he?"

"Well, actually, he was black."

We chose our sundaes and then went out to sit at a picnic table in front. Sheila hunched over her ice cream in a manner that evoked memories of her early days in the class, when she would clutch her lunch tray up close to her, wary, like an animal, in case someone tried to take it away from her before she finished. She began to stir her sundae. The ice cream, chocolate sauce and whipping cream all went together in a gooey mess.

"So how's school?" I asked.

"All right, I guess."

"What courses are you taking?"

"Just the usual stuff."

"Anything good?" I asked.

"No, not really."

"Anything hard?"

"Not really," she said and stirred more energetically. "Boring, most of it."

Looking for some angle to get a conversation started, I resorted to an old trick I'd used in the classroom to stimulate a child to talk. "So what do you hate most about it?"

"Being youngest," she said without hesitation. "I *hate* that."

An accusation? She knew I had been responsible for moving her forward a grade. Was there a second meaning here? "What do you hate so much about it?"

She shrugged. "Just being youngest, that's all. Littlest. I was always so much shorter than everyone else, right up until just this last year. And always the baby of the class. Everyone picked on me."

"Yes, I can see where that might cause problems," I said, "but it was hard for us to know what was best for you."

Another shrug. "I'm not complaining or anything. It's just you asked."

Then silence. I wondered whether to draw her out on this issue and chance getting into something heavy, which I didn't feel would be appropriate just at the moment, or whether to soldier on searching for new topics of conversation. I felt amazingly uncomfortable. This wasn't the Sheila I had expected at all.

More silence. Taking small bites of my sundae, I concentrated on the flavors.

Suddenly, Sheila expelled a noisy breath and shook her head. "This is so weird," she said. "Like, I always think of you as someone

I know well." She looked over. "But really, we're no more than strangers."

That broke the ice, that admission. Truth was, we *were* strangers and neither of us had anticipated that. Once it was acknowledged, talking became far easier than it had been when we were pretending that the previous seven years hadn't intervened.

Spontaneously, Sheila began to talk about her school. She didn't like it. She was just finishing ninth grade and apparently doing well academically, but in listening to her I could tell virtually none of it had touched her. The authorities were getting after her about her hair and her clothes and her general attitude, and the way she related it, I suspected she was dealing with it by playing truant.

Perversely, the only subject that appeared to be engaging her was Latin, a language I didn't realize was still being taught in schools. The teacher, an elderly man, was unfashionably strict and held unenlightened views about girls' academic abilities, but this combination had somehow goaded Sheila into working hard enough to "show him." As a consequence, she talked animatedly about the class and the curriculum, even though she professed to hate it.

In turn, I told her what I had been up to over the interceding years, about my other classes of children since leaving the one we had shared, about my stints at graduate school, and about the change to the clinic in the city. And about writing the book.

"I have it in my car," I said. "I want you to read it."

"A *book*?" she said incredulously. "You wrote a book? I didn't know you could write."

I shrugged.

"It's got *me* in it? Our class? God. Weird." Then a slight smile. "That's, like, mega-weird, you know?"

"You need to be prepared for the fact that it's going to sound a little different to what really happened. Everybody's gone on from there, so it wouldn't really be right to invade people's privacy. Consequently, I've had to change the names and things and put some events out of order, but still, I think you'll recognize everything."

"This is so weird. A *book*? About me?"

"Anyway, I want your thoughts on it," I said. "It is your story, well, yours and mine, but you're the big part in it. I wouldn't want to include anything you didn't think was right."

She smiled. "It doesn't matter much. I hardly remember a thing about it."

"Oh, you will," I said and grinned back.

She shrugged, her expression still benevolent. "You got to keep in mind, Torey, that I was nothing but a little kid then. That all happened more than half my life ago. Like, I'm going to love to read this, but if you want to know the truth, you could write anything you want. Honest, I remember nothing."

nine

"God, did it really happen like this?" Sheila asked, a curiously amazed tone to her voice. It was the following Saturday. We were in her bedroom and she was curled up, the pages of the manuscript fanned out around her.

Smiling, I nodded.

"Wow, you were pretty brave to take me on, if I was like this."

"A lot of people thought that at the time. I did a bit myself, sort of."

"It wasn't your choice, was it? They just said you got to take . . . me." She looked back down at the sheaf of papers. "I think I might remember Anton now. I didn't when you first mentioned him the other day, when we were at the Dairy Queen, but reading this kind of brings him back to mind."

"You know what he's doing now?" I asked. "He's working on his master's degree in special education. He works with mentally handicapped children and has had his own classroom for three years now."

Sheila looked up. "God, you're really proud of him, aren't you? I can tell by your voice."

"I think it's amazing, what he's achieved. That's taken hard work. He's had a young family to support through all of this and his whole history had been with the migrant workers."

Regarding the typewritten pages, Sheila didn't speak for a few moments. "All I can recall is this really tall Mexican guy. He seemed like about seven feet tall to me then, but I don't remember a thing about what he did."

"Do you remember Whitney?" I asked.

"No. But I do recall that time with the rabbit poop. I remember painting all those little balls. God, it'd disgust me now. Imagine. I was actually picking up shit with my bare hands." She laughed. "What a disgusting kid."

I laughed too.

"The weird thing is, you never think you are when it's happening to you," Sheila added. "I remember being really serious about painting those things."

"What about Chad?" I asked. "My boyfriend, the one who defended you at the hearing? Remember him?" I asked, but before she could answer I grinned. "Guess what? He's married now and he has three kids. And guess what he's named his oldest girl?"

A blank look. "No idea."

"Sheila."

"After me?" she asked in amazement.

"Yes, after you. I mean, he thought the world of you. We had such a marvelous time that night after the hearing."

A pause followed. Sheila glanced down again at the pages in her hand and appeared to be reading the top one for a moment. "Shit. Shit. This is just so weird. I can't get over it."

"Weird in what way?"

"I dunno. Seeing my name here. It's somebody else here, really, but it's me, too."

"You don't think I've done it right?" I asked.

"Well, no, not that . . . Maybe it's just seeing myself as a character in a book. . . . I mean, mega-weird." Another pause. "*You* seem real enough. This is just like I remember you. Reading this makes me feel like I've been sitting down and having a nice chat with you, but . . . Was that class really this way?"

"How do you remember it?" I asked.

"Mostly, I don't. Like I said last week . . ."

Silence again.

What entered my mind as I listened into the silence was the horrible nature of some of the things that had happened to Sheila over the course of the time she was in my room. In bringing the book here for her approval, I hadn't given serious consideration to the possibility that she might have dealt with her past by forcing it from memory. Such a reaction seemed un-Sheila-like to me and I hadn't anticipated it from her. Now, suddenly, I feared for what I had done. It was an upbeat story, but that was from my point of view.

Turning her head, Sheila gazed out the window beside her bed. It was an insignificant view—the side of the neighboring house, its gray-green paint peeling, the neighbor's window, a venetian blind hanging crookedly across it. She seemed to study it.

I, in turn, studied her with her long, straggly orange hair, her thin, undeveloped body clad in torn jeans and a rather strange, clingy gray top that looked like a piece of my grandpa's underwear. This gangly punk fashion plate wasn't quite what I had expected to find and I was having to fight the disappointment.

"What I remember are the colors," she said very softly, her tone introspective. "As if my whole life had been in black and white, and then I went in that classroom . . . Bright colors." She made a little sound. "I always think of them as Fisher-Price colors, you know? The toys? Fisher-Price red and blue and white. All those primary colors. Remember that riding horse you could sit on and move around by pushing with your feet? *That's* what I remember. Every single color of him. Of sitting at the table when I was supposed to be working and looking at his colors. And where it said 'Fisher-Price' on him. God, I wanted that horse so bad. I used to dream about that horse, about how it was mine, that you let me take it home and keep it."

I probably would have, had she ever said it meant that much to her, but she never did.

"And that parking garage," she said. "Remember that? With all those little cars that'd go down the ramps and those little people who didn't even look like people. They were just plastic pegs with faces, really. Remember how I used to steal them? I was so desperate to have them. I used to line them up on the floor beside where I slept, this whole line of them—the guy in the black top hat, the guy in the cowboy hat, the Indian chief—do you remember me taking them?"

Over the years there had been so many toys in so many class-rooms. I remembered garage sets and riding horses, but they could have been any of a dozen such I had had.

"You never got mad at me for it," she said, turning to look at me. She smiled. "I kept stealing them and stealing them and you never got angry with me."

In the hurly-burly of that class, truth was, I probably hadn't even noticed she was doing it.

"That's what seems so weird to me about this book, Torey. You make out like we're always fighting. Like, in it you seem to be getting mad at me about every other page. I don't remember you *ever* doing that."

I looked at her in surprise.

Then she wrinkled her nose and grinned conspiratorially. "Are you just spicing it up, like? So they'll want to publish it?"

My jaw dropped.

"I mean, I don't mind at all. It's a terribly good story. And, like, it's brilliant, thinking of myself as a character in a book."

"But, Sheila, we *did* fight. We fought all the time. When you came into my class, you—"

Again she turned to look out of the window. Silence ensued and it lasted several moments.

"What exactly *do* you recall?" I asked at last.

"Like I said . . ." And then she didn't say. She was still gazing out of the window and the words just seemed to fade away. A minute or more passed.

"We *did* fight," I said softly. "Everybody fights, whatever the relationship, however good it might be. It wouldn't *be* a relationship otherwise, because two separate people are coming together. Friction is a natural part of that."

No response.

"Besides," I said and grinned, "I was a teacher. What would you expect?"

"Yeah, well," she said, "I don't really remember."

✻   ✻   ✻

I couldn't come to terms with the fact Sheila had forgotten so much. Driving home on the freeway that evening, I turned it over and over in my mind. How *could* she forget Anton and Whitney? How could the whole experience be reduced to nothing more than a fond recollection of colorful plastic toys? This hurt me. It had been such a significant experience for me that I had assumed it had been at least as significant for her. In fact, I had assumed it was probably more significant. Without me, that class, those five months, Sheila most likely would now be on the back ward of some state hospital. I had *made a difference*. At least that's what I'd been telling myself. My cheeks began to burn hot, even in the privacy of my car, as I realized the gross arrogance of my assumption. I was further humbled by the insight that those five months might well now mean more to me than to her.

She had been only a very young child. Was I being unrealistic in expecting her to remember much? At the time she had been so exquisitely articulate that it had given her the gloss of a maturity even then I knew she didn't really have, but I had been accustomed to associating verbal ability with good memory.

As I sped through the darkness, I tried to recollect being six myself. I could bring to mind the names of some of the children in my first-grade class, but mostly it was incidents I could recall. There were a lot of small snippets: a moment lining up for recess, a classmate vomiting into the trash can, a fight over the swings, a feeling of pride because I drew good trees. They weren't very complete recollections, but if I tried, I could identify the locations and the names and appearance of the individuals involved. Still, they were nothing akin to the clarity of my memories as an adult. I was probably being unrealistic in expecting her to remember more.

Yet, it nagged at me. Sheila wasn't just any child, but a highly gifted girl who had blown the top right off almost every IQ test the school psychologist had given her that year. Sheila's prodigious memory had been among the most notable of many outstanding characteristics. She had used it like a crystal ball for gazing in, as she spoke to us all so poignantly, so eloquently of love and hate and rejection.

Love and hate and rejection. It couldn't be all arrogance on my part to expect that she should be remembering more. Her amnesia seemed so uncharacteristic, but still, it was not hard to imagine what might be causing it. Although I didn't know any specifics about what had happened since Sheila had left my room, I knew these hadn't been easy years in between. She had been in and out of foster homes, had moved to different schools and coped with her father's instability. If these years only half mirrored the nightmare she

ten

At home, I rummaged through the things I had accumulated from the class, which I had used to write the book, looking for things to take with me on my next visit to see Sheila. The vast majority of the materials were just school papers and anecdotal records, neither very useful for the purpose. What I really wanted to share were the videotapes, but this was in the era of the old reel-to-reel videotapes and the only machine I had for playing them on was at the clinic; so those would have to wait for the time when Sheila came in to visit me. In the end, I resorted to going through my picture album.

I had surprisingly few photographs of that year. There was the class picture, all of us lined up against the blue curtain on the school stage, looking like felons in a group mug shot. The camera had caught Sheila full on, washing out her pale features. She wouldn't smile on demand in those days, so she had just a blank stare. Unfortunately, several others in the class had been equally uncooperative and many of them were consequently rendered unrecognizable.

In total, I had only three other photographs of Sheila and these included the individual school picture, taken at the same time as the group photo. I had kept this one, as her father had declined to buy it. It was the only one I'd ever had of her smiling. Normally, she'd simply refused to smile for cameras, but on this occasion, the photographer had tricked her into it while trying to get her to grab his pen. Taken only a short time after she had arrived in our classroom, it caught her full grubby glory and I adored it.

The other two photographs I had taken myself. One was to commemorate the first time I'd really gotten her cleaned up and she sat in deep solemnity on the school steps, hands clasped upon her knees. Her hair was combed smooth and put into pigtails; her clothes were washed; her face was cleaned; and the truth was, it didn't look like

Sheila at all. She was not nearly so engaging as the filthy character in the school photograph. The other picture I had taken on the last day of school when the class had gone down to the park for our end-of-school picnic. I had taken several photographs that day, but unfortunately, Sheila was in only one of them. She was standing beside the duck pond with two of the other little girls in the class. Both of them were neat and clean and beaming cheerfully, but Sheila, in the middle, stared back at the camera with a guarded, almost suspicious gaze. Despite the new orange sunsuit her father had bought for the occasion, she had come to school very scruffy that day, her long hair uncombed, her face unwashed, and she stood in stark contrast to her two classmates. There was a compelling aspect to the photograph, however. It was the wariness of her expression, which made her seem fierce and yet surprisingly vulnerable.

I decided in the end to take that photograph, as well as the others taken on that day, which showed the other children, Anton and Whitney.

The following Saturday, Sheila and I went to watch her father's baseball team play. They were an inauspicious-looking group, those boys. Grubby ten- and eleven-year-olds dressed in mismatched uniforms, they were almost all minority kids from a mixture of backgrounds, united, I suspect, only by their poverty. But they were noisy and cheerful in the way of all children, and they greeted Sheila's father like a returning champion when he ran out onto the baseball diamond.

From all I could gather, Mr. Renstad appeared to be doing well. He was enormously proud of the small duplex where they lived. It wasn't large; it wasn't in a particularly good part of town, and he didn't own it, of course; but he had *chosen* it himself, rather than have it foisted upon him by Social Services. Moreover, he was paying the rent himself out of the steady salary he now earned as a laborer for the parks department. He had taken me right through the duplex, showing me each and every thing he had managed to buy— the beds, the sofa, the television, the kitchen table. *He* certainly remembered the circumstances in which we had last met, and he was enthusiastic to show me how far he had come in the interim. These things were his and I could tell acquiring them meant a lot to him.

His real love, however, was the baseball team—"his boys." Again and again, he told me how it was they who had made him go straight for good. They depended on him, he said. The team had nearly been disbanded for lack of a coach until he took over. More to the point, he admitted, he would lose them if he messed with drugs again. He was still under the watchful eye of the parole officer.

I enjoyed that baseball game. They didn't win, but they played well and it was apparent that winning wasn't so important to them. They *were* a team, in the true sense of the word, and I identified immediately with that. Whatever his past, Mr. Renstad's present was going well.

I'd made plans to take Sheila out after the game. On the other two occasions I'd come to her house, so I thought it would be pleasant to go somewhere with her. Sheila, however, was unable to decide where she wanted to go.

I suggested we go for a pizza. I thought I might take her up to the city, partly to give her a change of scenery, and partly because there were nicer places to eat up there. So after the game, we got into the car and headed north.

Somewhere within the first five miles, I took a wrong turn. As I was still learning my way around this new area, this wasn't unusual; however, I didn't realize I'd done it until the thinning houses made me suspicious that I was not going toward the city. Normally I have an excellent sense of direction, and while I do take wrong turns, even then I can usually discern if I'm going in the right general direction. On this occasion, I managed to get myself completely turned around, because while I still felt that I was going toward the city, evidence outside my window said otherwise. I voiced my concern to Sheila.

"No, you're all right. I know exactly where you're at. Just keep driving this way," she said confidently. So I did.

Another fifteen minutes and I hit open country. I knew I was irredeemably lost and knew I wasn't going to right myself without taking drastic action, probably in the form of stopping and digging out the road map. I pulled the car over into a gateway to a field.

"What are you doing?" Sheila asked in surprise.

Reaching my arm over the backseat, I groped for my road atlas. "Looking for the map. I'm lost."

"No, you're not."

"We're lost."

"No, we're not. I've been out here millions of times."

I raised an eyebrow.

"Yeah, I have," she said. "I used to be in a children's home near here. Just down that road over there. I know exactly where we are."

"So, where are we then?" I asked.

"Well, here, of course."

"But *where's* here?"

Sheila looked out the window.

"Tell me. Where are we?"

"Don't get so bitchy."

"You don't know either, do you?" I said. "We are lost."

Unexpectedly, Sheila smiled. It was a beguiling smile. "I'm always lost," she said cheerfully. "I've gotten used to it."

I tugged the atlas over into the front seat and opened it. Locating us on the map, I discovered where I had turned wrong and figured out what I would need to do when eventually we headed back to Broadview. "Okay. I'm happy now," I said, closing the book. I started the engine.

"You're really a control freak, aren't you?" Sheila said. "I never realized that about you before."

"Not really. It's just I feel uncomfortable when I'm disoriented."

"Ah, not only a control freak, a defensive control freak."

*   *   *

If she wanted to go in this direction, I thought, well and good, we'd go. So we took off down a minor highway in a direction I'd never been before. The better part of an hour raced past, along with the scenery.

It was a pleasant drive. Sheila talked, launching into a most amazing conversation about Julius Caesar. She had read his account of the Gallic wars in Latin class and this caught her fancy, particularly his descriptions of the native Celts in Gaul. I had done Caesar myself when I had taken Latin in high school, but in those days I had been more interested to see if I could get good grades without having to read the assignments, rather than find out what the books actually said. Consequently, I had emerged from school clever but culturally illiterate and had spent most of my adult life catching up.

I hadn't managed to work myself around to Caesar yet in Latin or English, so for most of the conversation I just listened, which was probably no bad thing.

Passing through a small town, Sheila spotted a bowling alley. "Oh, look, there! Could we stop and play a game? I love bowling."

So we went in and had three games. Afterward, I bought us Cokes in the bar. "What about pizza?" Sheila asked. "You said we could get pizza."

"I'm thinking we might be better going back toward Broadview. We're quite a ways out and it's going to take a good hour and a half to get back. I'd probably find my way back better if it weren't pitch dark."

"God, Torey, do you get lost a lot or something? You are really hung up on it."

"I'm driving, that's why."

"So, relax. We're okay. And let's eat around here. It's late and I'm starving."

"I haven't seen a pizza place," I replied.

"Well, let's just keep driving."

I was hungry too and finding myself in a not particularly good mood. The day wasn't working out quite as I had planned. We had wandered from one thing to another, with none of it being very special. I became aware of wanting to impress Sheila. I wanted to win her over.

"There! There!" Sheila called out, interrupting my thoughts. "There's a pizza place."

Sure enough, there was. And like the rest of the day, it was nothing special. I thought of the old days and how my boyfriend Chad and I had taken Sheila out for her very first pizza after the hearing that had kept Sheila out of the state hospital. The place we went into now had none of the jazz-piano atmosphere of that pizzeria; this was just a branch of one of the faceless pizza chains found everywhere.

Too hungry to care, I stopped there and we went in. Placing our order at the counter, we then located a quiet table in the corner. Sheila pulled off her baseball cap, letting her long, crinkled orange hair spill down over her shoulders, and she sat down.

"I thought you might like to see some pictures from our class," I said, opening my handbag, "so I dug some out."

"Like, cool. Let's see."

"They're from that picnic we had on the last day. We went over to the park. Do you remember that park? It had that duck pond and the little stream."

Taking the photographs from me, Sheila bent over them, studying the faces. "Who's this kid?"

"Emilio."

"What's wrong with him? Is he handicapped?"

"He's blind," I said.

"Oh, yeah, the blind one. What did you call him in the book?"

"Guillermo."

"Oh, yeah, I know who you're talking about now."

Tongue protruding slightly between her lips, Sheila remained intent on the photos. "I think I remember that park," she said slowly. "Did it have trees that bloomed or something? They had a really sweet scent? Because I seem to remember that."

"Yes. The locust trees."

"Who are these girls?" she asked, handing over one of the pictures.

"Don't you recognize her? In the middle? That's you. That's Sarah and that's Tyler, but that there is you."

"*Really?* God, is that me? Shit." She craned forward to study it more closely in the dim light. "*Shit.* Did I really look like that?" She looked up in amazement. "My dad doesn't have any pictures of me when I was little . . ."

My heart sank. She didn't even remember herself. Watching her as she bent back over the photos, I felt so lonely. What was I doing here with this punky-looking adolescent? This wasn't Sheila. This was just some kid.

The pizza came just in time. We had ordered a huge one, loaded with everything save the proverbial kitchen sink, and we both tucked in enthusiastically. For several moments our attention was focused on the food.

"I've had so much fun today," Sheila said as she maneuvered most of a full slice of pizza into her mouth. "You know, I think it's brilliant that you live so close by now."

"Good, I'm glad."

"It's just like the old times, isn't it?"

"Yeah," I said, probably not too convincingly.

Sheila's expression grew rather sheepish. "I'm sorry I don't remember more about when I was in your class."

"Well, you were little."

"Yeah, but I can tell I'm, like, a real disappointment to you."

"Of course not!" I said a little too heartily. "You were *very* young when we were last together and nobody remembers much from that age."

"But you want me to, don't you?"

"Yes, if I'm honest, I suppose I do, but just because it was a meaningful year for me and it was you who made it meaningful."

This disarmed her. She smiled. "Really?"

"Yes, really."

"You liked working with little kids, didn't you?" she said.

I nodded. "I still do."

"It showed."

Silence came then and we went back to our food. Then Sheila looked up.

"Can I ask you something, Tor? It's from the book."

"All right."

"How come you didn't marry that guy Chad?" she asked.

"I was too young. I wasn't ready," I said. "If I had, it wouldn't have worked out."

Pensive over her pizza, Sheila picked at it, ferreting out the olives and eating them with her fingers. "Too bad," she said. "It would have made for a brilliant ending to your book."

"Probably, but this was real life."

"Real life never follows the script, that's the problem," she replied. "You and him getting married and adopting the little girl. That's how every single person who reads it is going to want it to come out."

"Yes, I know, but it isn't how it did come out."

"Yeah, I know." She smiled faintly. "But you know, his eldest daughter? The one called Sheila? Well, that's right. She should be called Sheila, but by rights, she should have been me."

eleven

The summer program at the clinic had been my idea. I had always felt there was a better chance of effecting change when I was with a child several hours a day, day in, day out, rather than in just one or two hourly sessions, which was one of my original reasons for choosing teaching over psychology as a career. This was borne out to me at the clinic, which was the first place I'd worked that stuck so strictly to the fifty-minute "psychiatric hour." I felt there must be some other way.

My office partner, Jeff, was intrigued with the idea of working with children in a different setting from the therapy room; so together we developed the idea of a morning summer-school program to run for eight weeks in June and July. We made plans to use a nearby school that was normally vacant over the summer, and from the clinic client list, we began to handpick the children we felt would benefit most. Because of the experimental nature, we decided to keep the number modest. It was just Jeff and I supervising, and I thought it was best to start out with something I knew we could keep in control. Thus, we settled on having eight.

In the group, three of the children were severely handicapped. Joshua, five, and Jessie, six, were both autistic and couldn't speak, and Violet, eight, was labeled a childhood schizophrenic. Of the five remaining, there were two girls, Kayleigh, a five-year-old who persistently refused to speak in group settings, and Tamara, eight, a startlingly beautiful girl with dark, exotic features, who suffered from depression and bouts of self-mutilation. Of the three boys, there was David, a bright, beguiling six-year-old arsonist, Alejo, a seven-year-old Colombian boy who had been adopted at four by American parents, and a six-year-old tornado named Mikey.

Experience had long since taught me that the higher the adult-to-child ratio, the more effective a program generally is. I didn't want a one-to-one situation, as I felt this would destroy the benefits of the group, but I felt we needed enough adults in charge to minimize the chance of any given situation degenerating into total chaos.

Jeff took umbrage at the idea that we couldn't handle eight children between us. He pointed out that he was, after all, a fully qualified doctor, ready to sit for his final board exams in child psychiatry, and well on his way to certification as a psychoanalyst. I pointed out in turn that this setting required rather different skills. Over the course of the three hours each day that the children were with us, they would need not only therapy, but entertainment, exercise, refereeing and nurturing, to say nothing of Band-Aids, drinks, snacks and taking to the toilet. This was more than two adults could sanely do, if we wanted to accomplish something more than baby-sitting.

Thus, together we approached Dr. Rosenthal to fund us more staff for the project. He agreed to do the best he could. As a result, we gained Miriam, a former teacher. She was an older woman, lively and decisive, with silvery hair and an enviable figure. I liked her instantly. She had a sensible, down-to-earth approach, but with that touch of class I admired but didn't possess myself. Yet, even with Miriam added to our staff, I was still eager for more help. With such young, handicapped children, we didn't need many expensive, highly trained professionals. We just needed *hands*, real hands, plain and simple.

I was editing *One Child* during the period when Jeff and I were setting up the summer-school program, and the contrast of reading about my situation with Sheila's class in comparison to the luxury I was currently working in struck me dramatically. There were eight children then, every bit as severely handicapped, and what did we have but a young, fairly inexperienced teacher, an ex-migrant worker without a high school diploma and a junior high student. Junior high student. *Junior high student!*

Sheila! Of course.

This seemed an ideal solution. Old enough to be responsible, yet young enough to be flexible and cooperative, Sheila was at an age to be very useful in a setting like this. In return, it would give her the chance to spend the summer in a structured, stimulating environment with supportive adults. Best of all, it would allow the two of us to spend time together in a natural way. I wanted to get to know Sheila again. The child I had loved so much had to be somewhere in that gangly adolescent. I wanted the chance to seek her out.

Sheila was delighted with this proposition. She had had no work lined up for the summer and even when I explained that the pay would be very small indeed, covering not much more than her bus fare and lunch, she remained enthusiastic.

Jeff didn't have a chance to meet Sheila before the first day of the summer program. We had discussed the need for an extra pair of hands and he had been pleased that I could come up with a volunteer so easily. I gave him a brief summary of Sheila's background and my previous relationship with her, but I didn't go into great detail, as it seemed inappropriate. If anything had become obvious to me over the previous weeks, it was that Sheila had moved on from her former self; and just as I would not have expected an employer to take into account what I had done when I was six, I didn't feel it was necessary to discuss her background.

Privately, I was looking forward to introducing Sheila to Jeff. In the summer-school program, Sheila'd find herself surrounded by adults who were all intellectually formidable, but among us only Jeff was probably Sheila's equal. I doubted she had previously encountered another person of her ability, and as a consequence, I was keen to acquaint them. Both showed similar personalities, given to quirky, somewhat unpredictable behavior, and both emanated that aura of isolation so common to highly gifted individuals. I was tickled to think of the possibilities in bringing them together.

*   *   *

On the first day, Sheila arrived forty-five minutes early. What she was wearing looked—honest to God—like thin white long johns. Over this she had layered a pale-colored, flower-sprigged shift. To complete the outfit, she'd laced on heavy, black work boots more befitting of a lumberjack. And, of course, on her head was the ever-present Cubs baseball hat.

I gaped. I'm embarrassed to admit it, I, who has cultivated the ability to disregard the most bizarre of behaviors, but my mouth dropped right open.

"Like it?" she asked ingenuously.

God, was I getting old? Was this what teenagers were wearing now and I hadn't noticed? I was dressed in a pair of Levi's and a work shirt and thought I was being avant-garde at the clinic. "Well," I sputtered, "it's unique."

"My dad doesn't let me wear things I like."

"Where did you get it?" I asked.

"Different places. I got this dress at a rummage sale and I got these down at the Goodwill place," she said, indicating the long-john things. "They didn't cost me much. My boots cost me the most."

I found myself startled. The ghost of that six-year-old in her ratty brown T-shirt and outgrown overalls still haunted me. I had been unprepared for this adolescent fashion plate.

"You don't mind, do you?" she asked and I realized that for her to ask, she must have read my surprise.

I shook my head. "No, I don't mind." And I suppose I didn't, really. The fact was, she looked surprisingly good in her long johns and little flowered dress. Weird, yes, but still attractive, if one suspended personal taste and just looked at her. And confident. That's what really struck me. For the moment, anyway, Sheila was clearly very pleased with who she was.

Jeff arrived shortly afterward. He was carrying a huge box of Pampers. "Yo, catch, Hayden!" he shouted and lofted the box at me. Sheila leaped back in surprise as I lunged to catch it. I set it on the ground.

"What are those for?" she asked.

"Help, help! Let me out!" came a little voice from the direction of the box.

Sheila looked alarmed and I thumped Jeff's arm. "This is Dr. Tomlinson's sense of humor."

"Jeff to you, sweetheart," he said and chucked Sheila under the chin. "Like your outfit."

Sheila recoiled from his touch.

I grabbed the box of Pampers and took them into the book closet alongside the room. Sheila followed.

"Is that your office partner you're always talking about? That's Jeff?"

I nodded and pushed the box up onto a shelf.

"Yuck."

"Oh, he's all right. Got a weird sense of humor, but he's good fun. You'll like him."

"Don't count on it." She leaned back against the wall. "How come you've got those diapers?"

"Because one little boy isn't toilet trained yet," I replied.

"You're kidding. You mean he shits in his pants?" she asked.

I smiled.

"Oh, gross. You didn't tell me this. I'm not going to have to change him, am I?"

"We'll see."

"We *won't* see," she replied. "We shall close our eyes!"

I laughed.

*   *   *

The first child to arrive was Violet. She was a large girl for her age, although not really fat, with pallid skin and pale, crumpled hair. Her clinical diagnosis was childhood schizophrenia, manifested by an obsessional interest in ghosts and vampires. She believed all the people around her were either vampires or the victims of vampires, hence, ghosts, and she had much trouble with invisible ghosts talking to her, teasing her and telling her awful things.

"Shhh," she said to me, as her mother brought her in. "I saw him in the hallway, the one with the rainbow-colored hair. He had his ghost cat with him."

"Sheila, could you show Violet where to sit down?" I asked.

"Not going with her!" Violet shrieked. "She's got fangs!"

Eyes wide, Sheila looked over at me.

"Here, I'll take her," said Jeff. She was his client and when she saw a face she recognized, Violet relaxed visibly.

Just then, in whooshed Mikey. Mikey was six, short and stout, and capable of moving at light-speed. This gave him the appearance more of a ball than a boy, rather like the sort used in pinball. Zip! Bang! Whoosh! He careered around the classroom, leaving all of us stunned in his wake. His mother looked only too relieved to be rid of him for the morning.

Next came Kayleigh, my elective mute. In contrast to Violet, Kayleigh was tiny for her age, her small features overpowered by long, thick bangs and a heavy mass of hair. It was in the back of my mind that Kayleigh might be a good child for Sheila to work with individually, as Sheila herself had been electively mute when she had come into my class at six. Moreover, Kayleigh had a sweet, loving nature, which made her easy to like and pleasant to work with. I was keen for Sheila to enjoy the challenge of being with us and longed for her to understand my own attachment to such children; so Kayleigh seemed an ideal choice.

"Sheila, do you suppose you could take Kayleigh over to the table and show her some of our toys?"

Sheila just stared at the girl.

"Kayleigh loves putting puzzles together. Perhaps you could help her do one while we're waiting for the rest of the children to arrive."

Uncertainly, Sheila held out her hand. Kayleigh responded with a delighted smile.

Joshua and David arrived together in a car pool driven by Joshua's father. Of all of our children, Joshua was the most severely handicapped. It was he we had the diapers for. Diagnosed at eighteen months as autistic, Joshua neither spoke nor engaged people in any other way.

David was Joshua's opposite number. Smily and gregarious, he could worm his way into the coldest heart. And he was such a lady-killer with his big blue eyes and curly blond hair. In truth, I think he was one of the most appealing-looking children I had come across. He was also one of the most disturbed.

Alejo came next. He was a new child at the clinic, having started only at the beginning of April, and he was seeing Dr. Freeman, so I didn't know him personally. His parents, a wealthy professional couple who had been childless through sixteen years of marriage, had decided to adopt a Third World orphan when it finally became apparent to them that they would not bear a child of their own. On a trip to Colombia, they found Alejo, then age four, in an orphanage run by a group of nuns. Adopted and brought to the United States, he had now been with his current family for almost three years, but he had never really settled into his new suburban surroundings. He was restless and aggressive and, although he had learned English, he spoke only rarely, preferring his fists to do his talking. His school performance had been uniformly poor and there was now a question of whether his deprived early life had caused permanent brain damage. Alejo himself was a small, rather unattractive boy with thick black-rimmed glasses. He had the flat features of the native South American Indians and a thatch of unruly dark hair that fell forward into his face. He appeared shy in the midst of so many strangers and clung tightly to his father's hand until Jeff came and knelt down beside him.

Behind Alejo came Jessie. A small black girl with her hair meticulously corn-rowed, she, like Joshua, was autistic. She was not as severely afflicted as Joshua and could talk after a fashion. Recognizing this as a school, she ran past us all to the table, sat down in one of the chairs and began drumming loudly with her hands while shouting out the alphabet song.

Last to arrive was Tamara. Of Mediterranean lineage, with long black hair and huge, soulful dark eyes, she reminded me rather uncannily of the opera singer Maria Callas, which gave me trouble the entire eight weeks in keeping her name straight. Now eight, Tamara had been coming to the clinic for over two years, ever since her parents had first noticed the myriad of small cuts along her arms. Despite intensive therapy, Tamara continued her obsession with self-mutilation. Consequently, she arrived that warm summer's morning wearing a long-sleeved T-shirt and jogging-suit bottoms to cover the myriad of sores and scabs on her arms and legs and to discourage her attempts to create more.

So we started. Like all first days, it was a bit chaotic; however, we had planned well to provide an engaging but low-key morning. Thus, there were no disasters.

Sheila befriended Kayleigh, or perhaps it was Kayleigh who befriended her. Whichever, Sheila spent most of the morning with the little girl, helping her with her activities, taking her to the toilet, finding good cookies for her at snack time. As part of my ongoing therapy with Kayleigh, I had insisted she speak to Sheila from the onset, which she did with only a little urging.

This is right, I thought, watching the two of them together at one of the tables, their heads bent over what they were doing. Sheila was talking to her, pausing occasionally to glance over at the child. Seven years earlier, she had been that small girl. There was something deeply rewarding in seeing her come full circle.

Indeed, as I stood there surveying the group, I became aware of how very happy I felt at that particular moment. The morning was going well; the program was off to a good start. The children were challenging but engaging. Jeff was my absolute favorite colleague to work with in the whole world. When we were getting fired up, the two of us could operate as one mind in two bodies, challenging, growing, building upon one another's ideas so easily that everything felt possible to me. Miriam, whom I had not known previously, was full of energetic initiative and had a far better sense of organization than either Jeff or I. Consequently, all the small things, like finding the paper cups at break time, happened as they should. Best of all, there was Sheila, back in the classroom with me and it was the first day, with all the future stretching ahead of us. I regarded her. It *was* Sheila there. For the first time since we had been reunited, I felt certain of that.

twelve

After the morning ended and all the children had gone home, the four of us went out to lunch. Miriam, who lived locally, suggested a whole-food restaurant down by the lake and so we found ourselves on benches gathered around a wooden plank table in the cool interior of the restaurant.

We discussed the morning's events, evaluating how the various activities had gone and making plans to adjust them as necessary. Sheila didn't say much, even when we went over our observations of Kayleigh in the group. She appeared absorbed in a tradescantia hanging in the window beside our table, its long branches stretching down to a point where she could fiddle with them.

After lunch, I offered to drive her the five miles down to Fenton Boulevard, where she could catch a direct bus back to Broadview.

"So, what did you think?" I asked, once we were alone in the car together.

Sheila was silent for several moments. "I don't like your partner very much. What's all this crap about regression motivating neuroses and stuff?"

"Jeff's a Freudian. You've got to excuse him that."

"It's crap. Why doesn't he just talk English?" Sheila asked.

"Freud's ideas have had very wide-ranging applications. While a lot of people don't agree with all of them anymore, they've still done a great deal to help us understand how minds might work. And people like Jeff, who have really studied the theories, seem to make good progress using them."

Sheila raised her lip in an expression of disgust.

We went a few moments in silence before I looked over again. "So, Jeff excepted, what did you think? Did you like it? Did you enjoy working with Kayleigh?"

"Yeah, pretty much. Why doesn't she talk?" she asked, her head turned away from me to watch out the window. "And not Jeff's kind of explanation. Not 'cause she's got an anal fixation or something."

"I don't know why."

"I told her that when I was her age, I didn't talk either," Sheila said.

"Did Kayleigh respond to that?" I asked.

"Dunno. She just kept coloring." There was a pause. "I wanted to ask you about that other kid. The kid with the Spanish name."

"Alejo?"

"Yeah. What's wrong with him?"

"He's very difficult at school. He fights with the other kids all the time, quite a vicious little boy, and he does very poorly at his work. We're trying to determine at the clinic whether this is as a result of psychological problems or a mental handicap."

"Jeff said he's adopted."

"Yes. He's from Colombia."

"Where are his real parents?" Sheila asked.

"I don't know. I don't think anybody knows. He was abandoned. The report I read said that someone had found him living in a garbage can and had then taken him to these nuns who ran the orphanage."

Forehead puckered, Sheila looked over. "Really?"

"Apparently there are a lot of street kids in some of these South American cities. It's a serious problem in some places."

"His folks abandoned him in a garbage can?"

"Maybe he was just sheltering in one. I don't know. The report's pretty scant and probably about fifth-hand."

Sheila was pensive a long moment, before turning back. "Did I hear you guys saying that the parents he's got now were going to send him back to where he came from?"

"I don't know. There's some talk of it. They're an older couple, both professionals, not very used to accommodating children, and he's been quite a handful."

"Can they really do that?" Sheila asked. "Just send him back to Colombia, like he was damaged goods or something?"

"I guess."

Then came silence. Plagued by red lights and roadwork, I wasn't making very speedy progress toward Fenton Boulevard. Sheila leaned her head against the window and gazed out. She looked tired. Had it been the rigors of the morning? Or had she come tired? The thought suddenly struck me that I was taking the stability of Sheila's home life for granted. Sneaking a look, I studied her. God, that orange hair!

"I think . . . well, I guess I can see now what got you attracted to this kind of work," she said, her voice quiet and rather distant-sounding. " 'Cause you hear about these things happening to people, and they are so unfair that they make you feel you just got to do something. That's my reaction, anyway." She paused. "Well, that's one reaction."

"What's the other?" I asked.

"I just want to put my hands over my eyes and my fingers in my ears and stop it from getting in. I mean, I already know the world's bad. I'm not sure I can stand knowing it's really worse."

*   *   *

Our first "incident" happened the next morning. The school was across the street from a small park. It wasn't an elaborate place, but there were swings and a large wooden structure built for climbing and plenty of room for running around. What made it particularly hospitable on a hot summer's morning were the trees. There were a dozen or more, with enormous trunks and long, overhanging branches. Some particularly forward-thinking person in the parks department had had attractive wooden seating built around three of the trees nearest the play equipment.

We decided to take our juice and cookies outside and let the children play on the swings and climbing frame during their break time. David and Mikey thought this was wonderful and went tearing off at such a rate that Jeff had to run after them and catch them before they went into the street.

Although I had agreed happily when Jeff had suggested that we take the children over to the park at break time, I realized the moment David and Mikey ran off that it was a mistake. We were all too new to each other. But by that time, we were already underway.

Right from the beginning, it was small-scale chaos of the sort that kids adore and grown-ups abhor. Joshua went into a self-stimulated frenzy on the swings. Jessie just stood on the grass, arms out, and spun dizzyingly around and around. David, Mikey and Alejo immediately fell into playing some dreadfully noisy war game that required an enormous amount of tearing around and much shouted large-artillery fire. Violet appeared to get rather turned on by this. I couldn't tell if she simply wanted to join in and did not have the appropriate social skills to get the boys to include her, or whether she found it all genuinely sexually stimulating. Whichever, she began to indulge in open masturbation, while shouting out cheers and gunfire noises to the boys as they tore by.

Needless to say, our break time was quickly turned into a rowdy, deafening affair. Only Kayleigh and Tamara did not join in. Clinging to Miriam's hand, Kayleigh watched the other children apprehensively. Tamara, on the other hand, didn't seem particularly frightened by the mayhem, but she withdrew away from all of us. Taking her paper cup of juice and her cookies, she went off into a cubbyhole formed by tires on the underside of the climbing structure.

After fifteen minutes, Jeff and I went to herd everyone back together, while Miriam sat down on one of the benches and tried to keep hold of those we had captured. Sheila proved fairly hopeless. Whether it was the noise or the sudden hyperactivity around her, I don't know, but she simply froze in the midst of it all and the more I shouted at her to go get one child or another, the more solidly she seemed to be rooted to her spot.

One by one, we rounded them up, until we only had David, Mikey and Tamara left. I was chasing David down when I heard Jeff cry out. "Oh, my God!"

We all stopped then and looked over. He was extracting Tamara from her tires and as she stood up, I saw she was covered in blood. While the rest of us had been absorbed elsewhere, Tamara had taken the opportunity her privacy afforded her to gouge long lines into the skin along her jaw with a small, sharp stick she had picked up from the mulch put down to cushion falls from the climbing frame. They were not particularly deep cuts, but they bled dramatically.

Then, abruptly, from the group of children with Miriam, frantic screaming started up. Instinct told me it was Violet and I spun around, but it wasn't. It was Alejo. Seeing Tamara's blood, he put a hand to either side of his face and screamed and screamed. I ran toward him, but this seemed to make matters worse. Shrieking incoherently, he fled across the grass until he came to one of the other trees and then, like a little monkey, he swarmed right up it and into the branches.

We all stood there, stunned. Even Tamara, Jeff's handkerchief pressed to her face, gazed up in amazement. Alejo kept climbing until he must have been the better part of fifty feet in the air.

"Oh, Jesus," Jeff muttered. "What now?"

I glanced around us and then back up in the tree. "Alejo? Are you all right?"

He wasn't screaming any longer, wasn't doing anything other than standing on a branch and looking down at us.

"It's okay. Everything's fine here. Nothing wrong with Tamara. She just scratched herself. But it's nothing serious. Why don't you come on down now?" I called.

"Alejo?" Jeff said. "It's time to come down."

He didn't budge.

"You reckon I can climb up?" I asked Jeff.

"Don't be stupid, Hayden."

Miriam was beside us now. She was holding Kayleigh in her arms. "How about the fire department? Do they do these kinds of things?"

I looked around at the others just in time to see Joshua strolling out into the road. "Oh, cripes. Josh? Come here, Josh." I ran after him. Snagging him by the T-shirt, I hauled him back into the group. It was then I noticed Sheila sitting on the ground. She was unlacing her work boots.

"I can get him," she said, and before any of us had a chance to protest, Sheila had leaped into the branches and was pulling herself up.

"Oh, God," Jeff cried, "*two* of them up there. Why did you let her do that, Hayden?"

"Well, at least we've got a doctor on the premises."

Then silence, as we all watched.

"We're gonna get sued out of our lives . . ." I heard Jeff mutter under his breath.

Sheila climbed the tree with no difficulty, shimmying up through the branches as easily as Alejo had done until she reached the one just beneath him. I heard her talking to him, but I couldn't discern what she was saying.

Minutes went by. All the while I was racking my brains for the best solution, as no doubt Jeff was doing as well. Should we call the fire department? The police? Dr. Rosenthal? Alejo's parents? Or could we risk just waiting him out? What about the other children? It was only ten forty-five and the program ran for another hour and forty-five minutes. Should Miriam and I take the rest back in and try to pretend everything was normal?

Then, just as I was about to suggest phoning for help, I saw Sheila begin to descend, and within a few moments, Alejo started down behind her. Jeff, Miriam and I all sighed a collective sigh of relief.

"Hey, you're a hero," Jeff said to Sheila as we all finally started back to the school. He reached an arm out and slipped it over her shoulder. "You really did great there. I bet you're proud of yourself."

Nodding, Sheila ducked to free herself of his touch.

*   *   *

"I hope you *are* proud of yourself," I said to Sheila as I drove her down to Fenton Boulevard after lunch. "What you did was very brave."

She shrugged. "Yeah, I guess." She put her hands behind her neck and lifted her hair up off her shoulders. "I didn't think about it."

"What did you talk about when you were up there? How did you convince him to come down?" I asked.

"I spoke Spanish to him. I didn't say anything special, just, like, I knew he was scared and I would help him come down, but I spoke in Spanish."

I raised an eyebrow. "I didn't realize you spoke Spanish."

"You don't know everything about me."

"No."

"I mean, like, you have been gone a few years, Torey."

"Yes, you're right."

There was a few moments' silence, while Sheila, her face turned away from me, watched out the window. Then she added, "All those years in the migrant camp and not learn to speak Spanish? Shit, I would never have had anybody to talk to."

I didn't answer. There was a sparky undercurrent to Sheila that showed itself more often than I was comfortable with. Much as she seemed to want to be with me, she also seemed easily irritated with me. Probably just adolescence. I wasn't particularly gifted with adolescents, so that didn't help any either. Whatever, I found it mildly upsetting.

Sheila seemed to sense this and came back with a conciliatory tone. "I thought talking in Spanish might make him feel better. Like, more secure. It was just an idea."

"It was a good one. And did he understand you?"

"I *am* fluent," she retorted.

"No, I mean, it will have been a long time since Alejo heard anyone speak Spanish to him, and even then it may have been a dialect."

"Yeah, he understood me. He came down, didn't he?"

Silence. I was approaching a major interstate junction on the freeway. There was the omnipresent roadwork and quite a lot of congestion, so for several minutes I concentrated on my driving. Once the traffic eased and I could relax, I listened into the silence.

"You know, Sheila, I get this sort of ongoing feeling that you're angry with me," I said.

"*Me?*" she replied with disbelief.

"If there are things or people I like, you seem to go out of your way to show you dislike them. If I say something, you seem to make a point of proving me wrong. And there's just this general tone of voice."

"Shit, you're just listening to, like, every little thing I say, aren't you?" she retorted. "And *judging* it."

"I'm not trying to."

"Well, you know, I don't think you're so great either," she said. "In that book you wrote, you come off sounding so patient with everything and you're not, you know."

I looked over. "What do you mean?"

"You get angry with everything. Like, you swear at all these drivers."

"I'm not *swearing*."

"You might as well be," Sheila said. "It's like 'Come *on*, lady!' 'Hurry up and get out there, mister,' every second sentence, Torey. And, like, you got mad at me when I tried to get in the car and had hold of the door handle so you couldn't unlock it."

"I didn't get mad at you."

"You did! You said, 'Let it *go*' in a really bitchy tone of voice. Not like you talk in your book at all. In there, you're so patient and kind. You wait forever in your book and never say a cross word, but now I can see how you really are and you get mad every other second."

"Not every other second, I'm sure."

"Seems like it to me," she replied.

"I'm human, Sheila. I get irritated sometimes. And irritable."

"That's not like you are in *One Child*."

"No, maybe not. That's a character in a book. People are too complex to be portrayed in their entirety on paper. And, in some parts, too boring."

Sheila snorted. "So you're saying it's *not* you."

"That character is the essence of me, but it isn't me, no. I'm me. Here. Now."

Sheila snorted again. "Hot shit."

thirteen

From dropping Sheila off at the bus station on Fenton Boulevard, I returned to the clinic. The conversation in the car had upset me, confirming as it did what intuition had already told me. She was angry with me. Why? Because I was annoyingly human, when she had expected the character from a book? I couldn't imagine that would provoke the strength of feeling I was sensing from her.

On the wall above my desk in the office, I'd hung the poem she had written me when she was twelve. Sitting down in my chair, I looked up at it.

> *. . . Then you came*
> *With your funny way of being*
> *Not quite human . . .*

Whatever she wanted from me, it was different from what she was getting.

Jeff opened the door and entered our small shared office. He was returning from a therapy session and had obviously had a close encounter with his client, because his hair was mussed and there was blue tempera paint on one cheek.

"You look like I feel," I said.

He set his notepad down on his desk. "I am never going into infant psychiatry, I can tell you that," he muttered none too good-naturedly. "Rosenthal can have that field entirely to himself. I am restricting myself to those who do not need finger paints."

"I don't think I'm going to go in for adolescents," I replied.

Jeff raised an eyebrow. "Who's getting to you? Your little orang-utan?"

I nodded and told him about the conversation in the car.

Although I had filled Jeff in about Sheila's past in general terms, such as the fact that she had been a student of mine, I had never gone into any great detail, including never having told him she was the subject of my book. Book publication being the lengthy process it is, *One Child* was not due for release for several more months; and being a little leery of how my venture into popular nonfiction would be received in professional circles, I had never talked much about it to any of my colleagues. Now I found myself not only explaining Sheila's darker past but also our complex relationship.

"Hoo," Jeff said when I paused. "You do land yourself in some tortured situations, Hayden."

"So, what are your thoughts?" I asked. "What have I done wrong with this girl? I've stirred something up unintentionally."

He smiled gently. "You know what I think the real problem is here? You and Sheila both have a dose of the same disease. All she remembers is this wonderful teacher who never got mad at her and now she's upset to discover just how ordinary and human you are; but, you know, Hayden, you're doing the very same thing. What's coloring your behavior toward her now is the fact that what you remember, too, is not Sheila as a real child, but rather the six-year-old character in a book."

"I do *not*."

"We all do," Jeff replied. "That's all memory is, our interpretation of what we've experienced. The only difference here is that most of us never get the book written."

*   *   *

"How much do you remember about your mother?" I asked Sheila the next afternoon, as I was driving her to the bus station.

"What do you mean?"

"Just what I asked. How much do you remember about her?"

Sheila didn't answer. Turning her head away, she looked out the window.

I listened into the silence, trying to discern what her emotions were. It had been a fairly good morning. After the drama of the previous day, everyone seemed content to keep things quiet. Jeff, Miriam and I were beginning to get a feel for each other's working style and weren't tripping over one another quite so often. Sheila still remained an outsider among us. She did not initiate much, either with the kids or with the three of us adults, and she didn't participate easily, preferring, instead, to hover on the perimeters. This was all right, to my mind, as this wasn't a field she was particularly familiar with and these were still early days. All in all, the day had gone quite well for everyone and we had gone off to lunch in high spirits, Sheila included.

"Have you ever seen your mother again? I mean, since leaving my class?" I asked.

Sheila shook her head.

"Do you know where she is?"

"No," she replied, her voice quiet.

Silence.

"Do you remember her?"

Again, Sheila did not answer me. Seconds rolled by and became minutes.

I glanced over.

"No," she said quietly. "I don't."

"Do you remember Jimmie?"

"Jimmie . . . ? You mean my brother?" A pensive silence. "I think I do. Maybe. I got this image in my mind . . . of someone with brown hair. It's a memory, you know, from long ago and when I try to place it . . . I think perhaps it's Jimmie." She looked over. "Why? Why do you ask?"

"Just wondering. Do you miss your mother?"

Sheila's eyebrows rose in surprise. "What's there to miss? I don't know her. I don't even remember her. How could I miss her?"

"Just wondering," I replied.

"You wonder a lot."

We had hit the roadwork section again and traffic had come to a standstill. Self-conscious of what Sheila had said the previous day regarding my attitude toward other drivers, I sat in silence.

"There's no reason I should miss my mother," Sheila said quietly. "She was a lousy parent. It's my dad who's done everything for me."

"Well, I was just wondering. It was a big issue for you when we were together last time."

"I was still a little child then. I suppose it mattered more to me when I was six."

*　　*　　*

The next morning, we broke the children down into three small groups. The idea had been initially to let one person be in charge of Jessie and Joshua, who needed the most individual attention, and then to split the other six by age, so that one of us would have Kayleigh, David and Mikey, who were younger, and the other would have Alejo, Tamara and Violet, the older three. However, after Alejo's extreme reaction to Tamara's behavior, it seemed unwise to put the two of them together just yet; so we substituted David for her.

I had this group of David, Alejo and Violet and I had decided on doing what I liked to call "guided drawing," the making of pictures after a short period of visualization. I found this a useful technique for bringing out children's emotions and it worked well with a small group. So we all sat down at one of the tables. I gave out large sheets of white paper and set in the middle of the table a variety of materials to choose from—thin felt tips, fat felt tips, crayons, colored pencils and plain pencils and pastel chalks.

Sheila came and sat down with us. I had hoped she would help Miriam, who had Joshua and Jessie, as they needed virtually one-to-one attention, but she seemed uncomfortable with these children. Feeling it was better to let her warm up at her own speed, I said nothing and let her take out the chair at the end of the table.

"All right," I said and looked with enthusiastic anticipation at each of the three children sitting across from me, "know what we're going to do today? We're going for a ride in space."

"Hey, cool!" David said.

"No, put your pen down, David. We don't need pens yet. Instead, I want everybody to close their eyes. Closed? Alejo? Close your eyes. That's right." I closed my own eyes to encourage the others. "Now, here we go: Keep your eyes closed so that you can see the rocket ship. Can you see it? Make a picture of it in your mind. This is *your* rocket ship, the one that is going to carry *you* into space. Can everybody see it?" I looked around to see nodding heads.

"Okay, here you go. You're strapped into your seat in the rocket ship. There go the engines. Feel them rumbling? They shake your seat a little."

David was very much into the fantasy. I saw his small body shake with the movement of his imaginary spaceship. I noticed, too, Sheila at the end of the table, her elbows braced on the table edge, hands interlaced to shield her eyes from my view. She was participating, I suspected, but didn't want me to realize she was joining in as another of the children.

"It's liftoff. Up, up, up you are going. The blue sky is rushing past you. It's getting paler. See it? Look out your window and see how the earth is falling away and you are zooming into outer space. Ooooh, there you are, out in space.

"Now, you can unfasten your seat belt and walk around, but ooh! What happens?"

"You're weightless," Sheila said without a moment's hesitation.

"That's right. You're weightless. You float. What's it feel like? Do you like it? Where are you going? Look around. What kind of rocket ship are you in? Is it big? Is it small? What colors are there? Is there lots of room to move around in? And where are you going? Where is the rocket ship headed? Look out the window. What do you see? Stars? Planets? Do you see Earth, or are you far away already? Is it crowded with things out there or is it very empty? Are there other spaceships out there? Look around your rocket ship again. Are you alone? Or is there someone traveling with you? Is it someone you like? What are you doing in the rocket ship just now?"

I paused, watching the children, all deep in their fantasy. "Okay, now, when you're ready, you may open your eyes and then I want you to draw me your spaceship."

As virtually always happened with this kind of activity, the children aroused from their imaginings excited and reached enthusiastically for the drawing materials.

"I seen Dracula, Torey," Violet said cheerfully. "And he had this big blob of blood hanging off his teeth."

"You're weird," David replied and reached across her for the felt tips.

As I would soon discover happened every time we asked Violet to create something, she made a cross, as this symbol kept her safe from vampires. On this occasion, she made one large black cross before going on to make several more smaller crosses and around this she dotted small round faces, all with pleasant, fang-toothed smiles.

David was drawing busily. He made a great red-and-white-striped rocket ship with a bright-yellow light shining out of its nose and was now surrounding it with an array of multicolored stars.

Alejo had reached quickly for a felt-tip marker, but once he had it, he paused a long time over the blank paper, then slowly he began to draw. His spaceship was a tiny speck in a huge, black universe.

It was this blackness that eventually got him into trouble. There was such a huge area of paper to cover that it soon became obvious he couldn't do it with the small black felt tip he was using. Setting it down, he surveyed the available drawing materials before spying a large black marking pen on the far end of the table. Rising, he reached across David to get it. In the process, he accidentally bumped David's hand.

"You spaz!" David shouted and flung his arm out angrily.

Within a split second, Alejo had him by the shirt. Indeed, it happened so very fast, I didn't anticipate it and was alarmed to discover Alejo had pulled David off his chair and down to the floor before I had even managed to rise. Grabbing David by the hair, he slammed his head down against the linoleum.

I dashed around the table, but before I could reach him, Alejo was off. In blind panic he ran. The room we had chosen in the school was normally a double classroom and we had picked it for its size. With so few children, however, we had not needed the many tables or chairs used by the ordinary pupils in the school; so we had shoved the large metal teacher's desk into a far corner and then nested all the other tables and stacked them around it, before piling the chairs on top. It was here Alejo went, sliding in through the tangled legs of the tables and under the teacher's desk to become virtually unreachable without moving them all.

David was my immediate concern. He had gotten a nasty bash

against the floor and was crying lustily, so I knelt to comfort him. Both Jeff and Miriam had come to my aid, and we all stood regarding Alejo in his hiding place. He, in turn, watched us with huge, dark eyes.

"What should we do?" I asked Jeff. I was unsure whether fishing him out and making him sit in our "time-out chair" would be the appropriate action or whether he was too frightened to benefit from that.

"Can I talk to him?" It was Sheila. "I could speak to him like I did the other day. Maybe I could get him to come out."

"Yes, I think that's a good idea," Jeff said. "You be in charge of Alejo, Sheila. You talk to him, and if you get him out, you keep him aside individually."

This seemed to surprise Sheila. "What should I do with him?"

Jeff gave her a reassuring smile. "What seems right. You'll know when the time comes."

The time didn't come. Alejo stayed under the tables for the remainder of the morning.

*   *   *

During the drive down to the bus station on Fenton Boulevard, Sheila was lost in pensive silence. "What was the point of that exercise with the rocket ship?" she asked after a long while in thought.

"To help the children experience themselves, I suppose. That's what creativity is all about, basically."

"So it was just an exercise in creativity?"

"In expression. Most of the children in this group find it difficult to express their inner feelings, and I've found these kinds of activities often provide a good way to start."

Again Sheila fell silent. We went for five or six minutes without speaking.

"Torey?"

"Yes?"

"I remember you doing that."

"Doing what?"

"In our class. I remember you taking us on one of those imaginary trips. We went under the sea." Her face suddenly lit up. "We were all sitting in a circle on the floor. On my knees. I was on my knees. You showed us these pictures of tropical fish in this magazine, and then you told us to close our eyes and we were going under the water. Under the sea to see the fish. And I remember all these fish swimming around, yellow-striped and turquoise, all colors." Sheila was smiling.

I smiled back and nodded.

"Suddenly, I can remember that. Really clearly. Like it just happened. I can see us sitting there in that circle on the floor. I can see the blackboard behind you."

"Yes, we did it quite a lot. It was a favorite activity with almost everyone."

She smiled broadly. "And now I remember it. I can really remember."

fourteen

Apparently Alejo felt we were too dangerous a group to deal with, because when he arrived the next morning, he wouldn't get out of the taxi. Jeff went out and tried to talk him into coming into the school, but Alejo was having none of it. He cowered in the small floor space of the backseat. Jeff, who was not accustomed to his clients so vehemently not wanting to see him, was inclined to let Alejo go home again. He felt Alejo needed more time to work through this matter and would only make positive therapeutic progress if allowed to move at his own speed. I disagreed, feeling that if Alejo left now, he would never come back. Sensing that any possible future of staying with his adoptive family hinged on his learning more appropriate behaviors over the course of the summer, I doubted we could afford that kind of therapeutic luxury. So, despite Jeff's misgivings and Alejo's loud protests, I extracted him from the back of the taxi and carried him in.

He was a really vicious little boy. Most children, when I had to deal with them physically, fought back in a reasonably predictable, "fair" way and I was able to hold them and move them without hurting either one of us. I got the odd knock on the shins, but that was about all. Not so with Alejo. When he fought, it was with fierce, no-holds-barred desperation, biting, scratching and squirming so violently that I found it almost impossible to hang on to him.

Both Jeff and Miriam tried to help me move the boy up the steps and into the school, but, if anything, Alejo struggled more as each additional pair of hands took hold of him. In the end, I asked them to let go and just make sure the exits were guarded, in case I accidentally let go of him before we got into the classroom.

Once we reached the classroom doorway, I did release Alejo and he bolted off to the same far corner that had succored him the day before. Dropping down, he slid back behind the stacked chairs and tables and under the teacher's desk.

"Oh, good," muttered Jeff and turned to me. "You're the expert in these kinds of things. Now what?"

What came back to me was my own first encounter with a seriously disturbed child. I was eighteen at the time and a volunteer in a preschool program. There had been a small girl there who, day after day, spent the whole time hiding behind the piano. The director of the program, a marvelous, innovative individual who was to serve as my mentor for several years afterward, had set me the same kind of task. I was to go spend time with this little girl and get her to come out. He didn't tell me how to do it or what to do, just that this was my task and that he had faith in me. He said, whatever I chose to do, it would make the child's life better than it was at the moment. Whether or not he realized that the months that followed would change my life forever, I never knew, but my entire career in special education could be traced straight back to that one small girl.

What had affected me indelibly in this encounter had been the director's faith that I, a rather awkward and self-conscious teenager, had the ability to think for myself, to discern what needed to be done and to do it. Looking at Sheila, I thought how much I wanted to give her that same gift.

"You go with him," I said to her.

She looked disconcerted. "And do what?"

"He must be terribly frightened. Talk to him. If he wants to come out, great, but otherwise, just use your judgment."

For a long moment, Sheila regarded me, her expression flickering between puzzlement and uncertainty, then she glanced over at Alejo behind his barricade.

"Remember how you felt when you first came to my class?" I asked. "Talk to him as if he were you, then."

"I don't remember," she said. "So I don't think I can do that."

"I'm sure you can."

Going down on her stomach so that she could see under the tangle of chair and table legs, she spoke softly to him in Spanish throughout the morning. Not fluent myself in the language, I could not understand most of what she was saying, but her voice grew gentle and encouraging.

Alejo didn't come out. Safe behind his barricade of metal legs, he kept himself curled up and resisted Sheila's charms. Indeed, I don't believe he even talked to her that first day. Sheila, however, proved just as persistent. She got up a couple of times and came and joined me, working with the children I had that morning, but she always went back to sit on the floor beside Alejo's den. I was impressed with her concentration. It was the first time, I think, we had managed to fully engage her.

*　　　*　　　*

For the following two weeks, Alejo continued to take refuge among the table legs. Each morning he would arrive, be carried in from the taxi, shoot across the room and under the tables to lurk until extracted again at lunchtime to go home. Jeff and I discussed the merits of hanging on to him when we got him inside the door of the classroom and not allowing him to get into his hideaway, but in the end felt it was perhaps better that he be allowed this form of security. So each day went the same.

Sheila accepted the ongoing challenge of trying to charm Alejo out. For several days she lay on her stomach on the floor and talked to him, sometimes in Spanish, sometimes in English. She was surprisingly good at keeping up these one-sided conversations. I had never perceived Sheila as particularly garrulous and would not have expected her to tackle the situation in such a manner, but she did, maintaining a pleasant chatter full of questions to him about what he might like in the way of food or sports or other activities, what he did with his day when he wasn't here, what his preferences were in regards to animals, school subjects and a host of other areas.

Occasionally, Alejo could be drawn into answering, although he never said much. He seemed to appreciate her efforts at Spanish, as we often heard him murmuring back to her then. And so they went, three and a half hours a day, five days a week.

*   *   *

As she continued to share floor space with him, Sheila grew intensely interested in Alejo's circumstances. Nothing was known about his real family, not even their names or whether or not any of them were still alive. Repeatedly, Sheila queried the possibility of finding out. I tried to explain the impracticality of it, and most likely the total impossibility of it as well, but Sheila's curiosity remained.

The tale of how Alejo had been found, living in the garbage can, provoked a particularly large amount of conversation from Sheila. She mused on everything from how cold and hungry he must have been to the logistics of a young child's actually surviving in such circumstances. My suspicion, of course, was that in some unconscious way, Sheila was relating this to her own abandonment. I could recall how, at six, she used to recount over and over and over again the incident where her mother had left home, taking her and her younger brother Jimmie, and how her mother had stopped the car and pushed Sheila out onto the verge of the freeway, before speeding off into the night, never to be seen again. Sheila's need now to recount Alejo's abandonment caused all those long-ago conversations to echo in my mind.

Whatever was happening psychologically, Sheila became increasingly committed to Alejo. She was desperate to reach him, to convince him that he could trust her, and it was this desire that engaged her so completely in her work with him.

Despite this newfound intensity in her work, however, there were still plenty of hot moments with Sheila. One of the most dangerous areas was her appearance.

Having known her as a child, I must admit Sheila did not now look at all as I had expected she would. She had been a very pretty girl, even through the dirt and grime of her early days in my class. Her long hair, a dark honey-blond in color, had been very, very straight, of the sort to slide off the fingers in a fluidlike motion when lifted. Her features were bold, with a cheeky little cleft in her chin and a particularly attractive mouth.

The chin, the mouth, the bold features were, of course, all still there, but the permed, brightly colored hair diminished them, and everything was overshadowed by Sheila's wardrobe. *Where* she got her fashion sense I could only guess at. It was so far out as to be almost in.

We had been treated to various combos involving the white long johns and an assortment of dresses and T-shirts. Indeed, one of her favorites included wearing nothing over the long johns except a very baggy peasant-style shirt, which made her look like an extra from *Fiddler on the Roof* who'd been interrupted in the changing room. She also had an assortment of what appeared to be lacy, white Victorian nightshirts, which she wore as dresses, usually layered over long-sleeved striped T-shirts in loud, occasionally neon, colors. And all of these were complemented by the thick black lace-up workman's boots.

She had had her ears pierced, the left one five times, the right one twice, although, thank God, no other parts of her anatomy seemed to have received this treatment. She wore nothing more than thin gold rings in her ears, but the sheer quantity made up for their simplicity.

Admittedly, it did all take a bit of getting used to, but the fact was I didn't mind it. In fact, as I did grow used to it, I found some of the sartorial combinations attractive, if a little bizarre. She did have an obvious flair for clothes, and, moreover, she had the slim, waiflike build needed to carry such outfits off. Had Sheila been among people a little more in the fashion vanguard than Jeff and I could lay claims to, I suspect her imagination would have been admired.

Sheila's father, however, did not appear to admire Sheila's dress sense whatsoever, and from what I could make out, there were many arguments over the matter. Moreover, her school hadn't taken a very enlightened view either and she had, on more than one occasion, been sent home to change. This, I assumed, was what accounted for Sheila's touchiness over the matter, because it became obvious from the first day that she wanted to wear these things and look the way she did and not have a single person even allude to the fact that she might appear a smidgen peculiar.

Jeff was always landing himself in it. He had nicknamed her the Orangutan as a result of her orange hair and her climbing feat on that second day and this was guaranteed to make her shout, just by his saying it. Worse, he could never resist commenting, "Shall we turn the air-conditioning down for you so you won't have to come in with your nightgown on over your clothes?" or "Isn't Grandpa missing his underwear yet?"

Sheila reacted to these comments, like most of his tongue-in-cheek humor, with the spitting rage of a wildcat kitten, and I was quite certain the rage was genuine. Whatever hopes I had had about bringing two such powerful minds together had long since evaporated. Sheila appeared to feel nothing short of hate for Jeff and Jeff was never much help. I tried to get him to turn off his undisciplined mouth, but it made no difference whatsoever. He enjoyed winding her up.

Once I'd adjusted, I didn't find it too difficult to keep my own mouth shut regarding her appearance. I'm fairly unshockable and can screen out unwanted sensory information quite easily, so except for mediating over the matter between her and Jeff, I could generally steer clear. This was just as well, because on the few occasions when I accidentally got drawn in, Sheila came out with all guns firing. In fact, I suspect there was a provocative aspect to Sheila's appearance, which, when I didn't react to it, made her have to come after me occasionally.

On one such time, we were at the back of the room after the session ended. Some of the children had done painting and Sheila was helping me wash out the paint pots. The sink was full of soapy water and Sheila had her arms plunged into it almost up to her elbows.

"Could you get my hair back?" she asked, as I came around the side with more paint pots. "I got a ponytail holder in my left pocket. Could you just pull it back and fasten it for me?"

I reached in her pocket, extracted the holder and began smoothing the hair back to fasten it. What came immediately to my mind were memories of doing Sheila's hair when she was little. It had been wonderful hair, so silky straight that it was lovely to feel, and I had always enjoyed our mornings before school when I had brushed it. What I felt now was quite a different matter. Treated and colored, it was a crinkly mass.

"I'm thinking of doing my hair yellow this weekend," Sheila said.

"I saw this stuff at the drugstore and it was only two dollars and ninety-nine cents."

"Do you ever think of letting it grow back like it was?"

In a split second, Sheila had whirled around and whacked my hand down, soapy water flying everywhere. "Stop it! Just stop it!" she shouted in fury.

I jumped back in surprise.

"That's what you want, isn't it? To control me! To make me back into your little darling. Well, I'm *not* her. I'm me! And you can't tell me what to do anymore."

She had gotten so angry so quickly that I was stunned into silence. Both Jeff and Miriam were in the room too and they stopped short and stared.

"I'm not your property anymore. You don't own me. You didn't create me!"

fifteen

The following Monday morning, I was playing "empty chair" with David, Tamara and Violet. A variation of the therapeutic technique developed by the renowned psychiatrist Fritz Perls, it involved setting an empty chair in the middle of the group and talking to it, as if a person were sitting in it. We were discussing angry feelings and sad feelings and how the two sometimes got mixed up. I had asked the children in turn to think of an occasion when someone had made them each feel that way, then to imagine that that person was sitting in the empty chair and to talk to him or her, telling that person about their feelings. It took us a while to get going. I gave an example, placing in the chair a neighbor of mine who disliked my cat, and then telling the empty chair how angry it made me feel when I saw him abusing my pet. Then the children had turns. It wasn't until we were on our second round that everyone began to pick up the right mood.

Tamara's second turn came. "I'm going to put my mom in that chair," she said.

"Okay," I replied. "And what do you want to tell your mom?"

"I'm fed up with the baby."

"Okay."

Tamara looked over at me. "I want to tell her I don't want to take care of the baby anymore. Why did she have so many kids that she can't take care of them all herself?"

"Can you tell her that?" I asked. "Imagine she's sitting just there and you tell her how you feel."

"I don't want to take care of the baby anymore," Tamara said. "I'm sick of the baby. He's not mine. It's not fair, just because I'm oldest. Why do I have to take care of him?"

Tears came to her eyes and she stopped. Looking over at me, she said, "I'm too little to take care of him."

I pointed to the chair. "Why don't you tell her you feel like that? That you feel too small for such a big responsibility?"

Tamara nodded tearfully. "I'm just little, Mama. I need you to take care of *me*."

She sat down, and for a long moment everyone was absorbed in a pensive silence.

"Okay, Violet?" I said gently. "How about you?"

Violet lumbered to her feet. She approached the chair, walked around it, all the while regarding the seat. During the first round, she had seated a girl from school in the chair. Violet told me that she wanted to ask the girl why she always treated her in such a mean way, but when redirected to imagine the girl sitting in the chair and to address her comments there, Violet had degenerated into silly chatter about ghosts. I wasn't holding out much hope for this new attempt. Violet's problems were so all-pervasive that she didn't appear able to cope with such a direct approach.

"I'm going to put Alejo in the chair," Violet said, much to my surprise.

Alejo wasn't far away. We were in a circle only feet away from where Sheila had been lying prone on the floor and talking to him; however, over the course of the empty-chair exercise, Sheila had gotten caught up listening to us and was now sitting cross-legged on the edge of the circle. She ducked her head slightly to see Alejo under his tangle of furniture when his name was mentioned.

"All right," I said. "What do you want to say to Alejo?"

"Why don't you come with us, Alejo?" Violet said, approaching the chair. She cocked her head and regarded it closely, as if really seeing the boy. "Why do you keep hiding from us? It isn't scary here and I miss you. I wish you would come out."

She circled the chair and then came to stand on the left side of it. "I feel angry with you when you go hide, because I think you don't like me. I feel sad, because I want to be your friend. Why don't you come out? I want you to be with us."

"All right."

Stunned, we all jerked our heads over to see Alejo standing beside the stacked table.

"He's come out!" David shrieked with such loudness that I fully expected Alejo to bolt back under, but he didn't.

"Do you want to join us?" I asked. I snagged a chair from an adjacent table and pulled it into our circle.

Alejo remained right where he was.

"Would you like to play too? Do you want to talk to someone in the empty chair?" I asked.

He shook his head.

Sheila, still sitting cross-legged on the floor, reached her hand out. "Come here, Alejo. Sit down beside me."

Without hesitation, he went over to her and sat down.

"Let's change things. You've had a chance to talk to the empty chair. Now, let's pretend the empty chair can talk back," I said. "Tamara, you just talked to your mom, sitting in the empty chair. Now you go sit in the empty chair."

Hesitantly, she rose from her place, walked across the circle and sat down in the empty chair in the center.

"Now you're your mom. You just heard what Tamara said. You answer her back."

Tamara sat silent a long moment. "I don't mean to make you work so hard," she started quietly. "I just got too many children." She paused. "Don't get married, Tamara. Don't have babies." Then she stood up and walked back to her place.

"My turn now. I get to be Alejo," Violet said and beamed at him. She went over to the empty chair and sat down. "I'm glad you asked me to come out, Violet. I was tired of being under there. You acted good to me. Now I'm going to be your friend."

I smiled at Violet and then looked over at Alejo. "Can you share with us how it made you feel, when Violet said how much she wanted you to come join us again?"

"Good," he said.

*   *   *

Sheila and I didn't join Jeff and Miriam for lunch as we usually did. I had a client meeting very near the school in the early afternoon, so I'd brought my lunch with the idea of eating it over in the park across the street. Deprived of her usual ride down to Fenton Boulevard, Sheila needed to make the rather complicated set of connections from the main road two blocks over. She left immediately after the program ended that morning and I assumed she was headed for the bus stop; however, she returned, a McDonald's bag in hand, and joined me on my picnic bench in the park.

"I don't have to go home right away," she said. "It's just an empty house anyway."

"I'm always glad for company," I said, as I unwrapped my sandwiches.

We spent a moment with our food.

"What do you usually do in the afternoons when you get home?" I asked.

Sheila shrugged. "Depends."

"Do you get together with friends?"

She hesitated over her food, then shrugged again. "Not usually."

"I don't hear you mention friends very often," I said.

"Doesn't mean I don't have any, if that's what you're asking," she said a bit testily. "Just I don't do much with them, that's all." She took a bite of her hamburger. "It's a dorky school I go to. There's not really anyone there I'd want to be friends with, if you want the truth."

"What do you do?"

"Like I said, depends. I always got the housework, you know. My dad sure wouldn't do it. If it's left to my dad, we'd live in a pigsty. And the shopping. And the cooking. Who do you think does our cooking?"

I nodded.

"He's very lucky he's got a daughter, you know. Somebody to do all this for him. He'd have been stuck, if I was a boy."

"How's it work out? Does he give you the shopping money and you make the decisions about what the meals will be?"

"I got to get it off him." She finished her hamburger in two big bites. "I learned that, like, ages ago. I got to get the money off him within minutes or it's not there to get."

I regarded her.

"Mostly he gives it to me when I ask. He's getting used to me doing it now, but if he doesn't, I'm still pretty good at getting it. I tell him I'm going over to the Laundromat and I got to have the pants he's wearing right away, so would he change? Then he takes his wallet out. Or sometimes I just wait till he's asleep."

"I thought he was done with the alcohol and stuff. I thought all that was in the past."

She snorted derisively. "Don't kid yourself."

"He's still drinking?" I said in dismay. "I thought the baseball team . . ."

"People don't change. Didn't you know that? Circumstances change, but people never do."

✳   ✳   ✳

Now that Alejo had come out from his hideaway of his own volition, Jeff and I decided to take definitive measures to prevent him from returning there; so we arrived early the next morning and humped the extra tables and chairs down the hall to a room we were not using. This had the added advantage of leaving us with a much larger working space.

When the taxi arrived, Alejo again showed reluctance to get out, but Sheila climbed in and sat with him a moment before finally coaxing him out with her. For the first time in three weeks he did not have to be dragged into the room, but instead walked in, holding Sheila's hand.

"Can I just take him and work with him on my own?" Sheila asked.

"If you'd like. Do you have something planned?" I replied.

She shrugged. "All that time I was with him on the floor I was thinking of different things. And I thought maybe he would find it easier than being in a big group."

They went to the far end of the room near a small, low bookcase and sat down on the floor. I saw Sheila tip out the canister of Lego bricks in the middle between them and then both bent forward to begin building.

It was my day to take Joshua and Jessie, our two autistic children, and between them, they were a full load, so I did not get much of a chance to oversee what Sheila and Alejo were doing together. They remained absorbed in the Lego bricks all the way to snack time and the break.

While they were outside, I took the opportunity to walk over and see what they had been building. It didn't appear to be much. There were several rectangular forms, looking like half-started houses or the like, and a few long strings of bricks clicked together.

"Should we let them continue?"

Startled, I jumped at the unexpected voice and turned to see Jeff. He crossed over to where I was standing. Bending down, he picked up one of the rectangular structures. "I think they'll go back to this after the break. Do you think we should leave them to it?"

"What do you think?" I asked.

"I was eavesdropping. It was quite an interesting conversation. They seemed to be building jails with the Lego and putting the little Lego people in it. From the sounds of it, Alejo was putting his mother in jail. He said, 'She says No! No! No! You do that again and I will lock you in your room. I won't talk to you for two days. You are a wicked boy to do that and you can't watch TV.' And Sheila says, 'Lock her in the jail. This is the bad moms' jail. Put her in there and we'll give her punishment. What shall we do to her?' And Alejo says, 'Cut her throat. Make her bleed. Drop bombs on her till she's dead.' So that's what they were doing, dropping hunks of Lego." Jeff looked over. "It was a little difficult to tell who was leading whom."

"So it sounds," I replied.

"I think we should let them go on, if they want," Jeff said. "He's talking more than I've heard yet, but . . . I want to keep an ear tuned."

I felt unnerved by the content of the conversation. As much as I wanted to give Sheila a positive experience here with us, she was an untrained teenager and not a therapist; moreover, she still carried plenty of her own emotional baggage. Was she encouraging Alejo's play in an effort to imitate Jeff's and my therapeutic activities? Or was she fulfilling her own needs? Or both?

We didn't get a chance to find out. When Miriam and Sheila came back in with the children after break, Alejo quite happily joined the others at the painting table and Sheila retreated to the back to clean up the things from snack time and to polish off the remaining cookies.

When the morning was over, Sheila came over to me as I was

putting things away. "Let's not go to lunch with them," she said, as she handed me the materials to put up on the shelf.

"You don't feel like it?"

"Let's do what we did yesterday and eat in the park. I liked that. It's so nice and sunny out and then we spend it sitting around in that dingy restaurant," she replied.

"The problem is," I said, "I haven't brought my lunch today, so I don't have anything to eat. Moreover, I have an appointment back at the clinic at two, so if I don't eat promptly, I won't be able to take you down to Fenton Boulevard before I have to be back."

"I don't care. I can take the bus from here." She bent down and unlaced one boot. Lifting the boot up, she tipped it and out spilled a five-dollar bill. "If you don't eat too much, I could buy you something from McDonald's."

"All right. McDonald's it is, but I'll buy," I said. "You can provide the delivery service and go get it when we're done here."

We'd had a messy morning, using finger paints at the table, soft colored chalk on the blackboard and water in the sand tray. In addition, there was the usual debris. Jeff was at the back sink washing out paint pots, while Miriam was sorting through books and putting them back into the bookshelf.

"Have you told them?" Sheila asked, coming over to where I was wiping down a table.

"Told them what?" I asked.

"Well, that we're not going out to lunch with them," she replied, a little exasperated.

"No, but I will. Let's just finish the cleaning up. We were really mucky in here today."

"We can clean up," she said. "Why don't you tell Jeff and Miriam they can go now. Then you and me can clean up." When I didn't respond immediately, Sheila continued. "This is the only problem with this work. You and I never get to spend any time alone. I thought we would more, but there's always them around. Sometimes I just want to be with you."

I smiled. "Well, go tell them we'll do the room on our own then."

* * *

I was hoping that Sheila's request to be alone with me was an indication that she wanted to talk. The conversation Jeff had reported earlier between her and Alejo still disconcerted me a little and I was anticipating that she might want to discuss it or at least discuss Alejo with me; but this didn't seem to be the case. Once there were just the two of us, we continued to clean up the room.

Taking a set of fresh erasers from the cupboard, Sheila erased all the colored drawings from the chalkboard, while I tacked up the finger paintings on the bulletin board. When I next looked over, she had a box of the colored chalk in her hand and was drawing on the board. I didn't say anything, but Sheila quickly became aware that I was watching her.

"The only other problem with this place is that I don't get to play too," she said and grinned sheepishly. "I keep wishing, like, I was one of them instead of one of you guys. God, it looks like so much fun, what these kids get to do. Like a dream school."

I grinned back.

"Can I make a picture with these?" she asked hesitantly, holding up the box of chalks. "Like, maybe it could be decorative? For when they come in tomorrow? It'd look better than just a blank blackboard, don't you think?"

"Yeah, sure. Go ahead."

Sheila threw herself wholeheartedly into making an enormous picture that took up a whole section of the chalkboard in the classroom. This intensity of concentration surprised me; she worked as if it had been bursting to get out of her all along. As I finished my work and the time drew near to go for lunch, I was reluctant to pull her away, as she was so deeply involved in what she was doing.

"Shall I go for the hamburgers?" I asked.

"Would you?" she replied in surprise. "God, like, great."

When I returned about twenty minutes later, Sheila was putting the finishing touches on the blackboard drawing. It was an intriguing picture: a desert of gold sand stretching the full length of the board with hardly anything above it. There was one lone saguaro-type cactus and a couple of branched, leafless bushes. Below the level of the sand, however, were an incredible number of little burrows filled with snakes, mice, scorpions, rabbits and beetles. And at the very far end was a female backpacker in hiking boots and shorts with a red scarf on her head.

"Hey, that's good. I didn't know you were such an artist," I said.

"There's lots you don't know about me, Torey."

"It's really good. You have the woman's expression very realistic. But I especially like all these things down under the sand. Look at the rabbit burrows. A regular warren, with all those individual rooms for the rabbits to go in. And I could never draw a scorpion just out of my imagination."

Sheila grinned. "I like doing things that surprise you."

I regarded the picture. "She looks lonely, though. This lone hiker with everything hiding from her."

"Now, don't go into your psychologist mode. It's just a picture."

"So," I said, "*you* tell me about it then."

"It's just a picture. She's walking in the desert. It's the California desert. I've seen pictures of it, of bushes like those."

California, where Sheila's mother had fled, I was thinking, but I didn't say that. "It still looks lonely from the hiker's perspective."

"Well, yeah, there's a lot of loneliness in deserts. You kind of feel like there's this big stretch of emptiness ahead of you," she replied.

"And everything that's alive is hiding from you?" I ventured.

"Well, yeah, that, or . . ." She turned and looked at me, a knowing smile crossing her lips. "Or everything is hiding just below the surface, waiting to be discovered. Touché? I caught you at it? I can interpret pictures too?"

I shrugged good-naturedly.

"You're dying to get your hands on me, aren't you? What you really want is for me to say that this person is me and this desert is my life, isn't it?"

"Only if it's true."

"Oh, it's true," she said. "And you should know it."

sixteen

Sheila's fourteenth birthday came in early July, just before the program broke up for three days over the Fourth of July. I told Jeff, saying that as it was the only birthday to occur over the course of the eight-week program, it would be nice to have a little party. All the time I was teaching I had always made a special effort to have class celebrations, in part because they provided a pleasant change from routine, but mostly because the handicaps, the emotional dysfunction in the families and/or the financial circumstances often prevented these children from experiencing parties elsewhere. Many were the boys and girls in my classes who had never been invited to a single birthday party or been the center of one for themselves. So I baked us a huge chocolate cake and decorated it with Sheila's name, while Miriam made up an assortment of small party foods. Jeff provided the paper hats and honkers.

Sheila made no pretense at sophistication when she saw the streamers and balloons, the colorful Pink Panther paper plates and hats, and the cake. Absolutely delighted, she picked up each and every item and inspected it.

"God, you did this for *me*? *Shit*," she said, trying a hat on. "God, I've never had one of these. How does it look? Where's a mirror? I've got to see." She went over to the corner where the dressing-up clothes were and took up the small hand mirror. "I've always wondered what I'd look like with one of these hats on."

The children were equally delighted, squealing with enthusiasm when they spied the bright decorations and the array of party foods. Having lived through dozens of classroom parties before, I knew what a recipe for disaster they generally were. Everyone got a little too excited, the noise level was unbearable and nothing of measurable worth got done. However, there was magic in this sort of chaos, to my mind, and I always enjoyed the ferment.

We started with party games and ended with a feast of goodies, the finale being the cake. All the children were amazed by the number of candles Sheila got and even more amazed that she had the ability to blow them all out. After cutting the cake and passing out a slice to everyone, Jeff said, "Well, now must be the time for presents."

I had gotten her a gift certificate from a local department store, so that she could have the leisure of picking what caught her fancy. Miriam, who was an accomplished craftsperson, had made an attractive woven belt. Then Jeff handed her a small package, prettily wrapped. It was obvious from its shape that it was a book. Taking the gift from him, Sheila paused to look at it. The wrapping, a shimmery gold, was quite unlike anything I'd seen before and I found it amazing to think that Jeff would take time with things like wrapping birthday presents.

Carefully, Sheila prized the sticking tape off. Inside was a paperback copy of Shakespeare's *Antony and Cleopatra*. Sheila lifted it up and regarded the cover. At a loss for words, she just stared at it.

"Torey said you liked Caesar," Jeff said. "This is set in the same time period." He regarded Sheila's face. "Have you read it?"

Curling her lip in undisguised disbelief, she shook her head. "This is Shakespeare."

"Yes, well, don't hold it against him. Forget who wrote it and just take it home and read it. There's one of the best stories in the world between those two covers and you're going to meet a soul mate."

Sheila looked up, astonished. "Me? Who?"

"You read it and find out."

✳   ✳   ✳

En route down to Fenton Boulevard after lunch, Sheila was full of ebullience.

"Thanks for that, Torey. That was really nice of you and Miriam and Jeff to do all that for me today," she said.

"We thought it'd be a bit of good fun. I'm glad you liked it," I replied.

She smiled. "That's what I always hated about having a summer birthday. All the other kids at school got some kind of fuss made, you know, like they sang 'Happy Birthday' or something, and I never got anything. And I always wanted it. Just once. You know, just once, so you could stand up and everybody'd think *you* were special." She paused. "It's funny how such a silly thing can matter so much when you're little."

I nodded.

"If you want the actual, honest-to-God truth, this is the first birthday party I've ever had."

I nodded again. I had suspected as much.

"Once, when I was in this one foster home . . . I was eight, I think, and turning nine . . . they said they were going to let me have a party and she took me out to look at paper plates and junk, but . . ." Turning her head, she gazed out the window. "I didn't get it. I did something or another, I don't remember what now, and she told me I wasn't going to have anything for my birthday because of it. But, you know, I don't think she was going to do anything anyway, 'cause she never bought the paper plates. I think she was just winding me up."

"That must have been disappointing," I said.

"Yeah, but then what's new?"

Silence.

Sheila looked down at the presents in her lap. Pulling out the gift certificate I'd given her, she examined it, then put it back in its envelope. Then she felt the weave of Miriam's belt. Finally, she began to page through the play Jeff had given her.

"Why on earth do you suppose he gave me this?" she murmured. "It's a weird gift."

I didn't answer.

"Have you ever read it?"

"Yes, long ago. I did a report on it at school once." I paused, then giggled. "To be truthful, I *didn't* read it. I was about your age and my sole goal in life in those days was to figure out how to short-circuit the work and still get the grades. I was a world-class skimmer. I don't think I actually read a whole book cover to cover until I was about twenty-two."

"*Torey!*" she said, absolutely appalled.

I turned and grinned.

"God, and I thought you were so perfect," Sheila said.

A pause.

"So, you don't know what's in it either?" she asked.

"Well, not other than it's about *Antony and Cleopatra*. You know who Cleopatra is, don't you?"

"Vaguely. A queen in Egypt a long time ago, but that's about all," Sheila replied. "I can't imagine why Jeff thinks I'll want to read this. Holy shit, *Shakespeare*."

"I guess you'll have to read it and find out."

I was coming to the roadwork again, so I slowed the car down.

"I remember that other book," Sheila said. "From your class. *The Little Prince*. Do you remember reading that to me? It was my best book in the whole world for the longest time. I just couldn't get enough of it."

"Yes, I remember it very well," I said.

"I can still quote all my favorite parts." She smiled over at me. "You know who I liked best in the book?"

"The prince?" I ventured.

She shook her head.

"The fox?"

"No, the rose. I loved that rose. It was so conceited, so full of itself and yet . . . Remember how it had those thorns, four thorns, and thought itself so brave? Remember that one bit? The rose said to the little prince, 'Let the tigers come with their claws!' " Sheila boomed out in a deep, fierce voice. "And the prince said, 'There are no tigers on my planet, and besides, tigers don't eat weeds.' 'I am not a weed!' " Again, the dramatic rendering. Sheila's voice squeaked over the word "weed." "She was so put out. And then she just kept going on, 'Let the tigers come! I am not at all afraid of tigers!' " Sheila smiled. "I can just imagine that brave little rose."

"I can see why you liked her," I said. "You were a bit of a little rose yourself in those days."

She wrinkled her nose. "Oh God, I wasn't, Torey. God. That's no compliment. A *flower*? No, it's the tigers I identified with. Rrrowrr!" she said and struck playfully out at me with fingers arched as claws. "I was the tigers' kid."

seventeen

Over the Fourth of July weekend, I asked Sheila if she would like to come with me for a brief visit to Marysville, where she had been in my class all those years previously. It was a two-hundred-mile journey and I thought it would fit well into the four days we had until the clinic summer school-program resumed.

Sheila accepted enthusiastically. She had been back on only one previous occasion five years before, when her foster family had taken her to visit her father at the penitentiary. It had been almost as long since I'd been there. I'd passed through on one or two occasions since but I hadn't stopped. With the exception of Chad, all the people I had been closest to were now gone.

The plan was that I would pick her up early on Thursday morning and we would work our way across the state to Marysville at a leisurely pace. Friday and Saturday we would spend looking around. Chad and his family had invited us to celebrate the Fourth of July with them on Saturday evening, and then on Sunday we'd return.

Sheila was waiting outside on the front steps of the duplex when I pulled up. It was very early, only just after six, and the sun was not high enough to dispel all the shadows. Even so, I squinted hard at the figure by the door. Sheila?

"I've done this *just* for you," she said emphatically, as she flung her duffel bag into the backseat and got in beside me. She buckled the seat belt. "I hope you appreciate it."

What could I say? The orange hair was gone, replaced by bright-yellow hair that stood up all over her head, as if it had a life of its own. Sort of Marilyn Monroe meets Bride of Frankenstein.

"You said I looked better blond," she replied to my stunned silence. "I thought, well, *just* for you, since you're taking me someplace nice."

*   *   *

I set off in a high mood. I love to drive, and it was a super time for driving, on an early summer morning. Although we had been in the midst of a string of quite hot days, the air was still cool and the humidity was low, making the far horizon sharp.

"I wonder what we're going to find," Sheila said. "Can we go to the school?"

"It'll be closed, but we could look at the playground."

While I negotiated the last of the freeway interchanges necessary to get us out of the city, Sheila amused herself trying to tune in a rock station, but my radio wasn't very good and she finally gave up.

"After you left my class, where all did you go?" I asked.

She shrugged. "Lots of places. I was in, like, three foster homes. Four? I can't remember now. See, we were in Marysville and then we moved to Broadview and my dad got in trouble, like really soon after we moved. So, I went in this one foster home and then I got in another one and another. Then I got sent to a children's home for a while."

"How come?" I asked.

Another shrug. "Just the way the system works."

"What made you move from Marysville in the first place?" I asked.

"Don't know. Don't remember."

"Do you remember being in Sandra McGuire's class the year after my class?" I asked. "When you were seven?"

"Sort of." She paused pensively. "Actually, I have exactly one memory. I was sitting at a table and we were getting assigned lockers. We had to share and so I got assigned to share with the girl sitting across the table from me. I remember her, this girl. She was the smartest kid in the whole class, you know, the one that always got the best grades, and I was excited to think I was going to have a reason to talk to her now and she was going to have to talk to me; but then, I was also sort of scared because I knew she didn't like me very well."

"*You* were the smartest kid in the whole class, Sheil."

"No, I wasn't. She got the best grades. I tried, but she got them."

"You were the smartest kid, regardless of who got the grades."

"Yeah, I read about what you said my IQ was in your book. I read it and thought, God, you faked that one. That's not me," she replied.

"It is."

"It isn't."

"Has no one ever told you in all this time that you were gifted?" Sheila shook her head.

Shocked, I looked over. "You're kidding."

"I'm not gifted, Torey. I know I'm not."

"What makes you say that?"

"Well, just 'cause. I mean, I'm me. I know. And I'm not smart. I'm stupid."

"You're not!"

She didn't respond, but I could tell I had not convinced her.

"So, give me one example of why you think you're stupid."

"Well, like, in class, for instance, everybody else gets the information the first time the teacher gives it out, but I never do. I hear it and I think I understand it, but then I start getting questions. I think, what about this? Or, like, oftentimes, I'll think, well, that's true in this instance, but is it true in another instance? And every time I'll see there's a time when it *isn't* true, but then it *is* true some of the time. Then I realize there's this big huge area of junk I don't understand at all, but everybody else is sitting around me, writing like mad. *They* understand it and I don't. And if I ask the questions, then pretty soon the teacher says, 'We've got to move on now. You're holding us up.' And then I know for sure I'm some kind of mega-dumbhead, because I only understand a weensy bit of it."

Her cheeks grew blotched, making me realize the intensity of her emotions over the subject. Pushing the shaggy mass of hair back from her face, she rested her hands against her reddened skin. "And the kids . . . Whenever I try to ask something, everybody groans. They say, 'Oh, God, not her again.' Or, 'Shut her up, would you?' This one kid who sat in front of me in math, he turned around to me and said, 'Shit, can't you just *do* it, for once?' I wanted to die, I was so embarrassed. I never asked anything again in there."

Pointed silence hung between us. Sharp, it was, like a small dagger. Sheila turned to me. "It's because I'm the youngest in the class.

I haven't had as much school as they have and it isn't fair." Her voice was heavy with accusation. "How can they expect me to know as much?"

"You're youngest in the class, Sheila, because you know *more* than they do, not less. The other kids aren't asking questions, because their minds don't throw up so many possibilities so quickly as yours. They don't even realize questions are there."

She chewed her lower lip a moment. Staring ahead at the far-stretching road, she sighed wearily. "If I'm so smart, how come I feel so stupid then? What kind of gift is it that turns the world upside down, so that less is more and more is less?"

*   *   *

We arrived in Marysville in the midafternoon after a leisurely journey across the state. The day had grown very hot, the sky going white with the heat, and coming into the shady streets of the town was a relief. I booked us into a motel on Main Street that, much to Sheila's delight, had a swimming pool. Unfortunately, she didn't have a swimming suit, so we made a jaunt out to find one at the shopping mall. The mall hadn't been there when I had last been in town, and as with all such places, Sheila was keen to explore. Consequently, we wandered around for an hour or two, by which time we were ready for an evening meal; so we stopped for supper in the mall food court before returning to the motel. Feeling overcome with nostalgia as I drove through the familiar streets, I would have preferred going out then and there to visit some old haunts, but Sheila was desperate to go in the pool. Thus, we spent the evening swimming.

The next morning, it was raining steadily.

"Oh, geez, would you believe it?" Sheila said in dismay, as she pulled the curtain back from the motel window. "In July? It never rains in July."

It certainly did that particular July day and by the looks of the clouds, it was not close to stopping. "Come on," I said, "it won't matter. Let's go."

Sheila wanted to go out to see the migrant camp. I thought I remembered the road, but it turned out I didn't and we were soon lost. This left me feeling a bit irritable, which wasn't a good start.

When we did finally locate it, we found the camp full to bursting with seasonal workers. Several types of crops were at a harvestable stage, which had caused the usual swell in camp numbers, but as it was raining and some crops could not be worked, many of the workers were milling around the various buildings.

The camp itself had changed considerably from what I remembered of it. Two large new housing units had been erected. They were great green-painted aluminum structures reminiscent of the calving sheds I was used to in Montana, and they dominated the camp. Many of the old tar-paper buildings that made up my clearest memories of the migrant camp were gone and the layout of the old roads in the camp had been disrupted by the new buildings.

What Sheila was thinking, as we drove through the rutted tracks around the housing units, I do not know. She had become increasingly silent as we approached the camp. Face turned away from me, she looked out the window.

There was a different atmosphere here to when I used to come out to see Anton. It didn't strike me as a particularly safe place for two young white women to wander around alone and a lot of people were noticing us, even in the car. As a consequence, I didn't suggest we get out of the car. It was with a sense of relief that I drove through the gates and back up onto the main road. Sheila still didn't speak.

Back in town, I took the car slowly down a few of the streets I knew best. I pointed out where my old apartment had been. The pizzeria where Chad and I had taken Sheila after the hearing had been replaced by a bar and lounge, but I showed her where it had been. We had an invitation to Chad's house for a picnic supper and fireworks for the next day, and I mentioned that I hoped the weather would improve.

Down a quiet, tree-lined suburban street I located our old school. A low, one-story brick building with white trim, it fit in attractively with the neighborhood of ranch-style homes. This wasn't a wealthy suburb by any means, but it was solidly middle class, the type of area that so embodied the American Dream of the fifties and sixties. Most of my teaching career since had been spent in drafty, old, turn-of-the-century buildings in the less-affluent parts of large cities, and I had forgotten just what a small, attractive school this had been. The contrast with the migrant camp struck me forcefully.

Pulling the car over to the curb, I turned off the engine. "Recognize this place?"

Sheila nodded faintly.

"See that window there, three along on the left? That was our room," I said.

Absorbed silence.

"Do you remember any of this?"

"I don't know," she murmured quietly.

I certainly remembered. All the little moments came crowding back, grappling one with the other to reach my consciousness first. There was the door where I lined the children up, observing the military precision my principal had loved so well. There were the seesaws the kids always fought over. There was the wide expanse of asphalt where Anton and I had struggled to teach them dodgeball and kickball and . . .

"Are there still special-ed kids in that classroom?" Sheila asked.

"The room isn't a classroom anymore. They've made a counseling center out of it," I said. "I suppose we could get out and walk around, if you want . . ."

"No."

I started the engine, then paused, hoping for what I'm not sure. Finally I pulled away from the curb and drove off.

After another half hour of cruising up and down the back streets, I began toying with the idea of visiting the shopping mall again. It was still raining heavily and my mood was going from wistful to something less comfortable, making me realize I'd had enough nostalgia for one day.

"You want to do something?" I asked. "I think I saw where there are movie theaters out at the shopping center. Shall we go see what's on?"

Sheila shook her head. "Let's go to that park," she said, "the one where you took those pictures of the last day of school."

"Why don't we wait until it stops raining? Maybe tomorrow, before we go see Chad."

"No, let's go now."

The park was just as beautiful as I remembered it, with its broad winding entrance road lined with locust trees and flower borders. I parked the car on the street and we walked slowly down amidst the flowers. The floral display being quite stupendous, I was entranced. I am very fond of gardening and was curious about the plants used, so I stopped along the way to examine them. Sheila, however, was totally lost to the here and now. She walked as if bewitched.

The lane ended at the duck pond. When we reached the point where it met the path circling the water, Sheila stopped stock-still. Her brow furrowing, she watched the ducks and geese noisily announce our arrival. One by one, they clambered out of the water and waddled over until we were surrounded, and all the time, Sheila never moved. She just stared down the path to the water, her expression inward, and I suspect she never saw the ducks at all.

The ghosts rose up before my eyes also. With an intensity I hadn't experienced elsewhere, the past came back to me. The rain disappeared and the air was full of children's voices. "Look at me, Torey! Look what I can do! How big the trees are here. Do you see the bunnies they got? Down here, come this way, so I can show you. Can I feed the ducks? Can I wade in the pond? Let's roll down the hill. Torey? Torey, look at me!"

And there on the path around the duck pond was Sheila, little Sheila in her bright-orange sunsuit, running, skipping, laughing. She threw out her arms and spun around, letting her head fall back, her long hair sail out in a sunlit halo. Around and around and around she turned, completely oblivious to the other walkers on the path, the other children, us. Eyes closed against the sun, lips parted in a half-smile, she satisfied some inner dream to dance.

Did she remember? I glanced sidelong at the gangly adolescent beside me. Intuition told me she was remembering something, and I longed to know her thoughts just then, but I dared not ask.

"I was happy here," she whispered after a long silence. It was said so softly that I couldn't detect the emotion it held. Finally she turned away from the duck pond. Crossing the grass to reach the lane again, we started back to the car.

We were soaking wet by then. It was warm summer rain. I wasn't particularly uncomfortable, but everything was dripping. Sheila bent to pick up a long, brown locust pod that had fallen on the walk.

"When I think of Marysville, I always think of locust trees," I said. "I remember how they used to scent the air when they were blooming. I remember driving into Marysville the first time. I'd come along the highway and as it dips down the hill into the valley, I can recall having my car window down, and I could smell Marysville before I got here. And when the blossoms start to fall, it's like snow. I remember coming out in the mornings and my car would be covered."

Sheila stopped, turned and looked back down the lane toward the duck pond, no longer visible. Pausing, she slit open the locust bean with her fingernail and took out the seeds, letting them drop to the wet pavement. "These are poisonous, did you know?" she asked and threw the empty pod out into the road. "They can actually kill you."

*　　*　　*

Sheila grew increasingly moody. Keen to rescue the situation, I suggested we go for a couple of games of bowling, a sport I knew she enjoyed very much. No, she didn't want to do that. An ice-cream cone at Baskin & Robbins? No. Was she sure? I'd pop for a banana split with extra nuts and whipped cream? No. A browse around the bookstore? No. All she wanted to do was just drive around more.

Having more or less exhausted the town, I tried the countryside, heading north along a network of small rural roads. We were soon into open countryside, comprised mainly of corn- and wheat fields. The area was hilly and Marysville had quickly disappeared from view to leave the fields stretching away from us in an undulating fashion for as far as the eye could see.

I made a few efforts at conversation, but they were useless. Sheila sat absolutely silent. Arms folded across her chest, she gazed out the passenger window so motionlessly that I could have been driving around with one of those inflatable dolls in the front seat beside me and no one would have discerned the difference.

The rain lessened, then finally stopped altogether, and very slowly the clouds began to break up. It was already early evening, so when the first patches of blue sky began to appear in the west, the sun came slanting across the hills.

"Stop!" Sheila cried. Not only was it the first word she had spoken in the better part of an hour and a half, which made it startling enough, but she said it with such suddenness that I fully expected to hit something with the car. I slammed on the brakes sufficiently hard to throw us both sharply forward. This made her smile briefly in my direction, before pointing to the east. "Look at that."

For a short, shining moment, color was sovereign. The wet asphalt of the road gleamed black against the sudden gold of the sun-lit wheat. Beyond the ruffling grain rose the dark remains of the storm clouds, pierced through by a rainbow. Only a very short part of the rainbow was visible; there was not even enough to form a clear arc, but that small section shimmered brilliantly above the restless wheat.

"Oh, God," Sheila murmured softly, as she regarded the sight, "why do beautiful things make me feel so sad?"

eighteen

Back at the motel, we had our evening meal and then went out to enjoy the pool. The rain had cleared away entirely to give a cloudless night, the stars dimmed by the town's lights but still faintly discernible.

Sheila remained subdued. There was a heavy, almost depressed feel to her quietness. For the first time, she put aside that smoldering anger I always sensed just below the surface. In its place was nothing, just a great emptiness.

The exercise did me good. The pool was cool enough to let me swim hard and I did, blocking out everything except the feel of the water rushing over me, until at last I surfaced, tired and relaxed. Sheila wasn't a very good swimmer. I suspect she had never been taught and just got by on what she'd figured out over the years, but she kept at it almost as long as I did. Then we both retreated to the warmth of the Jacuzzi.

Back in the motel room, she stood before the mirror toweling her hair dry. She studied her reflection as she worked.

"Do you like me?" she asked.

Having finished with my shower and changed into my nightgown, I was lying on my bed and inspecting the TV schedule. Her question caught me unawares. "Well, yes, of course I do."

"I know I look stupid," she said to her reflection. "I know you think I do."

"No."

"Yes," she said. "You do. Everybody does. I do too." She ran her fingers through her hair, smoothing it down. "You see, I just don't want to look like me. That's why I do it. I can put up with looking stupid, if there's a chance that it might make me into someone else."

* * *

Once she was in her bed, I turned the light out. It wasn't all that late, only a little after eleven, but the swimming, combined with the emotional rigors of the day, had left me exhausted. I was ready for sleep and drowsy almost immediately.

Sheila turned restlessly in her bed. The room was very dark, so I could only hear her, not see her, but the sound of her movements kept intruding.

"Torey? You asleep?"

"No, not quite."

Silence.

"You wanted to say something?" I inquired.

A second long pause. She turned again. "A lot's changed," she said quietly.

"In what way?"

"In the migrant camp. It's a lot different to what I remember it."

I didn't answer.

"I do remember it. I haven't forgotten everything." A pause. "My memory's like Swiss cheese. It's got big holes in it. But other things . . . I saw the camp today and it was, like . . . well, like I'd never been away. I can remember it so good."

Silence then, long enough that I felt myself growing drowsy again.

"You know what I used to do at night, when we lived in the camp?" Sheila asked into the darkness.

"What's that?"

"Well, my pa used to always be out drinking," she said, using her old name for her father for the first time since we'd been reunited. "He used to leave me. Nearly every night. He'd give me, like, a bag of corn chips or something and tell me to go to bed, and then he'd go out. And once he was gone, I used to get up and go out into the camp and walk around. It was dark. It was, like, really late at night, and I would look for places with lights on. We didn't have any electricity then, just a kerosene lantern and a flashlight. So, I'd look for these places with lights and then I'd go peek in their windows. All the time. Every night."

"Why? Because of being alone? Or the light?" I asked.

"Yeah. I wanted light, I remember that. But mostly just to see what they lived like. A lot of the people weren't a lot different than us, but I just wanted to see."

A pause.

"I got in trouble for it. My pa catch me and I'd be whipped red for it."

Catch. I heard the word in its present-tense form, echoing Sheila's old childhood speech patterns. We never had found out why she spoke like that and since we had been reunited, she had used remarkably impeccable grammar for an adolescent. It was eerie to lie in the dark and listen to these long-ago words and speech patterns begin to reemerge.

"The police got me once. More than once, I think. People thought I was stealing things, but I wasn't. I'd just been looking."

"I can understand," I said softly. "It must have been lonely, being left on your own so often, when you were such a young child."

"Yeah," came the quiet, disembodied voice through the darkness. "It was."

A long silence followed. I had woken fully up by then and lay staring up. The curtains were heavy to shut out the motel security lights, but the occasional car turning into the parking lot shot a brief spear of light over the top. This threw the stucco ceiling into sudden relief.

"Can I tell you what happened sometimes?" she asked.

"Here? When you were little?"

"Yeah. When we lived in the migrant camp. When I was in your class."

"Yes, of course," I said.

"I had a mattress on the floor. That's where I slept. My pa slept on the couch. But he'd go out boozing and when he came home . . . there were always people with him. Women, usually. And they'd fuck on the couch."

"Yes, I can remember you telling me once," I said.

"But sometimes . . ." She stopped.

I listened into the darkness. She was breathing shallowly, her breaths audible to me in the next bed.

"Well, he was doing drugs. You knew that too, didn't you?" she asked.

"Yes."

"Smack mostly. And these guys got it for him. There were two. Sometimes he'd come home with them. Sometimes it was one or the other, sometimes both of them, but he never used to have enough money to pay them. I can remember lying there listening to him pleading with them. Begging them to give him the stuff, telling them how he was going to get them money. He'd even cry some of the time; I can remember hearing him."

I watched the patterns flash black and headlight-yellow across the ceiling.

"Well, this one guy, he used to give it to my dad cheap if . . . He liked me to lay down with him . . . He didn't fuck me or anything; it's just he liked little girls. Like to feel them over. And if I sucked his cock, my pa got his stuff cheap."

My blood ran like ice. "Why didn't you tell me?"

"How do you say that when you're six? Besides, it was my life. I was used to it."

I lay awake long after Sheila fell asleep. Memories came back to me, one after another, of the days in our classroom. Things had been *so* bad for her. She had been such a deprived, neglected child that there would have been no way of doing everything that had wanted doing, of undoing all the harm. I had known that then and had approached her one small issue at a time, changing what I could. Yet somewhere between then and now I had come to believe I had saved her from the worst. To realize now that even while in my room she had continued to suffer hurt me; that I had never even perceived it hurt me worse. Over and over and over I pondered on what more I should have done.

*　　*　　*

The next morning, Sheila was back to her usual, rather off-the-wall self. She spent ages in the bathroom doing her hair to emerge looking not a whole lot tidier than when she had arisen from bed, and her outfit, a cute little number involving exceptionally ragged cutoff jeans and a shimmery green top that would have been more at home in a Las Vegas floor show, needed to be seen to be believed.

It was the Fourth of July and our agenda for the day included the picnic with Chad and his family. I was very much looking forward to this. Chad and I had remained on good terms throughout the metamorphosis of our relationship from the physical to the platonic, and in the last few years it had matured into a genuine friendship. We were now in contact frequently, exchanging stimulating letters and lengthy phone calls, but the fact remained that I had never met his wife nor seen his three young daughters. Bringing Sheila with me created the prospect of an even more enjoyable reunion.

We drove over to Chad's house at three. He lived down a quiet, unpaved lane on the very edge of town. His was a beautiful house, new and huge, with a three-car garage and a tennis court to the side. I must confess to a twinge of remorse, or perhaps it was jealousy, when I saw it, knowing that this could have been mine. Not that I was particularly keen on houses of that sort or wanted that kind of lifestyle, and I didn't even play tennis, but it was impossible to ignore his level of success.

"Wow," Sheila murmured as we pulled into the drive and summed the whole matter up in that one word.

Before we were out of the car, Chad was at the door, opening it wide. "Welcome!" he said and children came spilling out around him.

His wife, Lisa, appeared beside him. Of Latino descent, she had the most exquisite eyes, dark and sparkly. She was a lawyer too and I had heard so much about her reputation as a killer in the courtroom that I had been expecting something quite different from what I saw. She was sweetly pretty and quite petite, rather the way one imagines fairy-tale heroines.

"And here," Chad was saying, as he pulled a small girl in front of him, "here's my Sheila."

His Sheila and my Sheila eyed one another. Like her mother, Chad's daughter was pretty in a girlish sort of way. Her hair was dark and curled naturally in long, loose ringlets down over her shoulders. She was dressed impeccably in a two-tone green designer-brand outfit that beautifully showed off the rich color of her hair.

"Sheila's five," Chad said, lovingly clasping her to his side. She smiled up at him. "And these . . . girls, come here. Stand still a moment. This is Bridget, who's four. And this is Maggie. How old are you, Maggie?"

Laboriously, Maggie worked at holding up two fingers.

"That's right. Clever girl! Maggie's just had her birthday last Saturday."

Like their elder sister, both Bridget and Maggie were blessed with dark curly hair and laughing eyes, and both were attractively dressed in practical, but expensive clothes. All three girls were friendly, open children, chatting easily with Sheila and me, inviting us to come around to the backyard and see the picnic table and the box of fireworks.

At the back of the house, we found a large redwood deck ingeniously laid out to include a sandbox near the patio doors and to progress away on one side to a large wooden swing set and climbing frame and on the other to a large, landscaped garden that ended with a fence that overlooked open fields.

"Come see our horses," Chad's Sheila called cheerily and ran down the grass ahead of us. "Do you like to ride, Sheila? Do you want a ride on my horse? I'll take you."

"Thanks," Sheila replied, her voice hesitant. "Thanks, but not just now, okay? Maybe later."

"Well, come down and see them. Mom? Mommy, give us apples." She came running back up to the deck. She took Sheila's hand. "Come on. We'll get some apples and go down. I want to show you."

Chad and I, sitting in chairs on the deck, watched the two girls go off down the lawn toward the fence at the bottom.

"There's something I never thought I'd see," he said, his voice thoughtful.

"No."

There was a long moment's pause. "She's changed, hasn't she?" he said.

I didn't know quite how to respond. That had been my first impression too, but increasingly I was realizing that, no, Sheila hadn't actually changed much at all.

"I mean, that *hair*," he continued, when I didn't speak. "And those clothes! She's going to scare the horses." He laughed. "I suppose it's just adolescence, but I must admit, I didn't expect it of her. She always seemed such a practical little thing."

"She didn't have much choice in those days."

"How's it going for her?" Chad asked.

Sitting in my deck chair, I watched her with little Sheila, feeding apples to the two horses. "I don't know," I replied. "I haven't quite figured that out yet."

*   *   *

I sensed there was trouble fairly early on. Sheila mooched around on the outside of the crowd almost from the beginning. The little girls tried to engage her in various activities, ranging from riding the horses to grilling hot dogs on the barbecue, but for the most part, Sheila resisted their efforts. Initially, she wasn't unpleasant about it, just distant. However, as the afternoon progressed into evening, she became increasingly detached from the group. Long periods were spent wandering around the perimeter of the yard or swinging listlessly on one of the swings.

Feeling responsible for her, I tried to gloss over her behavior, especially to Lisa, who was going out of her way to try and include Sheila. I think perhaps things might have worked out better if Lisa simply could have ignored her and let her join in at her own rate, but this seemed to go against Lisa's innate way of dealing with children. It had become apparent very early on that Lisa was a doer and a joiner. Wanting to see Maggie, Bridget and Sheila sufficiently stimulated and socialized, she had provided schedules so full of lessons and extramural activities for her daughters that they probably maintained their own Filofaxes. Likewise, the picnic had been planned with exquisite attention to detail aimed at giving everyone a Very Good Time. That Sheila was refusing to join in implied she was not having a Very Good Time and this troubled Lisa to no end.

Sheila contributed to this. Discerning that she could bug Lisa so easily, she began to go at it wholeheartedly as the evening went on. Her ennui grew more obvious. The little girls irritated her, making her frown evilly at them when they came around her, and worst of all, she turned her back on the fireworks. Chad would light one, up it would go. Flash! Bang! Then all the oohs and aahs, while Sheila, bored, leaned against the deck railing and stared through the patio doors at Chad's dining-room table.

In turn, I got drawn into this too. Mortified by Sheila's rude behavior, I first tried making excuses, then tried tugging her off to the privacy of the bathroom for a quick word. She was having no quick words. She was having no words at all.

"Why are you so angry?" I hissed.

"You're the one who's angry," she replied in a sensible sort of voice.

"You've been angry with me the whole frigging time we've been back together. You act like everything is my fault."

"Well, isn't it?" she replied.

*   *   *

How we managed through the last hour at Chad's I don't know. I *was* angry. As far as I was concerned, the evening had been totally ruined. Here was my first time of meeting Chad's wife and his daughters, my first time face-to-face with Chad in many years, and what a jolly affair this had turned out to be. I felt like dumping Sheila off at the nearest bus station and buying her a one-way ticket back to Broadview.

The silence during the ten-minute ride back to the motel was lethal. Sheila was gloating, or at least that's what it felt like from my perspective. Having stirred all of us up into a lather, she appeared calm and detached, if not even a bit superior. I got the distinct sense that she thought she was above all this. With each passing minute, my feelings grew fiercer.

"Well, this evening was a write-off," I said crossly, as we got out of the car at the motel. Fumbling with the keys, I unlocked our room.

"You are really a control freak, you know that?" Sheila said. "God, you have got to be in charge of everything."

"I do not."

"You think you own my life. You think you created me. You think I'm just a character in your book."

"I do not!" I retorted.

"You do. I didn't say I wanted to go there tonight. You're the one who arranged it and you didn't ask my opinion of it. Why should I want to go over there? I don't even know those people."

"You *do*. That's Chad, for God's sake."

Sheila shrugged insolently. "*I* don't know him. Could have been anybody and his stupid kids there, as far as I knew."

"That was *Chad*. Who kept you out of the state hospital. Who stood up for you when nobody else would. All he did—"

She cut me off with one fierce downward movement of her arm, like a sword stroke. "And I'm supposed to be so grateful, aren't I?" Her voice rose. "That's what you want. I'm supposed to be so god-damned, fucking grateful to all of you guys for what you did for me. That's it, isn't it? That's what you want."

"*No.*"

"It *is*. Don't go fucking me around, Torey. That's what you want. To make yourself into such a good guy. That's the only reason you came back."

"It's not!" I cried.

Seeing her face, I realized a monster had been unleashed. Her face went from pink to red to a deeper scarlet, the veins becoming prominent at her temples. Her eyes dilated and her lips drew back against her teeth. Warning bells went off somewhere far back in my mind, alerting me to my own physical safety.

"You think you made my life better, do you?" she yelled, her voice growing louder with each word. "You think you *fixed* things? You didn't. You made them worse. A million, million, million times worse than they ever were before!"

"Whoa, whoa, whoa," I said.

"*No!*" she cried passionately, "you whoa. You're the one who can't stop meddling. You leave my life alone!"

I regarded her.

"You set me up, Torey. You took me in that room and you let me play with all those toys and read all those books and you just made me feel like a million dollars, and then what did you do? Did you stay? Did you take care of me once you got me?" Her mouth drew down to where I thought she was going to cry and there was one very long, shuddery intake of breath. "You set me up, knowing all along you were going to leave."

"I didn't mean—" I started.

"You *did!* You meant every goddamned thing you did with me, Torey. I never knew how fucking awful my life was until then, and then you came along and suddenly there's this whole other world. And you *meant* that. You controlled the whole thing. You created me out of shit and made me think I smelled like flowers."

"Sheila, listen to—"

"You made me believe you loved me."

"I *did* love you, Sheila. I still do."

"Oh, shit, don't give me that. How could you? You left me."

"Sheila—"

"You had so much power, Torey. I loved you such a terribly lot, *so much.* And what did you do? You pushed me out that door and left me."

"Sheila, *please.*"

"But you're never the fuck going to do it again!" she cried, and before I realized what was happening, she had opened the door to the motel room and was gone.

nineteen

I stood, shell-shocked, for only a moment or two before running to the door to see where she was. In that short time, she had disappeared into the night.

"Sheila? Sheila, where are you?" I called.

A door down the way opened. "Could you keep it down out there?" someone shouted.

Gripped with real fear, I closed the motel door and went back inside. What now? I looked around the room. Her meager possessions lay strewn around her bed. What should I do? Would she come back of her own accord? Should I go looking for her? Or leave well enough alone? I felt paralyzed with helplessness.

Sitting down on my bed, I tried to pull my thoughts together. Where would she be likely to go? The migrant camp came first to mind, but surely not. Surely she would have more sense than to go there, alone, in the middle of the night. And why? Would there still be anyone there she'd know? I doubted it. She had given no indication of still having connections with anyone in Marysville.

Where else? The only places I could think of were those where we had spent time together and I couldn't imagine, given the circumstances, that she would go to any of them. Most likely, she would head for the town center, simply because shopping areas were the places many teenagers escaped to when distressed. Obviously, little was likely to be open so late at night, especially in a community the size of Marysville, but it was Fourth of July night . . . Worried, I gathered up my car keys and set out to search for Sheila.

Around and around and around I drove, the streets becoming increasingly familiar again, until old, long-forgotten journeys through Marysville started coming back to me. It was a very still place that late at night. There were a few cars "turning the point" down on

Main Street, but otherwise, mine was the only vehicle for blocks, sometimes miles, at a time.

I went downtown three or four times and found no sign of her. From there, I followed the main road leading out to the shopping district that had grown up around the mall. I circled the whole town, using the highway to connect outgoing roads, and finally went out to the migrant camp.

There, unlike the rest of Marysville, people were up and moving around. Indeed, it was lively in certain parts, making me suspect that, as in the old days, not all the residents spent their days in hard labor. There were numerous drugged or drunken men lying about in one area on the lower end and I found myself feeling very ill at ease. Unwilling to roll my window down, I didn't stop and ask anyone if they had seen a girl of Sheila's description.

All my fond recollections of Marysville came crashing down to dust in those early hours spent driving around the town. I hated it by the end and only wanted to reach the highway and head home; however, worry kept me at the ceaseless midnight circling.

At long last, about two in the morning, I saw Sheila. She was in quite an unexpected area of town, walking along one of the larger arterial roads out in the residential part not far from our old school. It was only by chance I happened to be coming that way, as I had had an idea of a different part of downtown to search and was taking a shortcut to get there. I pulled the car up along the curb and rolled the window down.

"Look, I'm sorry. Can we go back to the motel and sort things out?"

Her eyes were wide and dark in the dim illumination of the streetlight, which gave her a wild, almost animalistic appearance. I sensed she was very frightened and not likely to be predictable.

"I am sorry," I said in my most contrite voice. "Come on, please? Come back with me."

She shook her head. "No. Go away. I don't need you."

"Please?"

She regarded me.

"Well, look, let's go get a hamburger or something, if you don't want to go back to the motel. Okay?"

Sheila hesitated, which encouraged me to keep on.

"We could go over to Lenny's. They're open all night. Come on. Please?"

Much to my relief, she opened the passenger door and got in. Indeed, she almost fell in, giving away just how very tired she was. I glanced over at her with her yellow hair and her silly clothes, crumpled in exhaustion. God, how hard it is to be fourteen.

Once in the restaurant, Sheila tucked hungrily into a whole plate of food, while I nursed a cup of coffee and a stale doughnut, but she didn't talk. I didn't press her. We were both too tired for that.

Afterward, she came back to the motel with me without any protest. Once in the room, she sat down on her bed and began to pull off her heavy work boots. "I'm not staying," she said quietly. "Tomorrow comes and I'm getting out of here."

"Yes, I think I'm ready to as well."

"No, Torey. That's not what I mean," she said, looking up. "I'm not going with you. I'm not going to sit in a car for four hours with you. I'm going home on my own."

I regarded her.

"And you can't stop me," she added to my unspoken words.

"No, I won't stop you. If that's what you want, I'll take you down to the bus station tomorrow and we'll get you a ticket. And you can take the first one out."

"*I'll* get me a ticket," she said.

"No, Sheila, I'm quite happy to get it. Save your money."

"No, I said, *I'll* get it, Torey. You don't own me, so don't try."

Wearily, I nodded. "Fine. Do it that way."

✳   ✳   ✳

Once in bed with the lights out, I lay staring into the darkness. What had gone wrong? What had happened between last night, when we had seemed so close, and tonight, when we felt worlds apart? As if she were reading my thoughts, Sheila spoke.

"You left me. Don't you know how much that hurt me?" Her voice was soft, almost inaudible even in the nighttime silence.

"I didn't want to, Sheila."

"Then why did you?"

"Because it was simply the way things were. I was a teacher. My end came in June when school finished and there was nothing I could do about that . . ."

"It wasn't right, what you did," she said so softly. A long pause followed. "You left me behind."

"I'm sorry. I truly am."

"And it wasn't just that. You took it all with you when you went— the sun, the moon, the stars. Everything. What right did you have to give it to me, when you just took it all away again?"

✳   ✳   ✳

Sheila did not return to the summer-school program on Monday, when we resumed after the Fourth of July break. I had neither seen nor heard from her since putting her on the bus in Marysville. Although I longed to phone, if for no other reason than to reassure myself she had made it home all right, I knew instinctively that I had to stay away.

Jeff, ever keen to perceive my moods, cornered me back in our office after lunch. "Okay, so what's going on?" he asked. "Where'd the Orangutan hie off to?"

I gave him a brief synopsis of what had happened on our visit to Marysville.

"Ooh," he replied, as if touching a bruise. There was a pause while he put away a medical journal that had lain open on his desk for the better part of the last week, then he looked over. "I can see where she's coming from, though. She's already been abandoned by one mother. Then you come along, provide all the attention and nurturing she was so desperate for. Then *you* disappear. At six it's going to be difficult for her to discern that what you've done is any different from what her mother did."

"Yes, I know that, but it *was* different. I was her teacher."

"Okay, so you were her teacher," he said. "But what was on your curriculum, Hayden? Math? Reading? Or was it love? Confidence? Self-esteem?"

"What should I have done with her?" I asked. "Left her alone? Seen this incredible kid in this even more incredible situation and done nothing?"

Leaning back in his desk chair, Jeff pursed his lips.

"*Are* you saying I shouldn't have done it?" I asked.

"Are you?"

Turning away, I sighed. "That's a pointless question, actually. I can't turn back time and change anything. The real question is: what do I do now?"

Balancing a paper clip on his thumbnail, Jeff aimed and then flicked it into the pencil holder on his desk. "You do what all of us do in this business: pray that in the end you've helped more than you've hurt."

*   *   *

Sheila remained absent from the program for the rest of the week and also the following Monday. Late Monday afternoon, when I was in my office at the clinic, there was a soft knock on my closed door.

"Yes? Come in."

Sheila gently pushed the door open. "Can I talk to you?"

I nodded.

"Is Jeff here? I want to talk privately. I don't want him walking in," she said.

"No, he won't. He's over at the hospital and won't be back tonight," I replied.

Sheila closed the door behind her and came across to Jeff's desk. Pulling the chair out, she sat down. She looked around. "So this is your office, huh?"

"Yup." I had been marking a file and returned to finish it off.

She studied Jeff's bulletin board. "You guys sure are alike. Look, you got your junk arranged just like his junk. You even got the identical same Pink Panther things. 'This is where Jeff lives it up' this one says. 'This is where Torey lives it up.' Where'd you get them?"

"Jeff got them," I replied.

"Do you love him?" Sheila asked, rocking herself idly back and forth in the desk chair.

"I *like* him. A great deal. But if you mean romantic love, no. I've got somebody else."

"Oh? Who? I haven't seen you with anybody."

I looked over. "Surely you haven't come all the way up here from Broadview to talk to me about my love life."

"Yeah, well, I was just trying to get your attention," she said. "You've hardly looked up since I walked in. The whole time you've had your stupid nose stuck in that thing you're writing."

Closing the file, I laid it up in the basket and turned in my chair toward her. "I'm all yours."

"Gosh, look. You got my poem up there. You never told me you put my poem on the wall."

"I wasn't hearing from you very much then," I said. "I didn't have your address."

"Yeah, I was in the children's home then, when I wrote that."

Her tone was light and breezy, her attitude, as she lazily rotated the chair, relaxed. One would never have known anything had happened between us. It would have taken her forty-five minutes on the bus to get up here from Broadview, plus a good ten-minute walk from the nearest bus stop, so this was hardly a casual visit. Yet Sheila was giving nothing away.

"Is there anything I can do for you?" I asked.

"Well, it's almost five o'clock. I thought maybe you would like to go out for Italian with me or something. It doesn't have to be pizza. We could go for spaghetti. Or something else, if you want."

I grinned.

"Or you could take me over to your house. I've never been to your place. I got to thinking that if we stopped at the supermarket first, I could get things and make you supper. I make this really good thing with tuna fish and a can of mushroom soup."

"I'd loved to," I said, "but unfortunately, I've already got plans for this evening."

Her face fell. "Is it with this guy?"

I nodded.

There was an enormous silence.

"Look, I'm sorry," I said. "I really would have loved to, it's just I didn't know in time. Maybe we can some other night."

Head down so that the yellow hair fell forward, obscuring her features, she sighed heavily. "I'm *trying* to say sorry to you," she muttered. A pause. "And I wanted to come over to your house."

twenty

Tuesday morning found Sheila back with us. As with me the afternoon before, she behaved as if nothing in particular had happened and there had been no absence. I had threatened Jeff to keep him from making an issue of it. Miriam inquired politely and Sheila blithely lied through her teeth, saying she had been ill.

Alejo was charmingly pleased to see Sheila. When she came through the door, his small face lit up and he ran across the room to throw his arms around her in an enthusiastic hug. This caught all of us by surprise, as Alejo had remained an aloof, unpredictable boy throughout the weeks, but none of us more so than Sheila. An expression of alarm crossed her face first, when the boy so eagerly grasped hold of her, but then she smiled and bent to hug him back.

Throughout the summer program, Sheila, like Alejo, had been a guarded soul. It was apparent by now that this was not a particularly natural setting for her. She did not innately respond to young children in the way that some teenaged girls do, and she found some of the more difficult situations unsettling, because, I suspect, they still came just a little too close to home. Jeff and I had discussed this and felt it was best to let her continue to the end, as we were not that far off now, but we agreed that to expect more in the way of help from Sheila was probably unrealistic.

She appeared genuinely happy to be back with us. Her mood was positive, if not downright sunny. Thus far, among the children she had only responded in a relaxed and natural way to Alejo and occasionally to David. The girls, in particular, she had shunned, which was a pity, as we could have done with a good role model for Kayleigh, Tamara and Violet. However, on this morning, she showed genuine warmth and generosity toward several of the children. Even Violet.

Over the course of the summer, Violet had developed what could only be described as a crush on Sheila. She had struggled vainly to catch Sheila's attention, to sit near her, to hold her hand. A big, ungainly girl with plain features and annoying persistence, Violet wasn't very easy to accept, even in the best of circumstances. Sheila had found her obsessional fervor irritating and Violet's repeated efforts to touch her horrid. I tried to explain to Sheila that such crushes were fairly normal in girls of Violet's age and implied nothing serious, but Sheila, not fully comfortable with her own sexuality, continued to find these advances revolting. On this morning, however, Sheila listened patiently to Violet's various ramblings, and while not allowing Violet to go so far as touch her, she did let the girl sit next to her at snack time.

After snack time, we took the children over to the park across the street and Sheila continued to play actively with them, pushing Kayleigh on the swing, boosting David and Mikey up to the uppermost reaches of the climbing frame.

I realized what was happening. Like the swan, so graceful above water and paddling like hell below the surface, Sheila was working actively on serenity in hopes that all the turmoil brought up between us would disappear, or at least no longer be apparent. Watching her through the morning, I pondered on how much of a behavior pattern this was for her.

Feeling the need to confront this issue, rather than allow her to bury it, I cornered her during the ride down to Fenton Boulevard.

"This might be a good time for us to talk," I said, as I pulled away from the school.

"Oh? About what?"

"About us. About the Fourth of July weekend. There were obviously some very strong feelings and I think it would be better if we cleared them up."

Sheila shrugged, as if I were talking about something completely unknown to her.

"I get the feeling you think I walked out on you when you were little."

"I never said that."

"What I heard was how angry you felt. How you felt that I set you up, how it seemed to you that I didn't care and I just left you."

"It doesn't matter. I'm not angry now," she replied.

"These things need facing, Sheila. If you have such strong feelings, they won't go away just because you pretend they have."

She shrugged. "I don't know. Sooner or later everything else in my life goes away, why not them as well?"

"*Sheila.*"

"Okay, okay, so I was upset," she said wearily. "So what? People get upset. I'm over it now, so let's just leave it at that."

I didn't answer.

Looking over, she smiled beguilingly. "You want me to say I'm sorry, okay? I was stupid. I didn't mean it."

"It's all right to be angry with me," I said. "I don't mind, but let's just be up front about it."

"No, I wasn't angry. Just stupid, that's all. I get like that. So let's forget it. Let's go on like it didn't happen."

"But it *did* happen."

"Not if I say it didn't." She looked over at me. "Things only exist if you believe they exist. That's true. I've read it. And it's true, because I know it."

"So, you're saying that if you don't believe we had the argument, we didn't have it?" I asked.

"Things can only bother you if they exist. And they can only exist if you let them."

Silence came then. I was drawn back abruptly across the years to a dark school closet where I had retreated with Sheila after she had gotten into serious mischief in another teacher's room. That teacher had sent her to the principal, who gave her "swats," the form of corporeal punishment acceptable in my school at the time.

Distressed to have lost control of the situation myself and have a child who I already knew was physically abused at home, then experienced swats at school, I had withdrawn with her into the only private place I could find to try and sort the matter out. Sheila, however, had seemed to take the whole experience in her stride. Indeed, she pointed out with some pride how she had not cried at all when the principal struck her.

"Don't you feel like it?" I had asked in amazement. She was six and I was twenty-four and I felt like it.

"Ain't nobody can hurt me that ways," she'd replied matter-of-factly. "They don't know I hurt if I don't cry. So, they can't hurt me."

Seven years later and I realized Sheila was still operating under a variant of that theory.

*   *   *

We had only two full weeks of the summer program to run. Both Jeff and I were immensely pleased with how it had turned out. There had been hiccups, to be sure, and plenty of things we would do differently the next time around, but in general, it had worked well.

One obvious advantage to providing a program of this nature for our clients was the opportunity to work with them in such a natural milieu. Some of the children, among them Kayleigh and Mikey, had responded well to the group situation and the supportive setting and were well on their way to putting their problems behind them.

Equally useful were the diagnostic advantages of such a setting. A few of the children had been with the clinic for some time without any marked sign of progress. Being with them for three hours a day, five days a week, in such varied circumstances allowed Jeff and me to assess their problems much more accurately than had been possible in the confines of the clinic and its psychiatric hour.

Tamara was a good example of such a child. She had first come to the clinic when she was six on referral from her family doctor. He had treated sores on her forearms, which refused to heal, despite all his efforts. His suspicions that Tamara was inflicting the injuries herself and then preventing the wounds from healing were soon confirmed.

Initially, Tamara had seen one of the other psychiatrists at the clinic, but after eighteen months of therapy, she was referred to Jeff in hopes that she might progress faster with a male therapist. Jeff had been seeing her weekly in play therapy for a further ten months and felt he was still no nearer to helping Tamara control her destructive urges.

The summer program showed us a complex, deeply unhappy little girl, who had difficulty relating to just about everyone, young and old alike. There probably was an element of depression in Tamara's behavior, just as her copious files said, but then depression is a fairly natural reaction to sensing no one likes you. Unable to get the attention she needed through more traditional means, Tamara had discovered that injuries received a lot of notice. Over the course of the program, we saw her draw blood on several different occasions when things didn't go her way. Jeff, armed with these insights, was now working with Tamara to help her improve her interpersonal skills and felt at last that they were moving forward in therapy.

Alejo was another child who had been included for diagnostic purposes. Unfortunately, he wasn't enjoying such a happy ending. Increasingly, Jeff and I were having to acknowledge that the majority of his problems stemmed less from emotional trauma than from low intelligence and, most likely, brain damage. There was no doubt that his traumatic early years had had an effect on him, and this showed itself in his abrupt, sometimes violent, responses to actions around him; however, many of his more trenchant behaviors were simply the result of a boy mentally incapable of coping with the usual demands of school and home. This had become particularly apparent in the ebb and flow of daily activities in the program and Jeff and I were making preparations to discuss the matter with his parents.

I was dreading telling Sheila this, even more than Alejo's parents. Of all the children, Alejo alone was special to her. There had been a natural affinity between them, right from the beginning, and we had encouraged it. Now I regretted having involved her so closely, because I knew Sheila would find the final verdict on Alejo unacceptable.

Unfortunately, I didn't get a chance to tell Sheila. Instead, she overheard Jeff talking to me at the end of one session when we were cleaning up.

"What do you mean, he's got a low IQ? You mean he's retarded?" Sheila asked, coming back to where we were standing.

"Jeff did the official workup last week," I replied.

"Last week? When I was gone? You just waited till I was gone, didn't you?" she retorted.

Jeff turned away, unwilling to get drawn into an argument with her.

"He's not got a low IQ. He's perfectly normal," she said.

Miriam, who was coming back to us with the boxes of crayons and marking pens, said, "He's still a lovely boy."

"He's *not* retarded. That's not why he's not talking. You think he's not talking for that reason, don't you? But it isn't that. He talks to me."

"He talks to us too, Sheila," I said. "But he doesn't say much and why he doesn't say much is because some of the areas of his brain aren't working quite like they should. It's called aphasia."

"I don't care what it's called," she snapped back. "He hasn't got it. He's perfectly normal. He just doesn't talk to *you*. He talks to me just fine. He talks in *Spanish*. So how do you expect him to tell you things when you don't even speak the same language as him?"

Jeff tapped my shoulder. "This isn't worth getting into, Hayden," he murmured quietly.

"Yeah, sure, you'd say that," Sheila said to him. "It's not you they're calling stupid." Throwing down the rag she'd been wiping the tables with, she stomped off.

✳   ✳   ✳

"You can't let that happen to Alejo," Sheila said to me in the car afterward. The anger had gone from her voice, to be replaced by urgent concern.

"No, it's a very difficult situation."

"But you realize what they're going to do, don't you?" she said. "Send him back to Colombia."

"We don't know that for sure. His parents have discussed a lot of different alternatives and that's just one of them."

"You mustn't let it happen."

There was silence between us then. I focused my attention on getting us out onto the freeway.

"You don't *want* it to happen, do you?" she inquired.

"No, of course I don't."

"So, Torey—"

"It isn't my choice, kiddo. He's a lovely boy, but he is brain-damaged, of limited intelligence and emotionally disturbed. That's a lot to cope with. I can encourage his parents to keep him and I certainly will do so. Both Jeff and I will, but we can't force them."

"But what if they want to send him back to Colombia?" she cried. "What if they put him in the orphanage again?"

"Sheila, I haven't got much control over this situation. In fact, he isn't even my client, or Jeff's. So, technically, we have *no* control. I do desperately hope they don't send him back. It would hurt him and I think it's wrong, morally; but I can't make them do anything they don't want to do. Nor stop them from doing anything they do want to do. They are legally Alejo's parents."

Sheila sputtered in angry frustration. "Look what's happened to him! He's been found living in some garbage can and brought here and people have been giving him nice toys and food and TV and everything. And now what are they going to do? Put him back in the garbage can. And you're going to just sit there and let it happen?"

"We're not going to 'just sit,'" I said. "We're going to *try* to keep that from happening. We're going to try to help Alejo change his behavior. We'll try to find an acceptable alternative for his parents."

"And what if you fail?" Sheila asked.

"I'll feel terribly sad."

"That's it? You'll feel sad?"

"That's all I can do," I said.

Folding her arms across her chest, she turned her head away from me. "You're shitholes," she muttered. "You and your kind. You really are fucking shitholes."

twenty-one

My personal life was in a state of flux that summer. I tended toward a pattern of exclusive, long-term relationships that often lasted several years, and was, at the time, "between men," as one close girlfriend so succinctly put it. I had actually been "between" for several months by that point and getting fairly fed up with it.

Synchronizing my life at work with my personal life had always been difficult for me. Although I'd mellowed from earlier years, when the intensity with which I'd thrown myself into classroom life left little room for other activities, I still loved my work profoundly. I still felt a thrill of anticipation on Sunday for the approaching Monday and I still found it nearly impossible to exclude the kids I was working with entirely from my thoughts. I didn't dwell on them, but they were simply there, turning over in the back of my mind. This made me a challenging companion, I knew, and it took a secure, tolerant man to cope. At the time, such men seemed rather thin on the ground.

To complicate matters, I preferred men from outside my profession. It kept me from talking shop twenty-four hours a day, as I was inclined to do with colleagues. And it kept rivalry at bay. I had a fiercely competitive streak, which served me well with the children, because it kept me determined to win even when the odds were not at all in my favor; however, it was lethal to personal relationships. I also enjoyed the slightly schizophrenic experience of maintaining separate lives because it allowed me to develop interests and talents that might otherwise seem mutually exclusive.

The newest contender was Allan. The downtown area of the city had been subjected to redevelopment a few years earlier and many of the old buildings had been rescued from decay and now formed part of a rather elite shopping district. Allan owned a small bookstore tucked into a tiny side street in the midst of this redeveloped area.

I had first met him when I was pursuing an obscure book of Greek plays. Intrigued, he had invited me into the back room to show me his classical collection, which was one of the better come-on lines I had heard. From there we went on to a series of rather nice dinners in restaurants quite unlike the greasy spoons I usually patronized.

Allan was, in a word, civilized. He enjoyed the opera, discussed literary novels in the enthusiastically casual way of one who had not only read them, but actually enjoyed them, and he could pick amazingly good red wines. His apartment was in an old, restored town house not far from the city center, and it was immaculately furnished with Indian rugs and antique furniture. He even had a tablecloth on his table, which indicated real class to someone like me, who seldom had enough of the clutter off the table to find the surface.

I knew right from the beginning that Allan and I were not soul mates, the way Chad and I had been. Allan was finicky, which got on my nerves. I was unpredictable or, as he termed it, "uneven," and that got on his. But there was still much to be said for the relationship, not the least the fact that I had met no one else.

Certainly Allan met the qualifications as far as being outside my profession went. Deep quests into the nether regions of human behavior might as well have been space probes into other galaxies from his point of view. Trying to talk with him about my kids was impossible. But this was all right. I had Jeff to talk to if I wanted to mull something over about work, and when I was outside it, I was perfectly happy discussing Greek poets or Australian Shiraz.

*   *   *

That Friday night, Allan and I had a picnic planned. This was no rude affair with Allan. He had European-style picnics, complete with wicker picnic basket, red-checked cloth to lay on the ground and real plates and glassware. This called for something rather grander than Kentucky Fried Chicken and barbecue beans, so I had spent Thursday roasting eggplants and fiddling with pâtés, while Allan sought out French baguettes and the right wine.

Friday night after work, I came home to put the final touches on the food. We were going to a local beauty spot on the lake that bordered the eastern side of the city. This required serious mosquito protection, so Allan was in the back room trying to get my insect lamp to work.

A knock at the door. Thinking it was the paper boy coming to collect his money, I slipped the check between my teeth and wiped my greasy hands before pulling open the door.

Sheila.

"Hi," she said cheerfully.

"Hi. What are you doing here?" I asked.

"I tried to look your address up in the phone book, but you aren't listed yet, so I called for Directory Inquiries," she replied. "Can I come in?"

"They're not supposed to give out addresses," I replied.

"No, I know it, but if you act like you already got the address, say, like, 'Is that the Hayden on Maple Avenue?' they always say, no, and give you the right address. Or at least part of it. Then you hang up, try again to get someone else and then use that part to get the rest. It always works." She looked past me. "Can I come in?"

She didn't wait for an answer, but came on in anyway. Smiling, she looked around at the walls of my apartment. "Wow, this is neat. I like the way you've done this." She flopped down in a chair. "I came over 'cause I thought maybe we could talk."

I didn't want to make her feel unwelcome, but her visit was totally unexpected. It left me momentarily floundering.

"You're always trying to talk to me in the car when you take me down to Fenton Boulevard and I hate that," Sheila said. "It's too short. I know the ride's going to end and I never can get my thoughts organized fast enough. I didn't have anything to do tonight, so I thought I'd come over here and we can talk."

Was this manipulative? I wondered. Did she know that I would normally give over what I was doing to allow her to talk?

Just then, Allan appeared from the back. "Torey? Oh . . ." he said, seeing Sheila.

"Oh," said Sheila in return.

"I had plans tonight," I said gently.

"Oh. I see." A long pause followed as she regarded Allan. "Is he the one you're fucking now?" She said it casually, as if she expected it to be normal conversation.

"Sheila, I think you'll need to go," I said. "I'm sorry you came all this way. I wish you'd let me know first."

Her expression hardened. *I know that look*, I thought. Flashing back across the years came the face of six-year-old Sheila, thwarted, angry, bent on revenge. So much about her had changed, but with that expression she became instantly recognizable.

"You know, he isn't as good-looking as Chad," she said to me, her voice still pleasantly conversational. She glanced at Allan. "That was her last fuck. Well, probably not her last. I don't know how many others have been in between."

"*Sheila.*" I put a hand on her shoulder and turned her toward the door. "I'll see you on Monday." I got her through the door and shut it.

"Maybe you will, maybe you won't," she muttered.

As I turned from the door, I saw Allan's face, pasty-white with shock. "Sorry about that," I said.

"*Who* was she?"

"It's too difficult to explain."

*   *   *

Sheila was back on Monday with no indication that anything had happened. She joined in with the children in a helpful manner and chatted pleasantly with Miriam at break time. I was aware of being on my guard with her, expecting I'm not quite sure what from her, but it never materialized. Sheila behaved as any other teenaged helper might be expected to.

In the car down to Fenton Boulevard, I said nothing. If she wasn't comfortable with this as a time for talking, then I'd abide with that. There could be other times.

Her arms folded across her chest, Sheila sat in silence for a mile or two. Out of the corner of my eye, I caught her glancing at me occasionally. I leaned forward and turned on the radio.

Sheila gave a huge sigh. "Oh, God, now she's sulking," she muttered under her breath.

"I'm not sulking," I said. "The other night you said you didn't want to talk during this ride, because it was so short."

"I didn't mean not talk at all. You practically haven't said a word since we got in the car."

I studied the cars on the freeway before me.

Sheila was watching me. When I didn't respond, she let her shoulders drop. She sighed. "Tor?"

"Yes?"

"What's going to happen to me?"

"What do you mean?" I asked.

"Well, I mean when this summer-school thing is over. What will I be? I mean, what am I now? I'm not your student, really, am I? I'm not a client. At least I don't think I am. But you wouldn't treat a friend like you treat me."

That caught my attention. I looked over at her. "How do you mean?"

"You know what I mean, Torey. We're not friends. I don't know what you want to call it, but it isn't friendship." A pause. "And now this program is just about over. Are you going to leave me again?"

"No. I'm not going anywhere. I'll still be at the clinic."

She made a frustrated little clicking noise. "You are, like, so dense sometimes," she muttered. "I don't care where you're working, Torey. The thing is, *I'm* not going to be there, am I? What's going to happen to me?"

"What do you want to happen to you?" I asked.

Arms still folded across her chest, Sheila turned her head away from me and gazed out the window. Several moments passed in pensive silence. "We're going to run out of time," she whispered. "We're one point eight miles from the bus station. Shit."

Turning my car into the parking lot of a large discount store, I pulled over to the far side and turned off the engine. "There are other buses. If you miss the usual one, you can get a later one."

Her eyes had grown huge with the unexpectedness of my action.

"If you're asking what's going to happen in regards to our relationship, that's up to you. I like having you around. I've enjoyed this summer. I hope once the summer school is over, we continue to see each other."

The car quickly grew warm in the summer sun, so I rolled down the window and leaned on it.

"That's it?" Sheila asked. "We might just get to see each other sometimes?"

"There's a hidden agenda here," I answered. "You're asking me more than I'm hearing."

She didn't reply. In the heat, sweat beaded up along her temples and trickled down along the side of her face. Minutes passed. My mind began to wander, and as it so often did when I was with Sheila, it wandered back to the time we were together in the classroom.

Suddenly, I was awash with longing. It had been so much simpler then, when I was the adult and she was the child, when I was convinced my world was right and her world was wrong and it was only a matter of getting her to change sides. Never once had I questioned then the basic value of what I was doing.

"Do you fuck him?" she asked, her voice soft.

Pulled from my thoughts so abruptly, I looked over in surprise. "Who?"

"That guy who was at your apartment. Do you fuck him?" The question was not saucily put at all, as her references to such activities had been on Saturday night, but with genuine inquiry in her voice.

"That's a fairly personal question," I replied.

As if suddenly embarrassed, her head dropped and her cheeks colored. There was a deep intake of air. Then, unexpectedly, it crossed my mind that she was going to cry.

"I'm sorry," I said. "I'm not angry with you for asking it. It's just that it's one of those questions that I'm not prepared to answer."

She was going to cry. I could see her sucking her lower lip between her teeth to keep it from quivering. "You told me before," she said. Her voice was shaky, but the tears didn't fall. "When I was little. I asked you if you and Chad fucked and you said you did."

I wasn't sure I quite remembered that particular phraseology, so I paused, recalling what she might have said.

"You *did*," she insisted, reading my silence. "It was that time after my dad's brother Jerry had . . . had done what he'd done. You know. And I couldn't figure out what was going on. I couldn't understand why he'd done that to me, because I liked him so much. And you explained all that to me. 'Cause he'd told me it was how you and Chad loved and he was just teaching me, so you'd love me too. And I asked you. And you answered me without even pausing. I know, 'cause I remember you doing it."

"That was different, kiddo. I was explaining," I said. "It wasn't just conversation."

"Why do you call me that?" Sheila asked abruptly, looking over at me.

"Call you what?"

"Kiddo. When I was little, you called me lovey. And tiger. And sweetheart. What was I then that I'm not now?"

*   *   *

What occurred to me when I was back at the clinic and mulling our conversation over was that Sheila had clearly remembered our talking about the matter when she was six. She made precise reference to that early conversation, using real names and details that indicated a very clear recollection of the event. This stood in stark contrast to her hazy memories earlier or, indeed, to her insistence that she had no recollection of Chad. Were the memories coming back? And if that was so, what had happened to make them fade in the first place? Or was it possible that she had remembered all along and had told me otherwise? If so, why?

I was also becoming very conscious of a hidden agenda. Conversation after conversation with Sheila I sensed we were talking on two levels at once, that she was addressing another matter as well as the one at hand. I had the distinct feeling that she was aware of what this hidden agenda was and that it fueled a good deal of the sparky anger Sheila had demonstrated over the course of the summer.

Then again, maybe it wasn't so hidden. Sheila had spoken in no uncertain terms during our visit to Marysville about the pain and anger she'd felt when the school year had finished and I'd departed. Perhaps the fault had been mine in not bringing the subject up again. I had been so startled by the intensity of her feelings that night in the motel room and then distracted by the need to deal with the here-and-now of her running out, that I hadn't handled the issue as deftly as I might have in a more controlled location, like the clinic or the classroom. And she was right: the car after summer school was not the appropriate place for such a discussion.

I looked at my calendar. We were meeting with Alejo's parents on the following afternoon, so I wouldn't be able to see Sheila then. In fact, it was a very busy week, due to the ending of the summer program. Jeff and I had several evaluation meetings, in addition to our usual clinic commitments. Pulling the diary over, I penciled in Sheila's name on Friday. She seemed so desperate to come over to my house, I thought, so maybe Friday evening we could do something special together.

The next morning was one of chaos. It started with the minibus driver, who brought several of the children to the school, announcing to us that Violet had been sick on the ride over, and indeed, she had, everywhere and over everyone. This involved all four of us in cleaning up. Then, when I phoned Violet's mother, she explained that she couldn't come to get Violet, because her husband had the car. Miriam volunteered to take Violet home, but it was quite a distance, so that left us without Miriam for the first half of the morning.

Tamara, who had become quite reliable about not hurting herself, seemed to find all the attention the minibus children were getting was simply too much. While we were all distracted, she managed to locate a large pair of scissors and cut a long gash on her inner arm, almost from wrist to elbow. It wasn't deep, but it was bloody and by that point it was just Jeff, Sheila and I. The other children were becoming very unsettled with all this disruption, and frankly, we did not have control of things.

Jeff, being the doctor, got the job of bandaging Tamara back together, while Sheila and I tried to quell fears and get everyone reoriented. The summer school had not been running enough weeks to develop the very useful group camaraderie that I'd always cultivated in my classrooms. There was still no real center with this bunch, such that when disaster struck, things flew apart easily. I tried a few songs to keep up the cheer, but Joshua and Jessie, our two autistic children, both screamed and a couple of the others just kept wandering off.

The only humorous moment came when, in the chaos, I noticed David, Alejo and Mikey were gone. Panicked, because I realized that in all the commotion, we had not searched David that morning for matches, as we usually did, I dashed out to hunt for them. It took me five or ten minutes to locate them. The three boys were outside. I was still inside, when I heard their voices through an open window, and I approached cautiously because I wanted to see what they were up to before giving my presence away. Sure enough, David had started a very small fire of grass and twigs in the lee of the school building.

"See, there it is," he said to Mikey. "I told you I could do it."

I was just about to make myself known when, much to my pleased surprise, I heard David say, "But now we got to put it out."

"How?" Alejo asked.

David cast around a moment for something to use, then his small face brightened. "I know. Like this." And he unbuttoned his jeans. "Okay, all together. On the count of three, everybody *pee*."

*　　*　　*

Afterward, Jeff and I had the meeting with Alejo's parents, so I wasn't able to take Sheila down to Fenton Boulevard. Instead, she left on foot for the bus stop near the school, while Jeff and I headed back to the clinic.

Alejo was the only child in the group who was not a client of either Jeff or myself, so as a consequence, neither of us knew his parents, Mr. and Dr. Banks-Smith. Indeed, my only contact had been with his father, the first day of the program, when he had brought Alejo in. I had never met Alejo's mother at all. Jeff had had a little more contact, as he had done the full workup on Alejo a couple weeks earlier, but for the most part we had relied on Alejo's psychiatrist, Dr. Freeman, for our information on his family.

Alejo's mother was a doctor practicing family medicine, while his father was an insurance man. They were both tall, attractive and Nordic-looking, the kind of couple usually dreamed up by advertising executives. They greeted us warmly, shaking both Jeff's and my hand, and then turned to exchange pleasantries with Dr. Freeman before sitting down. What struck me forcefully as I watched them was the knowledge that a dreadful mistake had been made. This was the wrong set of parents for Alejo.

The second thought to strike me was that Mr. and Dr. Banks-Smith had not bonded with Alejo. As we passed out our various test results, papers and compilations of data, they each examined them in turn and asked articulate, intelligent questions, but they did so in the same thoughtful yet detached way that Jeff, Dr. Freeman and I did. They spoke to us not as parents, but as fellow professionals.

"So, you say Alejo is functioning at a lower level than his age group," Mr. Banks-Smith said to Jeff. "This translates into what, IQ-wise?"

"If you look at it as a bell curve, with the average IQ—i.e., most of the population being here in the middle where it's fattest—"

"No, just his score, please. What is his IQ?" Mr. Banks-Smith asked.

"I'm often reluctant to tie us down to specifics," Jeff replied. "IQ is a relative measure, and tests don't always reflect a true picture."

"Come on, just the numbers," Mr. Banks-Smith replied.

"Well, I gave him the WISC. He had a verbal score of sixty-five and a perceptual score of seventy-nine, which gives him a total IQ of seventy-four."

"That's in the retarded range, isn't it?" Mr. Banks-Smith said.

"We generally regard seventy as the cutoff, but really, sir, we don't like to put a lot of emphasis on single scores, particularly in a case like Alejo's, where cultural issues may have influenced the results."

"And you," Dr. Banks-Smith said, indicating me, "you said there are definite indications that he is brain-damaged?"

"Possible, not definite. It's very difficult to be definite about such matters," I replied.

"What caused it?" Alejo's father asked. "Was it inflicted? A result of his deprivations?"

"No way of saying. He shows indicators of aphasia, which involves an inability to use and understand words in the usual way. The majority of children I've seen with this disability have been born with it."

"So, he could have been damaged all along, is that what you're saying?" he asked.

I didn't want to be saying that, but unfortunately, it was probably the truth.

"Alejo's problems can't really be helped, can they?" Dr. Banks-Smith said.

"They can be helped," Jeff said quickly. "Alejo's made very good progress in the summer program in terms of his interpersonal relationships. He is getting on quite well socially and has made friends with some of the other boys. We've seen a nice change in him, haven't we, Torey?"

I nodded.

"I think if he continued at the clinic—" Dr. Freeman started, but Dr. Banks-Smith cut him off with a wave of her arm.

"No, what I'm asking is: he basically can't be helped. You can't make him more intelligent. You can't repair the brain damage."

"Well, no . . ." Dr. Freeman said.

I felt myself pulling back, as if slipping down a long tunnel. We'd lost. Perhaps we had lost even before we'd started. I suspect Mr. and Dr. Banks-Smith had already decided to send Alejo back to South America and, indeed, had already begun the process before ever coming in for the conference. Whatever, at that precise moment, I knew there was no hope. Alejo was condemned.

twenty-two

"I thought perhaps you would like to come over to my place tomorrow night," I said to Sheila as we drove down to Fenton Boulevard the next day. "It's Friday, so we don't have to worry about work in the morning. Maybe I could do us something on the barbecue."

"Barbecue? Where do you have a barbecue in an attic apartment?"

"I have a door out onto the garage roof. Wait until tomorrow. I'll show you."

Sheila smiled sweetly. "Yeah, I'd really like that."

There was a small period of silence before Sheila looked over again. "How did that meeting go last night with Alejo's parents?"

I shrugged.

"What are they like, his folks?"

"All right. Nice, in a way. If I had met them at a party or something, I think I would have liked them," I replied.

She pulled a strand of hair down and examined it. "So, what's going to happen to him? Are they going to try and send him back?"

"I don't know for sure. Dr. Freeman will cover it with them, because he's Alejo's therapist, but we didn't go into it."

"Yeah, but you're going to do something, aren't you? You and Jeff? You're going to try and stop them," Sheila said, an urgency coming into her voice. "I mean, like, you won't *let* them."

Pulling my lips back over my teeth, I sucked my breath in. "I don't want to let them, but I'm afraid if they want to, there won't be much I can do to stop them."

"But you won't let them?"

"Like I said . . ."

Bending forward in her seat, Sheila put a hand on either side of her head, as if in pain. "Oh, it can't happen. Oh, geez, he's been brought here. He's been given all these things. Everything's so nice."

I could hear the tears in her voice. Unexpectedly, I felt my own tears. They welled up without warning, blurring the road ahead of me. The enormity of what was happening to Alejo, and, through him, all unfortunate victims, suddenly overwhelmed me. "It makes me want to cry too," I said.

Startled, Sheila looked over at me.

I reached up and wiped the tears away. "I feel so helpless when something like this happens. I want to change things so badly and I just can't."

Her forehead wrinkling, she gazed in amazement. Unlike me, she had remained dry-eyed.

"Sometimes it helps," I said of my tears and wiped the last of them away. "In these circumstances, it's about all there's left for me to do." I smiled at her.

"I want to cry sometimes, but I almost never do," Sheila replied. "I feel it building up and then just when I think I'm going to, the feeling disappears."

I nodded.

"Actually, I make it disappear," she said. "Not that I necessarily mean to. It's just I suddenly think, what is this? It isn't real. What is any of it? A bunch of chemicals rushing around in our brain. A bunch of molecules. What kind? Carbon? Hydrogen? And what does that amount to? Nothing. It's all really nothing."

"Do you believe that?" I asked.

"Yes."

"*Really?*"

She shrugged. "It just comes to me, whether I want it to or not."

*   *   *

We celebrated our last Friday together with a special activity: finger painting using chocolate pudding instead of paints. Both Miriam and I had done this activity on previous occasions, so we were well prepared for the extraordinary mess it generated. Miriam arrived with an assortment of old shirts to protect clothing and we cleared back the tables and set out newspapers on the floor before putting down the large sheets of paper for painting. Then we mixed up huge bowls of instant pudding.

Both Sheila and Jeff were highly amused with our proceedings. Jeff with his Freudian training saw all too much meaning in the gloppy brown mixture, but he was the first one to plunge his hand deep into the bowl and scoop pudding out onto Violet's paper. Exuberantly, he provided all the children with generous splats.

The kids, of course, loved it. More went in their mouths than on the paper, and within a short time, there was chocolate pudding from ear to ear on most of them, but that was the glory of it. Of the various activities I had done through the years with my classes, this had become one of my favorites. All such terribly messy things are releasing, but there is a special freedom in those surrounding food. The squishy, cold feel of the pudding, the copious quantity, the permission to smear with the fingers, to slurp up from the paper with tongues produced an unhindered gaiety. Every child in the room was lively and open.

Sheila was seduced too. Indeed, she had been unusually outgoing all morning, chatting spontaneously with several of the children, lifting Mikey way up in the air above her head. Alejo had initially been reluctant to touch the chocolate pudding, so Sheila sat down beside him on the floor and started off his painting for him, encouraging him to join her. Scooping a fingerful of the pudding up from the paper, she held it out for him to taste. He wouldn't, so she ate it herself, smearing it playfully across her lips. Alejo laughed at this. He had a gorgeous laugh, very bright and boyish, and we all turned in surprise to hear it. Lifting up a finger loaded with pudding, he let it drip into his mouth, then burst into giggles.

I was delighted with the success of the project. Everyone was laughing and talking and I felt a deep sense of fulfillment watching them.

Sheila appeared at my right and said, "I'm going to take Alejo down to the rest room. He needs to go and he's absolutely covered with pudding, so I'll sluice him off." Through a coating of chocolate, Alejo grinned up at me.

"Yes, I think it's time we all clean up," I replied.

Giving the children a five-minute warning before terminating the activity, I went over to Jeff and Miriam and suggested that once we had the worst of the mess off the children, they could take them outside for break time and I would volunteer to clean up the classroom. This met with approval and I was soon left alone with what appeared to be the aftermath of an explosion in a pudding factory.

There was such a mess that I never made it outside at all. I could hear Jeff's voice filtering through the open window, as he supervised a game of Sharks and Mermaids, and it evoked far-off memories of my own childhood. The warm, dry summer heat, the light falling in across the floor, patterned by the cottonwood trees outside the window, the sound of children's voices all combined to lend a moment's transcendence to the mundane tasks I was doing.

A good half hour passed before the kids came back inside and we resumed normal activities. As everyone was getting settled, I surveyed the classroom. "Where're Sheila and Alejo?"

"I was just going to ask you the same thing," Jeff replied.

I looked at him blankly. "What do you mean?"

"Well, I'd assumed they were in here helping you during the break. I thought maybe you'd sent them down to the janitor's room to get something."

"What? They weren't outside with you?"

Jeff shook his head.

"Miriam?" I called. "Have you seen Sheila and Alejo? Weren't they with you outside?"

Surprise crossed Miriam's face. "I thought they were with you."

The meaning of that expression of one's blood running like ice came home to me just then, as a physical sensation of cold flowing down through my body suffused me.

"When did you last see her?" Jeff asked me.

"Ages ago. She took Alejo down to the toilets. I was in here all along and I just *assumed* . . ."

✳   ✳   ✳

I tried to quell the sense of rising panic I felt, as I went out into the hallway and down to the rest rooms. Bursting into the girls', I slammed open the doors to the stalls and looked around the corner where the trash bins were kept. Then I went next door to the boys' and did the same. Nothing and no one.

Back in the classroom, Jeff and I huddled in the back by the sink, discussing what to do next, while Miriam attempted to keep the children occupied.

"What's happened? Where could they have gone?" Jeff asked.

"I don't know. I have no idea what's going on. Sheila was fine when she came in this morning."

"Is she a runner?" Jeff asked.

"No. I don't think so," I replied. "Well, I don't know. She wasn't when she was six."

"That's a long time ago," he said acridly.

"But why would she go? She wasn't unhappy, not that I could see. She was delightful this morning, in very good humor."

"Yeah," said Jeff blackly. "The way suicides are, once they've made their minds up."

Silence then, as we regarded one another.

"But why's she taken Alejo?" he asked. "There's the dangerous question."

The moment Jeff voiced it, I knew the answer. "She was worried about Alejo, about the possibility that his parents might send him back to South America."

"Oh, God. So she's done a bunk with him, you think?" Jeff asked. A pause.

"Why didn't you tell me this *was* a possibility, Hayden? We should have been alerted that she was capable of this."

"I didn't think it *was* a possibility, no more than I would think it was a possibility that you would take one of the kids and go," I hissed back in an angry whisper.

"Well, you seem convinced enough of the reason now. You had no trouble coming up with that; so you must have known there was the possibility she might act on it."

"I *didn't*. Would I act on it? Would you act on it? We were both upset by the Banks-Smiths' reaction the other night; why not us? Why should I have suspected Sheila?" I cried.

Jeff looked at me darkly.

*   *   *

For all the times I had found Jeff able to keep his humor in adversity, on this occasion he couldn't. He was genuinely angry with me, acting as if I had kept great secrets from him about Sheila's mental stability. Because I hadn't, because this was coming as a big surprise to me too, I felt hurt and angry, as well. This did nothing to help our situation, because for the first fifteen minutes of the crisis, neither of us was thinking straight.

Jeff was right in saying that I was convinced that Sheila had run away with Alejo. While it had never occurred to me beforehand that Sheila might try such a thing, once it had happened, everything fell clearly into place for me. She was desperate, and desperate measures were called for. The first logical step was to search the school thoroughly; so once Jeff and I had gotten over the initial stages of accusing one another, we helped settle Miriam on her own with the kids and then divided up the school building between us.

I went methodically through every room, cupboard and storage area that we had a key for and some that we didn't. My hope was that even if Sheila was serious about taking Alejo away, she would try hiding in the school until we were all gone, so I tried to leave no area unchecked. When nothing turned up, I rejoined Jeff and we went outside to scour the playground and the park area across the road. Nervously, I kept checking my watch. I dreaded the moment when the minibuses and taxi arrived to take the children home, because we would then have to acknowledge to the driver who transported Alejo that we had no Alejo to transport. Jeff had settled down, but he was still prickly. Consequently, I kept my feelings to myself.

Unfortunately, search as we did, there was no trace of them. Twelve-thirty came and Miriam brought the children out front. When we saw the taxi pull in to take Alejo home, we had to acknowledge defeat. I explained nothing to the driver, just said that Alejo wouldn't be coming with him, which he accepted grumpily as an annoying last-minute change to his routine. Meanwhile, Jeff went inside to do the unwelcome task of phoning Dr. Rosenthal and Alejo's parents.

Miriam, who had other commitments after lunch, went home, leaving Jeff and me alone, regarding one another.

"Oh, God," Jeff muttered. "Why did it have to end like this? We were doing so well. This has been such a super experience. Why did it have to end like this?"

Dr. Rosenthal was next on the scene. When his gigantic frame appeared in the classroom door, the seriousness of the situation really came home to me. He had never visited our site. He'd followed the program closely, because Jeff and I had to submit weekly reports, and he had sat in on several parent conferences, but otherwise, this had been our project. Seeing him here now gave me a sudden sense of a stern parent come to sort out his children's mischief. Jeff and I were so much younger than anyone else at the clinic, so much less experienced that, in contrast to the other psychiatrists' suit-and-tie formality, we'd always seemed like kids. I'd gotten a bit of a kick out of it on other occasions, but now, seeing this tall man in his elegant dark suit and graying hair, all I could think of was what a stupid little twit I was.

He crossed the classroom to where Jeff and I were at the table and lowered himself into one of the small schoolroom chairs. "Did you know this girl was a risk?" he asked me.

Normally I'm quite cool under pressure, but just then I wasn't. It was past lunchtime and I was hungry. I was worried and I was worn down by the guilty suspicion that this might all be my fault. Dr. Rosenthal's question, although straightforwardly put, sounded all too much like those last ninety minutes of Jeff's questioning. Consequently, I started to cry.

This unsettled Jeff, who squirmed and turned away, but with surprising gentleness, Dr. Rosenthal rose and came around to my side of the table. He put a hand on my shoulder. "Don't worry," he said. "It'll come right."

I'm glad he thought so.

Alejo's father arrived at one-thirty. "What's this? What's going on? Who is this girl?" he asked. Like Jeff, his worry took the form of anger. He waved a fist threateningly at us. "Why weren't you watching?"

Dr. Rosenthal relieved Jeff and me of the necessity of explaining. "I understand you're contemplating returning Alejo to Colombia," he said to Mr. Banks-Smith.

This comment caught him completely off guard. He looked blankly at Dr. Rosenthal.

"Yes?" Dr. Rosenthal persisted.

"Well . . ." Mr. Banks-Smith foundered a moment, glancing back and forth among the three of us. "What does this have to do with anything?"

"The girl who has gone off with Alejo, she's formed a very close attachment to him. She was worried he might be returned to the orphanage."

Mr. Banks-Smith dropped his eyes to the floor.

"I don't think Alejo is in any danger," Dr. Rosenthal said. "From my staff's experience of her, she's a sensible, streetwise girl. So what I think we need to do is respond to this in a calm, rational manner. It's a very unfortunate thing to have happened, but I'm sure it will turn out all right."

I could have kissed Dr. Rosenthal just then, so grateful was I for his supportive approach. For the first time since it had started, I began to feel perhaps things weren't so bad.

* * *

There was one last thorough search of the school and its environs. Dr. Rosenthal contacted the school caretaker, who supplied keys to the areas of the school that we had not been able to get into; consequently, we were able to search every nook and cranny. Unfortunately, there was not a single clue as to their disappearance.

At four, we transferred back to the clinic. Dr. Banks-Smith met us there. Dr. Rosenthal had managed to dispel Mr. Banks-Smith's anger so successfully that he had become a supportive member of the search team at the school. Now his wife joined in the conversation in the conference room, giving us helpful suggestions on Alejo's anticipated behavior in this situation. Sheila's father had been contacted at his work and we all awaited his arrival.

Dr. Rosenthal came over to me as we milled about in the clinic corridor with our coffee cups while waiting for Mr. Renstad. "Come in my office a moment, please," he said.

In contrast to the bright lights and nervous bustle in the area around the conference room, Dr. Rosenthal's unlit office was dim and silent. As director, he commanded the biggest office, a room of late-Victorian elegance with a mahogany fireplace and corniced ceilings. There was a thick carpet on the floor and wonderfully squishy leather chairs—womb chairs, Jeff called them, for their propensity to envelop the sitter in comforting softness—as well as the obligatory psychiatrist's couch.

"Tell me more about this girl," Dr. Rosenthal asked me. "What's her background?"

"She's a former student of mine," I said. I'd already given a brief summary of Sheila's relationship to me in the conference room, but now I went into detail. I told him of her deprived background and her history of abandonment and abuse.

Nodding, Dr. Rosenthal reached across his desk and turned on a cassette recorder that was sitting on the window ledge. Mozart's Piano Concerto no. 20 began. He cocked his head and listened to it. The somber first notes of the allegro sounded foreboding to me.

"It's quite understandable, isn't it?" Dr. Rosenthal said at last. "Here's a child who was, herself, abandoned by her mother. She identifies with the boy, who was abandoned in Colombia. He's been rescued, but now he's about to be abandoned again."

I nodded.

He looked over at me. "It says a great deal for her, really. She's a good girl at heart."

"I think . . . if I'm reading my experiences lately with Sheila right . . . that there may be even deeper identification. You see, Sheila and I . . . well, I've gotten mixed up in the abandonment issue. I think she sees me in the same role as Alejo's parents, that I helped lift her out of her former life by bringing her into my classroom, accustoming her to a more stable environment, more reliable adult relationships, and then, when the school year ended . . ."

There was a deep silence. The music, which should have filled it, emphasized it.

"I didn't mean to," I said. "It's hard for me to come to terms with the fact that what I thought of as such a good experience she's interpreted as abandonment . . . She doesn't even remember being abandoned by her mother, but she remembers my doing it. And now this."

"Ah," said Dr. Rosenthal and he said no more. Leaning back in his chair, he looked up at the patterned design on the ceiling. The music washed over us.

*   *   *

Sheila's father was in the conference room when I came out of Dr. Rosenthal's office. He had been called over from work and was wearing filthy jeans and a sweat-stained shirt. His metal-toed boots clicked against the legs of his chair and the conference table. The moment I saw him, I knew having him present was a mistake. His scruffy appearance was off-putting, but worse was his mouth. I'd tried to downplay the more lurid aspects of Sheila's childhood, feeling that the things she had done when she was five or six were hardly to be held against her at fourteen. Without anchoring it to this early time, Mr. Renstad readily acknowledged that Sheila had been in trouble with the police. I challenged him and he admitted that, no, she hadn't been in trouble since being in my class, almost a decade earlier, but then he added that she had caused serious problems in her last foster home, because she'd kept running away, and had eventually been sent to a secure children's home. By the time he finished talking, the Banks-Smiths were wild-eyed and they insisted the police be called in.

*   *   *

At six forty-five, two police officers arrived. One was a big, burly fellow named Durante, the other a woman with short blond hair and a steel glint in her eye named Metherson. Still sitting around the conference table in the clinic were Dr. Rosenthal, Sheila's father, the Banks-Smiths and Jeff and I, and once again, Jeff and I recounted our tale. I was numb by then, my emotions having run on high for too long, so I just related it as it had happened and did not try to give meaning to any particular aspect. Afterward, Officer Durante stayed in the conference room with the others, while Officer Metherson, Jeff and I went into our office to review Alejo's file and discuss the summer program in more depth. We returned to the conference room to discover someone had ordered sandwiches from the deli on Nineteenth Street. Neither Jeff nor I had had lunch, so we fell upon them like dogs.

Time ground down, nearly to a halt. The police officers had come and then left, but we all remained, not knowing quite what else to do. In contrast to the hectic urgency of the afternoon and early evening, there was nothing left but to wait. And eat. Another order was sent out to the deli and someone popped across the street to the doughnut shop and brought in a dozen doughnuts. Dr. Rosenthal made fresh coffee and Jeff raided the pop machine. After not eating for the whole course of the working day, I easily overate while sitting there with nothing else to do. This only contributed to the murky, depressed sense of lethargy I felt.

On my way back from the rest room about 9 P.M., I met Mr. Renstad loitering around the front door of the clinic. He wanted to go home; I suspect he had wanted to go home from practically the moment he had arrived, but by now there was an urgency to his restlessness.

"I don't know what we're going to do," he said wearily. "Don't help none staying in this place. She's not going to come here."

I nodded.

"We just got to wait her out, that's all. That's all you can do with Sheila."

"How often has this happened before?" I asked.

He shrugged. "Often enough."

"Where does she go?"

He shrugged again. "She don't tell me and I don't ask. She's got her mother in her. Does what she wants, when she wants, how she wants, and I just sit home hoping it don't cause trouble."

"She *hasn't* been in trouble with the police recently, has she?" I asked, almost dreading his answer.

He shook his head. "No."

There was a small silence between us. I glanced out through the double doors at the summer twilight. "Could you tell me a little about these occasions when Sheila was in foster care? It's something she hasn't talked much to me about. How many has she been in?"

Mr. Renstad puffed out his cheeks and expelled the breath. "Quite a few. I don't know. Ten, maybe?"

"*Ten?*" I said in surprise. I had thought it'd been three or four. "On what occasions? When you were . . . away?"

"Yeah." He nodded. "Them times I was in Marysville. And I was down at the state hospital. Down twice, getting dried out. You know." He gave an embarrassed smile.

"But it was *ten* times in, what? Six, seven years?"

"She just didn't settle. She was okay the first time. She was, like, eight, maybe, when she went in the first foster home. And they seemed real good. They used to bring her down to see me. That's when I was in Marysville and they used to bring her down every month for a while, then all of a sudden, it stopped. Turns out he was fucking her, the old man. Showing this real good face to me and then fucking my kid at night."

I searched his face.

"She didn't say nothing about it, but she ran away from there. Actually, she never has said, but the guy got done for fucking the next kid they put in with him, so I reckon that's what he was doing to my kid too."

Oh, God, I was thinking, did this never stop?

"He made a runner out of her, that guy. She never run before that, but now anytime you get mad at her, she goes. And just like a hare she is. They keep putting her in different places, but nothing stops her. Got her mother's blood, I tell them. If she wants to go, she's gone, and no one the likes of who's in there," he said, gesturing toward the conference room, "is going to find her."

twenty-three

Nothing came of all our waiting, and at last we had to give up and go home, leaving the affair to the police. Once home, I couldn't sleep. Around and around in my head went all the aspects of my relationship with Sheila. It had been too easy to think that what I had done with her at six had been enough, that I had made a difference. Now sleepless in the gloom of night, it became too easy to think I had made no difference at all.

The next day was Saturday. I didn't go back into the clinic, as there was little we could do from there anyway, but I remained close at hand for the phone. Allan came over for a little while, but he had come with the intention of our going upstate for the afternoon to nose around in the small antique and secondhand places that dotted the sleepy rural communities of the corn belt. When I explained what had happened, he was astonished and remarked several times about never having known anyone before who got herself involved in such things as I seemed to get into. Although sympathetic, he was a bit disconcerted. I also suspect that he didn't want to spend such a bright summer Saturday afternoon in the city. As a consequence, Allan soon left and I spent the rest of the day on my own.

The phone rang a lot. Dr. Rosenthal rang three times to catch me up on things. Officer Metherson phoned once, as did Dr. Freeman, Alejo's psychiatrist from the clinic. Jeff rang twice. And I telephoned Mr. Renstad late in the afternoon to see if he had heard anything. The police were at his house when I called, so I had another opportunity to talk to Officer Metherson. There was still no news.

Making myself supper, I took it in front of the TV. That not holding my interest, I reread the newspaper and did the crossword. Restless, I toyed with the idea of going swimming at the health club. I could have used some exercise at that point and the thought of a hard workout and a soak in the Jacuzzi really appealed to me, but in the end I decided against it. Gathering my dishes up, I took them to the kitchen to wash them.

A knock at the door.

Sheila? The thought shot through my mind like a brightly sent arrow, lifting my spirits as it went. "Just a minute," I called, lifting my hands from the soapy water and drying them. The knock came again, louder, more insistent. I hurried to open it.

Jeff.

"What are you doing here?" I asked.

"Now there's a friendly greeting, if ever I heard one," he replied and came on in. He glanced around. "So, this is *chez* Hayden, is it? I like your paneling there."

"*What* are you doing here?"

"I just thought I'd come over. You're by the phone, I'm by the phone. We might as well be by the phone together. You play chess? I've got my chessboard along. Could do Trivial Pursuit, but it isn't much good with two people. But I'm wicked at Trivial Pursuit," he said and grinned.

"I just bet you are."

He scanned my bookshelves. "So where's this book you've written?"

"It's not published yet. Won't be out till next April, but that's the manuscript over there." I pointed.

Jeff went over and picked it up, while I returned to the kitchen to drain the sink and finish cleaning up. A few minutes passed before Jeff wandered into the kitchen, the pages of the manuscript in his hands.

"What's this, Hayden?"

"What?"

"Right here, Chapter One, page one. 'The article was a small one, just a few paragraphs stuck on page six under the comics. It told of a six-year-old girl who had abducted a neighborhood child.'" He looked up. "Is this Sheila?"

A sense of horror came over me.

He continued reading. "'. . . she had taken the three-year-old boy, tied him to a tree in a nearby woodlot and burned him. The boy was currently in a local hospital in critical condition.'" Jeff paused to regard me. "You never told us about this."

"I didn't think of it."

"Didn't *think* of it, Hayden? She's done this before and you didn't think of it?"

That wasn't quite the truth. I had thought of it, at great length, in fact, particularly during the night when I'd been lying awake, but I wasn't quite sure how it fit in. It sounded so horrible, that incident. It *was* horrible. Yet, did it have any bearing on what she was doing now? I doubted it. As with inadmissible evidence in a trial, to have mentioned it at this stage would only have prejudiced people without contributing anything useful. I said this to Jeff.

He raised an eyebrow. "Be careful. You're setting yourself up as judge and jury in this thing."

"So you think it needs to be brought out?" I asked.

"Well, to Dr. Rosenthal, at least. I mean, this was hardly a small incident, was it? All the things you've told me about her, you never gave me the impression she was up to this kind of thing as a child. Sounds like she almost killed the kid."

"It was a one-off. A cry for help. She never did anything else like it," I replied. That I felt was the truth, although this had been the one unspoken area between Sheila and me. When she was in my classroom we'd talked about every other aspect of her life, including her abandonment, her abuse and her difficulties adjusting to our expectations, but we had never once touched on that abduction. I'd thought of it often enough during those five months she was in my class, but I had never pressed the matter. I wasn't a trained psychologist at that point in my career and I didn't feel it was my place to press the issue, if Sheila showed no willingness to discuss it. And the fact was, she never did.

Jeff was uncomfortable with this new knowledge. "She *could* do something," he kept saying, as if it weren't true that we all "could do something" if the circumstances were right. Then came the lawsuit side of the matter. "They could sue us, if something happened and we hadn't told about this."

"They could sue us anyway, if they got the urge, just because we let Sheila in the summer program. She's been a risk all along," I replied. "But for pity's sake, she was a little child when she did these things. I mean, when I was six, I used to steal Hershey's bars from the grocery store. Does that make me a security risk now? Of course not. Because when I was old enough to know better, people expected me not to do it and treated me as someone who wouldn't."

"This is rather different from Hershey's bars, Hayden."

"No, the point is she shouldn't be treated like a criminal now for something she did when she was a very little girl."

Jeff shook his head. "No, Hayden, the point is that this girl already has a history of abducting little boys and harming them, and if we don't tell somebody we know that, we're talking big trouble here."

In the end, Jeff won the argument and we phoned Dr. Rosenthal. He listened solemnly. No, please, not the police, okay? I'd asked, but Dr. Rosenthal gently made all the same points Jeff had. Consequently, half an hour later, Officer Durante was sitting at my kitchen table with Jeff and me.

By the time everyone had gone home, I was well and truly depressed. What was it with this girl? She had so much to offer, so much promise, yet at every turn things went wrong. Running myself a hot bath, I tried to soak the problems away.

The door again. Glancing at my bedside clock, I saw it was almost eleven-thirty. Officer Durante had said he was going to check up the details of the abduction in Marysville and if he had any questions, he'd come back to me. Wearily climbing out of bed and pulling on my robe, I went to the door. Didn't this guy ever call it quits?

It was Sheila. Sheila and Alejo standing in the dim light of the apartment-building hallway. "Can we come in?" she asked.

"Oh, yes," I said in surprise. "Yes, come in." I stood aside to let them pass.

Sheila flopped down on my sofa, with Alejo dropping down beside her. He looked as if he had recently been crying. His eyes were puffy and red- rimmed. Sheila just looked tired.

"Where have you been? Do you know everybody's looking for you?" I asked. "Do you realize the police are involved?"

Sheila grimaced. "Could you make us something to eat? We're so hungry."

I made them tuna-fish sandwiches, and when they'd devoured those, they moved on to peanut butter and toast. All the time, I was trying to puzzle out how to handle this situation. It didn't seem inconceivable to me that Sheila might flee if I was too quick about telling everyone else she was here, but knowing how desperate Alejo's parents were, I was anxious to let them know he was safe.

Alejo answered the matter for me. I turned from putting the peanut butter away to find him sound asleep, face down on the table.

"Come on, lovey," I said and reached down to pick him up. Carrying him into my bedroom, I removed his shoes and slipped him under the comforter. He never really woke up.

Back out in the kitchen, Sheila, sitting slouched down in a chair at the table, looked in about the same shape as Alejo. She braced her head with one hand, her fingers shielding her eyes from my view.

"I'm going to have to call and tell them you're here," I said.

"I know," she murmured wearily.

"Why did you do it? We were so worried, Sheila."

Looking up at me, her face crumpled. "Don't be mad at me. Just do with me like you did with him, okay? Just say, 'Come on, lovey,' and let me know you're glad to have me back."

*　　*　　*

By the time Alejo's parents arrived, both Alejo and Sheila were asleep. I'd moved Alejo out to the sofa, because he was so far gone that lights and noise scarcely made him stir, and I put Sheila to bed in my bedroom. Alejo's parents roused him briefly with hugs and kisses, but he was asleep again before they had him in the car.

Officer Durante, just going off his evening shift, stopped by on his way home. I showed him the bedroom and he stood in the doorway, watching Sheila asleep in the darkened room. "Silly girl," he murmured and turned back into the living room.

"What's going to happen now?" I asked.

"Depends if the parents press charges or not. Depends what everyone does."

"Could it just end here?"

He shrugged affably. "Possibly." He met my eyes. "Is she really such an okay kid?"

"Yeah."

"Well, tell her to smarten up."

twenty-four

Sheila roused late the next morning and stumbled out into the living room like an old she-bear just coming out of hibernation. It was past eleven o'clock and I was sitting on the floor reading the Sunday newspapers. She flopped into the armchair and regarded me amidst my sea of newspapers.

"God, how many papers do you get?" she asked and sleepily rubbed her face.

"You want some orange juice?"

She yawned and rubbed her face again. "I'm all stiff. I don't think I moved all night." Then suddenly, realization crossed her features. She glanced around my apartment, then back at me. "I almost don't remember how I got here," she murmured. "But then again, how could I forget?"

"Yes," I said, "we have some serious sorting out to do."

"Yeah," Sheila muttered, "heap big trouble, eh?"

*   *   *

The one person I hadn't called the night before was Sheila's father. I know I should have, but it was very late by then and I reckoned he probably wasn't losing any sleep over his daughter's absence. However, once Sheila was up and moving, I insisted she phone him.

"Do I have to go home right away?" she asked, when I made it plain that she was doing nothing else until she let her father know where she was.

"Don't you want to?"

"Couldn't I just stay here for a little bit? Please?"

"Look," I said, "we'll get you sorted out first, all right? You have a shower and clean up. I'll make you some breakfast and then we'll see what's going to happen with this mess. Then maybe I can run you home later on. Okay? But *phone* your dad *now*."

Begrudgingly, Sheila agreed.

*   *   *

There was something unusually defenseless about Sheila that morning. Perhaps it was just the rigors of her experiences with Alejo leaving her so tired and hungry. For whatever reason, she left her neediness undisguised.

One of the most poignant moments came when she went in to get cleaned up. She had no clean clothes, so I suggested she put on an old jogging suit of mine, while I washed her things. Hearing she was out of the shower, I came into the bathroom to collect the dirty laundry. Sheila stood in front of the mirror, her hair dripping wet.

"Do you like my hair like this?" she asked, as she pulled the comb through.

I hesitated, wondering whether to lie for politeness's sake or gently tell the truth.

"You don't, do you?" she replied, reading my hesitation. "You think it looks stupid."

"No, not really. It's just that I always thought you had very beautiful hair. I've always wanted straight hair myself and had to put up with curly, and yours was so shiny and nice."

Pulling her hair back from her face and into a ponytail, Sheila regarded her reflection. She looked much more like her childhood self that way. For the first time, I saw the little girl I'd known looking back at me. "I don't know why I do this, why I make myself look like I do. Nobody likes it."

"I think you've got quite a good fashion sense," I said. "I rather like it. It's different, but there's nothing wrong with being different, and it is quite good."

"I wanted you to like me so much," she said quietly. "I want everybody to like me, but then just as I get to where I think I can do that, I stop myself. I don't know why. I think, I can put this on—like it's some dress or something—and everyone will think it's very pretty. But then some other part of me stops me. I put it away and try something different, something I know is going to drive everyone nuts. I *know* what to do. I *want* to do it. But I never can."

I smiled gently. "That's just being a teenager. It goes with the territory."

"No," she replied. "Maybe in most cases, but not in mine. Because I've done it all my life. Even when I was little, even when I was dying inside for people to like me, I never could do those things that would make it easy for them."

✳   ✳   ✳

Afternoon came and with it the need to confront and resolve Alejo's abduction. The phone had been ringing all morning and it was finally decided that everyone, including Sheila, would meet at the clinic. Feelings were still running high and I sensed that police action remained a distinct possibility, but I took it as a good sign that everyone wanted to meet and talk the matter through before turning it over to the authorities.

At home with me, Sheila was visibly worried. If the term "clingy" could be applied to a fourteen-year-old, that's what she was, trailing after me from room to room in the apartment. She worried about her hair and her clothes, bit her fingernails and wrung her hands, although she never directly addressed the matter on any more than a superficial level.

"We'll take it one moment at a time," I said, as we got into the car.

"I was just trying to do what I thought was right," she murmured. "That's what's so awful. I wanted to do the right thing."

"I know, lovey." Putting the key into the ignition, I reached across the seat to her. "Come here." I drew her in close in a hug. The years melted away when I did that. Suddenly she was tiny again and the need to protect her made me feel tigerish.

The hug had the same effect on Sheila. She looked at me as I started the car and pulled out of the drive. "Know what that reminds me of? Remember that time I got into that teacher's classroom and wrecked it?"

"Yes."

"Remember afterward? You took me into that little teensy room and I can remember sitting on your lap. I was so scared. What happened? Did the principal whack me or something? I don't really remember that, but I remember it being afterward and you took me in there and held me on your lap."

I nodded.

"I felt so horrible. Just empty inside, like someone had pulled all my guts out. And then you held me. It was dark in there, I can remember that, and I can remember laying against you and feeling your arms, and how you just slowly sort of filled me up again."

Looking across at her, I smiled. "Yes, I remember that well."

A silence came then. It was bright and sunny, the kind of summer day meant for going out on the lake or having a church picnic, and it contrasted sharply with the tense mood in the car. I was watching the traffic and thinking loosely about picnics and how hot it might get, while at the same time never losing completely the reverberations of Sheila's earlier conversation.

"You remember that well," I said suddenly, as the realization dawned on me. "I mean, given how little you were remembering."

"Yeah," she agreed. "It comes back to me. Not in continuous memories, but jigs and jags of it. I don't know why. Things just turn up in my mind."

*　　*　　*

The meeting included the Banks-Smiths, of course, along with Dr. Rosenthal, Jeff and Dr. Freeman, as well as Sheila's father. Much to their credit, Mr. and Dr. Banks-Smith greeted Sheila with calm understanding. Dr. Rosenthal presided over the small group around the conference table, his soft-spoken civility contributing significantly to the overall composure of the group, but Mr. and Dr. Banks-Smith impressed me.

From them we heard that Alejo was home, tired but safe and happy. He had spent a good night, eaten well that morning and was enjoying cartoons now at his grandmother's house. Dr. Freeman had stopped over just after lunch to chat with Alejo and he felt that

Alejo was none the worse for his ordeal. Indeed, he said he found Alejo friendly and chatty, wanting to show him a new toy.

"What we need to understand, Sheila, is why this happened," Dr. Rosenthal said.

Sheila, beside me, lowered her head. She didn't speak.

"It was wrong. I can see you know that already. Taking Alejo caused his parents a great deal of worry and we were very worried for your safety, as well as Alejo's."

"I know I caused a lot of trouble," she mumbled, her head still down. "I'm sorry. I didn't mean to."

"Why did it happen?" Dr. Rosenthal asked.

"Because I thought . . ." She lifted her head and looked pointedly across the conference table at the Banks-Smiths. "Because I thought they were going to send Alejo away."

"So you thought taking him would be better?"

Sheila nodded.

"Do you still think that?" Dr. Rosenthal asked.

For a long moment, Sheila didn't answer. Hands in her lap, she twisted them and watched as her knuckles went white. Then finally she looked back over at him. "Yeah, I still think so."

"What were you going to do with him?" Dr. Rosenthal asked Sheila.

She shrugged. "I'm not sure. But I wasn't going to hurt him, if that's what you're asking."

"No, I didn't think you would," Dr. Rosenthal replied.

Taking a deep breath, Sheila looked up. "I'm already in trouble, so I might as well say what I think." She turned to the Banks-Smiths. "Don't send Alejo back. He can't help the way he is. He's just a little boy. He doesn't know that not being smart isn't acceptable, that because things happened to him to make him damaged, he isn't as good as other boys."

It was the Banks-Smiths' turn to lower their heads. I saw Dr. Banks-Smith's eyes fill with tears.

"I didn't mean to cause a lot of upset. I didn't think I would, because I thought you didn't want him anymore anyway," she said.

"That isn't true," Dr. Banks-Smith said tearfully. "We do love him. We're not sending him anywhere."

Mr. Banks-Smith nodded. "I'm sorry we made you think we did-
n't love him, Sheila. I suppose if there's any good to come out of
this, it's been to show us how much we do."

*   *   *

In the end, the Banks-Smiths decided not to press any charges
against Sheila. Indeed, they responded generously to her throughout the meeting, making me suspect that perhaps Dr. Rosenthal had
had a private discussion with them about Sheila's own circumstances. Whatever, it was one of those rare occasions when pain and
fear give way to growth. I think we all came out of the experience
better people.

In talking to Sheila's dad after the meeting ended, I offered to let
Sheila come back with me for the rest of the day and said I would
drive her home to Broadview that evening. He had been totally
silent throughout the whole proceedings, and his reticence remained. I suspect he had been braced for trouble with the authorities and hadn't quite taken in the fact that things had come out all
right. Whatever, he appeared vaguely confused by the whole works
and seemed not to care too much one way or another where or
when Sheila turned up. It did cross my mind then to wonder
whether or not he was high or coming off a high.

Sheila, too, seemed stunned by the decision to let things drop. I
had expected jubilation from her and the desire to celebrate, but
found instead a deep quietness. That, and a desire to touch me.
Standing in the conference room as we talked to her father, she
slipped her arm through mine and leaned against me. Smiling, I put
my arm around her shoulder and she then grabbed me in a warm hug.

I hugged her back, but then started to pull apart. Sheila kept
ahold of me. "This feels good," she murmured. "Don't let go. I don't
want to lose you again."

*   *   *

I fell back on old favorites and took Sheila out for a pizza, then
bowling. I think she was probably still exhausted from her ordeal,

because she didn't play at all well, but she seemed to have a good time. Coming out of the bowling alley, I noticed Walt Disney's *Jungle Book* advertised at the multiplex theater across the street at the shopping mall. Impulsively, I asked her if she wanted to go see it. So we did.

By the time we came out from the movie it was dark, and I knew I ought to get Sheila home, particularly as it was a good hour's drive down to Broadview.

The first ten minutes of the drive passed in pleasant chatter, as we discussed the movie, but then silence descended on us. I could sense Sheila's tiredness by that point and, lulled by the ride, I felt no need to talk. The miles ticked by. I came to the outskirts of the city. The freeway lighting ceased and we plunged into country darkness.

I was thinking as we sped through the darkness, and it occurred to me that despite the traumas of the last few days, or perhaps because of them, my relationship with Sheila was the best it had been since we were reunited. While it had been a harrowing day in many ways, it had been emotionally rewarding as well.

"You won't do it again, will you?" Sheila asked softly. "That's all behind us now, huh?"

I looked over at her.

She sat with her head resting against the shoulder strap. She gazed ahead into the darkness. "I remember that night."

Racking my brain to recall what she might be referring to, I finally gave up. "I'm not sure I know what you're talking about," I said.

"Well, you know. That night you left me. When you went."

"When I went? Where?"

Sheila straightened up in her seat and looked over at me. "You remember, of course you do. Remember, I was fooling around in the car and you stopped it and made me get out."

"When?"

"When I was little. When I was in your class, when the class was over. That night." An agitated note had come into her voice. "You had me in the car, you had everybody in the car. What were you doing?" She asked this last question more of herself than me. "Taking us out? For a good time? Like tonight. Like you're doing tonight."

I puzzled a moment, trying to recollect what she might be talking about, but the only time I had ever had Sheila out in a car at night was when Chad and I had taken her for pizza after the hearing. "I don't think that was me," I ventured.

"Yes, it was. I remember it. And we were on the road. I can remember the lights going by, the streetlights, and then dark, like this. You pulled over to the side of the road and told me to open the car door and get out."

"That wasn't me, Sheila."

"It was, 'cause I can remember your car. That little red one. You called it Bingo. You used to take us all in it and we'd sing that song, B-I-N-G-O, for the little red car."

I smiled. "Yeah, I remember the car, because it was my first one. But I only took you kids out in it two or three times, and never at night."

"It was at night," she insisted. "We were all sitting in back. I had the door against me on one side, and on the other, I was next to . . . Jamie? No, there wasn't a Jamie, was there? Billy? No. Well, I can't remember his name, but he was next to me and we were fooling around, making noises. Fart noises, I think. And you said to shut up. Shut up or you were going to stop the car and make us get out. We were just fooling around, but you got really angry and I got scared. *I* shut up. That's what made me so upset all these years, Torey, because *I* shut up. But Jamie didn't, he made this other big fart noise and you veered the car over to the side of the road. I remember that really clearly, because there was such a big jerk we all screamed. And you said, 'Get out.' I was crying by then. I knew it wasn't me, but you were so angry. I was scared to say it wasn't and I could tell I had to get out. And then you just drove off." She took a deep breath. "I mean, like, *that's* why it's been so hard for me to settle down since you got back. You kept saying 'Remember this? Remember that?' and if I tried to remember any of what happened then, all that came into my head was that you left me. You got me used to thinking I was special and then you just pushed me out."

Horrified, I looked over at her. "Sheila, that *wasn't* me!"

"It was you, because I remember your car."

"It was *not* me. That was your mother. And it wasn't Jamie sitting next to you, it was Jimmie, your brother. You've confused me with her."

Sheila's expression was one of utter bewilderment. "It was you. You were the one who left me. I don't even remember my mother."

Seeing a rest stop on the side of the road, I pulled my car in. There were bright overhead lights, which in contrast to the darkness in the car threw everything in sharp relief and I saw a look of genuine terror run across Sheila's features. Caught as she was between confused worlds of memory, I think she half expected me to tell her to get out now, so I hurriedly turned the engine off. The fact was, the conversation we were having was too powerful to carry on and still drive safely. I realized this needed my whole attention.

"Sheila, I never had you in my car at night. You were in Chad's car with me after the hearing and in my red car maybe two or three times when we had class outings, but otherwise, you were never in my car."

She sat as if paralyzed. Gazing straight ahead, her eyes unfocused, she remained stock-still for several moments, then slowly shook her head in a faint, confused fashion. "I *remember* it," she said softly, her voice perplexed. "Telling me to get out. Reaching back and opening the door. I was so scared. I was crying and so scared and I wouldn't do it. I could hear the cars going by and I was just crying and crying and no one came to get me."

"That wasn't me," I said gently.

"I was so sure it was," she replied, her voice going way up into a whimper. Tears came over her cheeks. Putting her hands up to cover her face, she bent forward. "No, oh no," she cried in dismay.

Leaning across the space between the seats, I took her in my arms and held her close against me. "That's because I left you too, didn't I? I'm sorry, lovey. I never realized how much it must have hurt."

twenty-five

In the end, the only consequence to come out of Alejo's abduction was the general feeling of Dr. Rosenthal and Alejo's parents that it would be better if Sheila did not return to work at the summer program. This was understandable and we all agreed. We were in our last week anyhow, so it didn't make much difference.

Because she didn't come back to the program, I didn't get a chance to see Sheila until the following Wednesday evening. She phoned me that afternoon at the clinic and asked if she could come over to my apartment. She was sounding cheerful but rather lonely, so I agreed to let her make me her famous tuna-fish-and-mushroom soup combo for supper. I arrived home to find her sitting outside on the doorstep of the apartment building, a brown paper bag full of groceries on her lap.

"You shouldn't have spent your money," I said. "I probably have all the ingredients."

"That's okay. I wanted to pay you back for Saturday night. And Sunday." Rising from the step, she followed me into the building and up the stairs to my apartment.

Sheila was ebullient that evening. The contrast between the silent, sullen teenager I'd first encountered in May and this eager, chatty girl was marked, and it was easy to be with her; indeed, to want to be with her. However, there was an undercurrent to her cheerfulness, something poignant that made Sheila seem terribly vulnerable to me.

We had much that needed talking about. The realization on Sunday night that Sheila had confused me with her mother and my departure with her initial abandonment had shocked me deeply, as, I suspect, it did her, and both of us were so overwhelmed with emotion that we were not capable of discussing it in any depth then. However, I definitely did want to discuss the matter with her. The insights from that revelation were causing me to see the whole situation with new eyes.

The problem was, the topic did not raise itself naturally that evening. Perhaps we were still too dazed by the discovery to be ready to discuss it. I don't know. Whatever, our conversation skirted around the edges of it.

Sheila repeatedly got off on complete tangents. She was *very* chatty and for the first time seemed keen to unleash the full extent of her brain power, describing to me the most extraordinary projects she had in mind. She was quite good with computers, for example, and told me at some length about working on programs on the school computer. Still keen on Roman history and Caesar, she had come up with the idea of trying to develop an extension to a program on one of the computers that would allow the machine to construct 3D models of Roman buildings that you could walk through. Knowing what school computers were like, I couldn't imagine what kind of program she might be thinking of modifying, but it was fascinating listening to her talk.

And so the evening passed pleasantly, as friend to friend, rather than teacher to student or therapist to client, and perhaps that's how it should have been. It was only toward the very end, when it was getting late and I knew I was going to have to send her home or I wouldn't be worth anything at work the next day, that Sheila touched briefly on matters at hand. She had grown rather melancholy toward the end of the visit. Deep down, I think she had been angling for an invitation to spend the night and was sad that this wasn't forthcoming and she'd have to go home.

"You know what?" she said, as I was rising to collect the odds and ends we had scattered around the living room and putting them away. "I don't even remember my mother. My mind is, like, absolutely blank. I've never even seen a picture of her. Dad hasn't got any. So she could look like anyone."

A silence came, gently fringed with the clinking of the mugs as I picked them up.

"I look when I go in crowds. I look at the different faces and think, Are you my mother? I wouldn't know. And she wouldn't know me. And that, like, strikes me as *so* weird. I mean, think of it, Torey. This woman carried me inside her. She made me. She *created* me and half of what I am is from her, yet I wouldn't even recognize her on the street."

Sheila remained in the armchair, the table lamp bathing her in a golden tungsten glow. I carried the dishes out to the sink and came back. All the time, Sheila kept her eyes on me. "Why do you suppose she left me?" she asked.

In the glow of the lamplight, I could see tears in her eyes. They didn't fall, but they shimmered, sparkling faintly as she moved her head.

I paused a moment to think of the best answer. Before I could say anything, she spoke again. "Tor? Do you think it's ever going to come right for me?"

"Do you mean, are you ever going to find your mother?"

She shrugged. "No, not necessarily. Just is it ever going to be all right? Do you think? Am I ever going to have a chance just to be normal?"

Slowly, I nodded. "Yes, I think so. It's going to mean coming to terms with things. Accepting that an appalling thing happened to you when your mother left you . . . two appalling things, because I left you too. I didn't mean to, or at least I didn't mean for it to feel like that's what I was doing, but I can see now that it did. And it means accepting that perhaps they both had to happen, that circumstances wouldn't allow otherwise, but that they weren't your fault. They happened to you, but you didn't cause them. And finally, you have to forgive and let go."

"Do you think I can do that?"

I nodded. "Yes. It'll take sinew, but then you always have been a tiger."

*　　*　　*

I didn't see Sheila for the rest of that week. We were busy with the final aspects of the summer program, with parent conferences and clinic evaluations. Then came the weekend and Allan and I had a flying trip out of town to the ballet planned. It wasn't until the following Wednesday that I realized how long it had been since I'd heard from Sheila and tried to phone. There was no answer.

I'm not particularly good at contacting people. I don't enjoy using the telephone and procrastinate phoning people for an embarrassing amount of time for just that reason. Most of my friends, aware of this bad habit, were accustomed to maintaining the lion's share of keeping in touch. So it had usually been with Sheila. She had almost always telephoned me. When it became my responsibility, another three or four days slid by before it occurred to me to try her again. Again, there was no answer. I did begin to wonder at this point, simply because since we had been reunited in May, two full weeks had never gone by without my hearing from her.

No answer. No answer. No answer. Then, on the Thursday three weeks after the night Sheila had made dinner for me, I tried her house again. This time a recorded message came back: the line had been disconnected.

My first thought was that Mr. Renstad had failed to pay his phone bill. This was certainly within the realms of possibility, knowing him. Nonetheless, I felt disconcerted. So, after work, I drove down to Broadview to investigate for myself.

Given the distance and the traffic, I didn't get to Sheila's house until after eight. The street was already in evening shadows, as I pulled the car up in front of the beige duplex. In the left-hand unit where another family lived, there were lights and the sounds of a television playing. In the Renstads's unit, there was only darkness.

I knocked. No answer. I knocked again. Still nothing. Going around to the side of the house to see if there was a second door, I tried that. Obviously, they weren't home. Coming around to the other side, I rose up on tiptoe and attempted to peer in through the window.

"Hey, what are you doing there?" a voice called.

Startled, I pulled back and looked over to see a man sticking his head out from the door of the other unit in the duplex. "Oh, hi," I said. "Do you know where these people are? No one seems to be home."

"You're not going to find them here," he replied. "They moved out about three weeks ago."

"Moved out?" I said in surprise.

"Yup."

"Where'd they go? Do you know?"

"Nope. No idea. Sorry." Then he shut the door and disappeared inside.

Utterly overcome, I just stood there on the sidewalk beside the house and stared at it. Moved? Sheila had said absolutely nothing about moving to me. And Mr. Renstad had given us no indication when we had seen him that weekend. He had a steady job, he had his baseball team. Why would they move? And where?

*   *   *

Sheila and her father had disappeared. I couldn't believe it. I ran through the whole gamut of emotions over the weeks that followed: shock, anger, dismay, regret, sadness. Very definitely sadness. It had taken me the better part of three months to re-form a relationship with Sheila, then it all evaporated.

I simply couldn't believe it. Over and over again I discussed the whole affair with Jeff and tried to puzzle out where they might have gone and what signs I had missed that were pointing to their leaving. Together, we endeavored to find out where they had disappeared to. This was much harder than I had hoped. We didn't have any legal reasons for finding Sheila or her father, so straightforward inquiry did not open many doors. I was reluctant to lie or otherwise falsify my intentions, so this left me with nothing more to fall back on than deductive reasoning, persistence and good luck. The first two I probably had enough of, but the third I simply had to wait for.

As much as I hated to consider it, the first thought to come to mind was that Mr. Renstad had committed a new offense and was back in prison. I couldn't find anyone who would willingly confirm this, given privacy laws. Chad seemed my only chance when I ran up against a blank wall, so I called him and asked if he could find out. A stickler for maintaining client confidentiality, he was reluctant to do much, but he did confirm that Mr. Renstad was not on his firm's client list. This seemed to decrease the chances that he was in the penitentiary again.

Jeff suggested that perhaps they had simply fled, from bills or maybe some dodgy loan shark or the like. If we were lucky, he said, perhaps they were still in the city and it would just be a matter of waiting for Sheila to contact me. That, I suspected, was what it was going to boil down to anyway—waiting for Sheila. She knew where I was, and unlike the previous occasions when we'd lost contact, she was now old enough to initiate the process of finding me.

Anyhow, that was the end of it. Sheila, once more, was gone.

part
three

twenty-six

Sheila didn't contact me. Summer turned to autumn. New children came. New relationships formed. My work went on.

Then, in October, luck caught up with me. Through a series of flukes, I found out that Mr. Renstad was back in Marysville at the state hospital detox center. I attempted to talk to him by telephone, but was unsuccessful. So, when we had the long Columbus Day weekend, I drove over.

It was a warm, bright fall afternoon when I arrived at the unit. The poplars and the birches had all turned to brilliant shades of yellow and gold, highlighted by long shafts of autumn sunshine.

Mr. Renstad didn't seem all that surprised to see me, nor all that happy, although he went willingly enough with me to the visitors' area.

"Why don't you just leave us alone?" he said, when I asked about Sheila. "You don't do her any good."

"How do you mean?" I asked.

"You stir things up. She was doing okay before you came in. She was settled down nice and we weren't having no problems."

I regarded him.

"It's you that's caused everything. You upset Sheila and I don't want you around no more. She was settled down nice till you stirred things up."

"I didn't mean to upset Sheila," I said. "I didn't realize I had."

"You put ideas in her head that don't belong there. She was happy before you came along."

"But the things we talked about were things Sheila wanted to discuss. I think she needs to talk to someone about what's happened to her."

"What's happened to her? What *has* happened to her? Nothing she ain't done for herself. And you put her up to it. Her stealing that little boy. It never would have come to that, if you hadn't gotten her going. She was *fine* till you came in."

"I'm sorry, but—"

"So just leave us alone, okay? Keep yourself to yourself. Sheila don't need your help and I don't want you seeing her anymore. I got the right. I can stop you." And with that he rose and walked back into the unit.

Chastened, I returned to my car. It was only after I was seated behind the steering wheel that anger began to overtake the effect of being reprimanded. Me? My fault? What a stupid man.

Still, what was undeniable about the outcome of that meeting was that he had no intention of telling me where Sheila was. If anything, he would make certain I didn't find her, or block my efforts, if I did. Disheartened, I returned home.

*   *   *

Winter came and the year turned. There were reminders along the way. Alejo's parents stopped by one afternoon in January to tell me that they had formally adopted Alejo. He was now in a special class for mildly mentally handicapped children and making good progress. On another occasion, my mother sent me a recipe that included tuna fish and mushroom soup. And Chad stopped by my office one frosty February afternoon with his Sheila. He was on a business trip in the city, and his daughter, now six, was enjoying her first solo trip with Dad. Immaculately dressed, bright, friendly and terribly polite, Sheila showed me a small handheld computer game her father had bought for her. The contrast between her childhood and the girl she was named after couldn't have been more profound.

I remained hopeful, scanning the mail each evening when I came home for something in Sheila's handwriting, but it didn't come. Winter turned into spring and eventually spring into summer.

We ran the summer program again. It was much less the amateur affair it had been the previous year. We had twenty-four children in three classrooms with three specialist teachers, four aides and rotating on-site psychiatrists. Jeff only came once a week, and while I was there daily, it was in a supervisory capacity, roaming between rooms. The program was excellent, I felt, but it lacked the gung-ho magic of its predecessor.

In early July, I noted when Sheila's birthday came. She would be fifteen now. And then the anniversary of her disappearance. I couldn't help wondering where she was at the moment and what she was doing.

When the summer school finished, I took a month off and went to Wales. The barren, mist-laden mountains in the north of that small corner of Britain had become a second home to me. I was never quite sure what it was that attracted me there in the first place, but there had never been any doubt about what brought me back. I found an innate rightness in being there amidst the heather and the slate-built stone walls. It was an organic thing, something from within me, and I returned for the peace it always brought when I did so.

I had a group of good friends among the locals by that summer and we all shared a love for the mountains. Days were spent spanning the rainy moorlands and communing with Wales's teeming sheep population. Evenings were passed around the coal fires of local pubs, where I could indulge a fondness for draft Guinness and Welsh accents. The city, the clinic and all my former life disappeared like the mountains did when the mist rose up from the sea.

*   *   *

Like all good vacations, this one ended with my returning so exhausted I could hardly see straight. I staggered down off the plane, caught a taxi into the city and then staggered up the stairs of my apartment building. Setting down my rucksack, I fished out my house keys and opened my door. Or rather, I tried to. The mail, pushed through the mail slot, had fallen to the floor and wedged itself under the door as I pushed it open. Several minutes passed before I successfully extracted enough mail from under it to get into my apartment.

Once in, I bent to clear up the rest of the mail when my eyes fell upon one letter. Immediately, I recognized Sheila's handwriting. I ripped it open.

Dear Torey,

I don't quite know how to start, but I think I'm going to kill myself. I got the pills. They're right here and all that I've got left to do is write this letter. I feel so alone, Torey. Nothing seems to work out for me and I'm just so damned tired of trying. This is the only thing to do that makes sense.

But I wanted to write you this first. I wanted to say thank you for everything you've done for me. I know you went the extra mile a couple of times and I'm really honored to think you would. I want you to know I always felt grateful. I'm sorry things just couldn't work out.

With love, Sheila

And across the bottom was a row of Os and Xs, indicating hugs and kisses, as in a very little child's letter.

Quickly, I looked for a date, but there was none. I flipped the envelope over to see the postmark, and to my absolute horror, I saw that the letter had been posted two days after I had left for Wales—a full four weeks earlier. Paralyzed with grief, I just stared at it.

There was an address on the letter, indicating that Sheila was in a group home near a community about an hour's drive east of the city. But what could I do now? Four weeks had elapsed. How did one handle this? Phone up the group home and ask if Sheila was still alive? Knowing Sheila's personality, I didn't think she was the type for gestures. If she said she was going to commit suicide, I had little doubt that was exactly what she would do, and I didn't know how I would cope with a phone call of this sort.

Unfortunately, this wasn't the only chaos to accost me on my return. Another youngster I'd been working with had assaulted a care worker, then run away, and he'd chosen this particular evening of my return to ransack Jeff's and my office in search of a homemade knife I had taken off him. The immediacy of this problem, combined with the pressure from the authorities to deal with this boy, and my general exhaustion after a twenty-hour return trip from abroad caused me to behave toward Sheila's letter in a way that I now feel deep embarrassment about. There I was, with the worst letter I had ever received, and, ashamed as I am to admit it, I did nothing.

*   *   *

I didn't forget the letter by any means. It preyed on me, night and day. Small, quiet moments, particularly those deep in the night when I would awaken, were nibbled by that letter. My problem was, I just didn't quite know how to handle it. I genuinely believed Sheila would do what she threatened, so I didn't know how or whom to ask to confirm this. Moreover, I was saddened and ashamed to think that she had written me in a moment of desperation and would never know that I had been unable to respond. She would think instead that I, like everyone else, had abandoned her.

All this provided an unexpected and rather unwelcome opportunity for intense self-examination. I had failed Sheila. That was the bottom line. Moreover, I couldn't help but feel I was the one who had set her up. I had opened up unimaginable worlds to her when she was six, and, as she had so rightly pointed out to me, I had made her think they could be hers. Young and idealistic at the time, I'd genuinely believed they could be. She was bright, articulate, attractive, charming when she wanted to be and full of grit. I thought I'd given her the passport to a better life. Older and sadly wiser, I now realized nothing was ever as simple as it seemed.

The months that followed were a difficult, disruptive time in several areas of my life simultaneously. My client list was very full, the children on it a more demanding assortment than usual. I was physically attacked on two different occasions and nearly raped on a third. Worse, more than a fair share of my clients were quite unrewarding to work with, requiring long hours of effort for very little response.

I was beginning to chafe under the capitalist ethos of the clinic, feeling uncomfortable knowing that I could only treat those children who could afford to pay for my services, not those who needed treatment worse. This caused me to waste precious time trying to secure special funding for some children, who I believed genuinely needed continued therapy, and to feel resentment toward those with mild problems that could have been dealt with easily in the school or home but whose well-off parents insisted on treatment.

The biggest blow, however, came in midwinter, when Jeff left the clinic in unfortunate circumstances. My colleagues' sexual behaviors were of little interest to me, as long as they did not impinge on work-related matters or my relationship with the individuals. Deep down, I think I was probably aware that Jeff was gay, although it had never been of any consequence to what we were doing together, and thus never something I'd paid attention to. Sadly, society did. When the board of trustees for the clinic found out about his sexual preferences, they felt it unwise for Jeff to be working one-to-one with young children. Jeff was given the opportunity to go quietly with good references, and feeling he had no alternative, he did. He transferred to a post in California working with alcoholics.

I was devastated. We had been sharing several cases and had built our treatment methods around the partnership. Jeff left very abruptly, having negotiated with the trustees right up to the end to stay. When they'd refused to budge, he'd stormed out in anger. Consequently, I had not been prepared for his departure and was left to clear up the damage. There was plenty, and I was kept unpleasantly busy.

The only bright spot in the winter had been the advent of a new boyfriend named Hugh. Allan had long since passed from the scene and I had been doomed to a number of months of the dreaded dating ritual. Then up popped this incredibly handsome man with a wicked sense of humor and a ten-year-old VW with dead bugs painted all over it. We were definitely an example of the old adage of opposites attracting each other, because Hugh and I couldn't have made a less likely couple. A complete antithesis to Allan and Chad, Hugh was a pull-yourself-up-by-the-bootstraps college dropout, who had set himself up in pest extermination at age twenty-one with the money that should have gone for education. He had a shrewd business mind and a genuine passion for crawling through people's cellars and attics killing small creatures, and after ten years, he owned one of the most successful pest-extermination businesses in the city.

What had attracted me most was his sense of humor, which was of legendary proportions. For me, in my deadly serious profession, humor was the lifesaver I often grabbed hold of just to stay afloat, so it was easy to love someone who was always capable of appreciating the funny side in life's unfunnier situations.

Spring came very slowly that year. It had been a dry, cold winter that lingered uninvited into March, and then the snowstorms finally arrived in April, burying us, paralyzing the city and destroying what few signs of spring there were.

At the clinic I argued with my colleagues over the fate of the summer program. Dr. Freeman had taken over much of Jeff's summer-program involvement and, without consulting me, he had applied for and gotten grants to expand us into two locations. We would now be serving forty-eight children, including a group of severely autistic children who were not clients of the clinic. I sensed a money-making scheme behind all of this, which annoyed me mightily, as I'd wanted to keep it confined to children whose progress we could continue to follow, but it didn't matter much. My position with the program had become almost tangential. In the end, I gave up the fight. It was probably a good enough program, but it was light-years away from what Jeff and I had conceived two summers earlier, so I decided to leave it all to Dr. Freeman.

May came and with it a new office partner named Jules. He was a dramatic change from Jeff in all respects, from appearance to demeanor. Having switched to child psychiatry after many years as a urologist, he was almost fifty, a short, round dumpling of a man with a few whiffs of white where his hair ought to have been. Unlike Jeff, with his rapier wit and showy confidence, Jules was soft-spoken and gentle as a bunny. I liked him. Indeed, the more I came to know him, the more I enjoyed his company. He was very easy to talk to and was a brilliant lateral thinker, which meant our conversations could go leap-frogging off in all directions. But he wasn't Jeff. Still missing Jeff enormously, I took a long time to get used to a new face at the other desk.

Then, one evening in June, I came home to find a thick envelope on the floor with my other mail. Sheila's handwriting was immediately recognizable. Astonished, I ripped the envelope open. There were thirteen sheets of notebook paper inside. The first one was a very brief letter to me:

Dear Torey

I've been wanting to write you, but after my last letter I didn't know how to start. I'm sorry. Anyway I'm still here.

    I've sent you these. I wanted to send them to my own mom, but I don't know where she is, so I've sent them to you. I hope you don't mind.

Love, Sheila

Lifting off the letter, I looked at the pages underneath. Each one contained a single, short letter addressed to Sheila's mother.

Dear Mom,

I wish I could see you. I wish I knew what you look like. I tried to get a picture of you, but Dad doesn't have any and nobody else seems to either. I want to know you. Do you have blond hair like I do? Is it straight? Do you have blue eyes? Every time I go out, I look at the women who go by me. I keep looking for someone who might know me. What do you look like? I think if I could find out, I'd feel better.

Dear Mom,

Why did you go? That's something that's always bugged me. I mean, how come you wouldn't take me? Was I that bad a kid? Was I, like, mouthy to you all the time or something? Did I fight with Jimmie? Or did you just get fed up with having two kids?

Dear Mom,

Did you go because of Dad? I know about him now, how he can't stay off the stuff. It makes me angry too. It makes me want to run away. Is that what happened to you? Could you just not stand it?

Folding the letters and putting them back into their envelope, I regarded my name on the front. Up in the corner was the name of the same group home her earlier letter had come from. Going into the kitchen, I picked up the telephone and dialed Information.

twenty-seven

Mr. Renstad's abrupt departure was, as Jeff had suggested, debt-related. What we didn't know at the time was that, contrary to his word, he was still using drugs regularly, and it was with some unsavory underworld characters that he had run up his debts. He and Sheila had escaped just ahead of trouble, as they had apparently done so many times before.

Trouble caught up with him a few months later, though, in the form of the law. He was convicted of a minor drug offense and sent to the state hospital detox center yet again, which is where I had caught up with him. Sheila, meanwhile, had been placed in a children's group home in the community where he had been arrested.

Unhappy with this new situation, Sheila had run away. This prompted her placement in a foster home, and when she ran from there, she was transferred to a children's home in a rural location about an hour's drive east of the city. This sort of place was known colloquially as a "children's ranch," a euphemism for a locked facility. It was from there Sheila's suicide note to me had come the previous summer and it was from there I had received this most recent group of letters.

Having located Sheila at last, I rang immediately and spoke with the director of the ranch, a woman named Jane Timmons.

"From the Sandry Clinic, you say?" she asked in amazement. "Sheila Renstad was treated at the Sandry? Who paid the bills?"

Annoyed with what seemed an unusually rude question, especially as I was a complete stranger, I explained that my relationship with Sheila went back a good deal further, but I did not elaborate on the fact that it was no longer a professional but a personal one. Thirty seconds on the phone and I could tell here was a lady for whom money and status meant much. That I was from the Sandry, a well-known and expensive private clinic, probably opened more doors than all my professional qualifications put together. If I had said I was only a friend, I would have been lumped with Sheila's father and probably not given the time of day.

Jane Timmons told me that Sheila had been at the ranch for just over a year and that for the most part she had been a difficult, uncooperative girl, who mixed poorly and seemed to have few, if any, friends. They had thwarted three different runaway attempts, including one where Sheila had gotten as far as the river and they'd needed to call the police.

I questioned her about the general philosophy of the ranch, and she confirmed for me what I'd already anticipated, that theirs was a program that relied heavily on behavior modification, with the children needing to earn all privileges through a point system. I also asked about Sheila's prospects for being released from the ranch. Jane explained that Mr. Renstad was due for parole near Christmas, and if social services felt it was appropriate, Sheila would go back to him then.

Because Jane Timmons assumed I was seeing Sheila in a professional capacity, our meeting was not subject to Sheila's earning sufficient points. Mercifully. As emotionally and intellectually complex as Sheila was, behavior modification was a system doomed to failure with her.

✳   ✳   ✳

I arrived at the ranch on the Saturday following Sheila's sixteenth birthday. It was a bright, hot day, following a long dry spell, when I came out. The ranch, a collection of low, modern buildings, squatted along the banks of a dry riverbed. There was not a tree on the property, and the grass had all burned yellow-brown in the summer heat. Only the barbed wire glinted in the sun.

As it was a weekend, Jane Timmons wasn't there, but I was greeted pleasantly by the young man in charge and then transferred to Holly, one of the counselors, who was responsible for the group of children that included Sheila. She took me back to the girls' wing, where Sheila was waiting in her room.

It was a genuine secure unit, with an endless number of heavy locked doors and windows sporting that thick glass with the chicken wire embedded in it that never gave you an undistorted image. Sheila's room was the third to the last on the left. The door, made of pale-colored oak with a small square window and a mortise lock, stood open. Sheila was sitting cross-legged on her bed.

"Hi," I said.

"Hi." There was a long moment's hesitation and then, abruptly, Sheila threw herself into my arms and clung to me tightly. I wrapped my arms around her and held her close.

In the doorway, Holly regarded us. Over Sheila's head, I looked at her. "Could you leave us for a little while?"

She paused, then nodded. "Yeah. Okay."

*   *   *

Sheila had changed enormously in the interceding two years. She had grown taller, but had lost weight. Too much weight. She looked frail. The wacky clothes had been replaced with nothing more exotic than a pair of jeans and a blue T-shirt. The brilliant hair was gone too, as was most of the permanent, and she had grown her bangs out—or mostly out. The result was not a style at all, but an untidy mixture of dark-blond roots, frizzy colored ends, and stray, sticking-out bits, all left to grow far too long without attention.

Sheila examined me as closely as I was examining her. "You're getting old, you know that?" she said. "You got wrinkles."

"Gee, thanks."

"It's just that I never thought about you with wrinkles."

"It happens to the best of us," I said and sat down on her roommate's bed.

The room was small and Spartan. It was no more than a cubicle, really, about eight by ten feet. There was a window at the far end, two iron beds with rather violent pink bedspreads, and a single desk at the foot of Sheila's bed. Her roommate, a girl named Angel, had posters of rock stars plastered on the wall above her bed and an assortment of stuffed animals against her pillow. Sheila had nothing.

I gazed around and then back at Sheila, who had settled again, cross- legged, on her bed. She was an immensely attractive girl, in spite of her thinness and her uncared-for appearance, but there was a melancholy about her I had never previously detected.

"So, are you married yet?" she asked.

"Married? Me?" I replied in surprise. "No. Why? Did you think I would be?"

"Yeah. You and Jeff."

"*Jeff* and me? Jeff and I were . . . I mean, not in that way. I was never involved with Jeff. We were just friends. Colleagues, really. Nothing more."

She tipped her head, her expression skeptical.

"What about you?" I asked. "Do you have any boyfriends?"

She didn't reply. There was a moment's pause, just a beat, and she looked back. "So, where's Jeff at? Is he coming out to see me too?"

"No," I said, and Sheila's face fell.

"Oh, I'd hoped he would," she said sorrowfully. This caught me off-guard, as I had never thought she'd felt anything but antipathy for him.

"He's in California now," I said and pondered briefly on whether or not to tell Sheila the whole story about what had happened to him. I decided I should, to make it clear that his departure had been forced upon him.

Sheila listened to the story with rapt attention, her brow furrowing. When I finished, she shook her head slightly. "Gone? He's gone for good?"

"I'm afraid so."

"Oh, Jeff," she murmured softly, shaking her head. "The breaking of so great a thing should make a greater crack. The round world should have shook lions into civil streets, and citizens to their dens."

Hearing those words, I realized they were a quotation, but I didn't know from where.

"You don't recognize that?" Sheila asked. Leaning over the side of her bed, she pulled out a flat under-bed box and tipped up the lid. Reaching in, she lifted out the copy of Shakespeare's *Antony and Cleopatra* that Jeff had given her for her fourteenth birthday. The cover was dog-eared and taped back together in places. I could see several pages were loose.

An enormous silence suddenly loomed up out of nowhere. Sheila held the book in her lap and regarded the worn cover. I just sat, all the words drained from my mind.

At last she began to speak softly. "I wondered why he gave it to me. I thought, what a stupid gift. I mean, who would want to read *Shakespeare?* For fun? Some dorky old woman in sturdy black shoes and support hose. Not me, that's for sure.

"Then I was stuck waiting at the police station one night. I didn't have anything to pass the time, so I started reading it. It was hard to get into, hard to get used to the language—which is weird to me now, because now when I read it, it seems so easy—but that first night I struggled. And I thought, why on earth did he give this to me?

"Then I got here, and it was, like, being in a desert. If you don't earn your points, don't play the game their way, you just sit. It's the boredom factor, you see, that they control you with." The smile was more enigmatic this time. "So I started reading it again. And this time I read it right through. And when I finished, I read it again. And again. I bet you I read it ten times straight through in about two days. And I thought, this is so beautiful. This woman is so wonderful. So *magnificent.* And this man gives everything for her. He gives away the world—quite literally. And yet . . . like, they don't even talk nicely to each other about half the time. They're in love in their minds, but in reality, they're always disagreeing, arguing, teasing.

"God . . . When I read this, it makes me . . . how does one describe it? Expand? No. No, that's not it." She paused, pensive. "It's like I'm in this little attic room—that's my normal life—and there's this skylight above me that I can see, but I can never reach. Then, when I read this, something inside me grows. Pushes me up, and for just a moment, I can lift the skylight and see out. Just glimpse the world beyond, know what I mean? But I can glimpse it. For just a moment I can tell there's something bigger than myself."

Listening to Sheila, I was deeply moved.

She went on talking, her words tumbling out ever more quickly, as

if she feared I'd stop her. All this thought, all these insights struggling
to light in a vacuum. I could sense her intellectual desperation.

"The story's all true, you know," she was saying. "I went and
checked the facts. The whole course of the Western world was affected by what this couple did. Did you know that? Cleopatra was,
like, this really incredible woman. She was very strong. A very powerful queen. And yet she is so human. So silly. So funny. God, Torey,
in places this is the funniest thing I have ever read."

All I could think was what the hell were we doing with this girl
locked up in a secure unit? Why was she here and not in some summer-school literature course at a college or studying the ancient history that obviously intrigued her so much? Where were the mentors
who should have spotted this girl along the way? My talents didn't
lie here. My knowledge of Shakespeare, like my knowledge of the
writings of Julius Caesar, was pedestrian. Where were the English
teachers whose hearts should have gladdened at the very idea of a
sixteen-year-old besotted with the poetry of *Antony and Cleopatra*?

Her expression slowly growing sorrowful, Sheila regarded the
book in her hands. With one finger, she gently smoothed the Scotch
tape back over a ragged edge. "You know, that's really sad about Jeff.
I'd wanted to see him. I'd wanted him to know I liked the book."

"Maybe I can give you his address, if you'd like to write him," I
suggested.

"I think I'd sort of fallen in love with him," she said. "I couldn't
tell him that then. Fortunately, I hadn't read this, because I could
never have told him I liked it. I wanted him to think I hated him."
She looked up. "Isn't that weird? I didn't. I never did. But I was
scared he'd hate me if I didn't hate him first." A pause. "Now I wish
I'd told the truth."

✳   ✳   ✳

We continued to talk for more than two hours that Saturday afternoon. Most of the other children, Sheila's roommate included, had
earned enough points for a trip into town, and after a noisy clatter
of activity while they got ready, we were left in peace. This suited
both of us.

Sheila, for once, was very open and talkative. I suspect this was the result of so much time spent on her own. Alone and lonely, she was susceptible to my familiar face. Depression played a part in it too. My overall impression of Sheila that afternoon was that she was quite seriously depressed. All the spark had gone right out of her, and with the exception of her relationship with *Antony and Cleopatra*, she showed interest in very little. As a consequence, I think she was too dispirited to disguise her thoughts as elaborately as in the past.

Feeling concern for her as a continued suicide risk, I felt obliged to bring up the letter she had sent me the previous autumn. "I'm sorry about last fall," I said, "about not answering your letter."

"Ah, yes," Sheila said and looked away. "That letter." She grimaced. "I'm sorry if I upset you. I feel stupid now that I wrote it."

"No, you shouldn't feel stupid. Those were very real feelings. It's my fault. I was gone then. I was in Wales and didn't even know about it until I got back, which was weeks later. I felt so terrible, Sheil, that you'd written and I couldn't answer."

"Let's just not talk about it, okay?"

I regarded her. She had her head down and was examining something on her fingernail. Sheila had always been a curious mixture of tiger and lamb, fierce and spirited on one hand, frightened and vulnerable on the other. I'd often felt utter exasperation with her when she was being tigerish, but it was also what had attracted me to her. Studying her rounded shoulders, her disheveled hair, I sought the tiger hiding there.

"I get to thinking a lot about my mom," she said softly. A pause. "That's your fault, too. Remember that last conversation we had? In the car? When for all that time I had you and her mixed up?"

I nodded.

"Well, I've been thinking and thinking . . . trying to pull the two of you apart, I guess. I don't know where I got the thing with you. *You* didn't abandon me. You were just my teacher. Only doing what teachers do. I was just being stupid, I think. Trying to survive."

"How do you mean?" I asked.

Sheila shrugged. "I dunno. By not thinking about those years. By forgetting them. 'Cause that's what I did. I forgot everything. I mean,

I *remember* forgetting. It was a conscious thing. I'd move on to somewhere new, like to a new foster home, or like back with my dad, and I'd think to myself, 'I'm going to start all over now.' And then I'd, like, go into my new school and stuff and people would ask me about my life before and I'd just say, 'I don't remember about it.' And really quickly, that'd be true. It's like I'd get reborn each time and all that went before was in some former life. Almost like it wasn't me."

"Did that help you not think of your mother?" I asked.

"Yeah. And not think of you. And not think of Miss McGuire, 'cause I was really happy in her class too. Because I didn't want to remember being too happy. I didn't want to think about those times, because I'd cry. Remembering bad things never bothers me. I think, 'Well, that's shit.' And that's all. But remembering being happy just guts me. So every time I'd do it, I'd just say, '*No*, don't do that.' And pretty soon it was gone."

I looked at her. She raised her head, glanced at me and then looked back at her hands. "Then you came mucking about. You really aren't one to leave things well enough alone, you know that?" she said. The tone was affectionate and she allowed a faint grin, but I knew there was truth in the words.

"You wish I'd left well enough alone?" I asked.

A long, pensive pause followed, with Sheila picking intently at her thumbnail, then finally she gave a slow shrug. "I dunno. I think my life would have been a lot easier if you had. One way or another, you've given me a lot of grief over the years, but . . ." She looked over at me. "The fact is, my life would have been a lot easier if practically everybody I've ever known had stayed out of it—my mother, my father, this place, the foster homes, Social Services. So you're no exception."

I smiled. This caused Sheila to smile back. "You don't mind me saying that about you?" she asked.

"No. It's probably true."

A silence came then. Sheila lay back on her bed and folded her hands behind her head. Staring upward, she regarded the ceiling for several moments. I turned to study Angel's rock posters. Most of them were of artists I'd never heard of.

"I think so much about my mom now," Sheila said softly. "I mean, about where she is and things. What she's doing. I don't even know her, Torey."

"Putting it down on paper was a good idea, I think," I said.

"I try to figure out why she did what she did when she left me on that highway. Maybe she didn't mean to. Maybe it was some sort of accident, like, perhaps the door handle came undone. Maybe I *fell* out of the car." Still regarding the ceiling, Sheila's expression had grown inward. "Maybe if she knew I was all right, that I wanted to see her . . ."

Not quite sure how to respond, I remained silent. Sheila finally looked over. "I'm not sending you those letters because I think *you're* my mom."

"No, I know that."

"I'm done thinking that. I just sent them 'cause . . . well, they're *letters.* They only mean something if they're sent."

"I understand and I'm glad to get them."

"Keep them for me, would you?" she asked. "Because someday, I'm going to find her and I'm going to give them to her. I want her to know me, to know how I've been feeling all these years. That's what I've decided. When I get out of here, I'm going to find my mother."

twenty-eight

Dear Mom,
Do you know how unhappy I've been? Do you know what kind of
life I've had? Why did you do this to me? I lay at night thinking
about it, trying to figure out why I wasn't good enough for you, but
do you know what it was like, being left behind?

Sheila concerned me greatly. Finding her isolated and depressed, I worried that suicide might easily loom up again as a possible solution. Moreover, her needs didn't seem to be well recognized by the group-home personnel. Like most such institutions, they were understaffed and overstretched. The staff turnover rate, in particular, was atrocious. Most of the care workers were poorly trained part-timers on minimum wage, who came and went on an almost weekly basis, which disallowed relationships of any depth to develop with the children. Among the resident staff, only Jane Timmons and her two deputies were specifically trained to work with disturbed children, and of them, only one had worked at the ranch for more than two years. Jane herself had been there only a little longer than Sheila.

This alone would have been cause for concern in Sheila's case, because none of the adults had been around her long enough to develop a meaningful relationship with her, but the strict Skinnerian approach used to control the children and bring about changed behavior seemed particularly inappropriate for Sheila. To begin with, it encouraged detached, impersonal contact between staff and children. Moreover, Sheila had the sort of personality that did not find it easy to accept coercion, which was how she interpreted the point system, and she was quick to dig herself in. This led, ipso facto, to prolonged isolation.

Unfortunately, I was not in a good position to do much, as I was not seeing her in a professional capacity. Jane Timmons did not know this and it seemed judicious not to enlighten her, which I didn't; however, I knew I'd better not overstep too much. Thus I confined myself to announcing my visits to Jane rather than requesting them, so as to ensure I could see Sheila when I wanted. That, and occasionally "conferencing" with Jane. I knew she would expect me, as a professional, to want to hear about Sheila's life at the ranch, and as I did, I took advantage of the opportunity.

When possible, I came out to see Sheila each Saturday afternoon. It was a fair drive from the city, but quite a pleasant one, and often Hugh and I would make it together. He'd bring his fishing gear along and would disappear off down the river for an hour or two while I talked to Sheila. Thus passed much of the rest of the summer.

Jane Timmons painted a rather bleak picture of Sheila's social behavior. I think I had already surmised that Sheila was no social butterfly. This had occurred to me clear back during the summer when she was working with Jeff and me, because there was never, ever any mention of friends, either male or female. I had never pressured Sheila on this issue, partly because I was not in a good position to do anything constructive about it, and partly because I felt her IQ interfered to some degree with normal peer relationships. This would be a difficult area to deal with, particularly in Sheila's circumstances, and I had ended up feeling that time and maturity would probably be the best solutions.

"Say what?" Jane asked. "What was that? Superior IQ?"

"Yes, you know."

"No, I don't know. What IQ?" she asked.

Shock hit me. All that effort my colleagues and I had gone through the year Sheila was six to confirm her extraordinary giftedness, and it wasn't in her records? "Sheila has an IQ over a hundred eighty," I said.

"Say *what?*" Jane's eyes widened. "One hundred eighty? You must be joking."

"You have no record of it?"

"*One hundred eighty? Sheila Renstad? Our Sheila Renstad?* You're kidding, aren't you? Who told you?"

"I was there myself," I said. "I know. I was working with her then, when the testing was done."

Jane fell back in her chair. "Boy, nobody ever said anything about this to me."

Filled with resentment at a system that treated lives with such appalling offhandedness, I went on down the hall with Holly, who unlocked the doors for me. Sheila, as always, was alone in her room.

"We've got to get you out of here," I said.

"You're telling me."

"No, I mean it, Sheila. This is no place for you. Why are you even here? You haven't committed any offenses. Why are *you* locked up? It's your dad who's supposed to be in prison."

Sitting cross-legged on her bed, she looked up at me. "Yeah, well, welcome to my world."

I pulled out the chair from the desk and sat down. A silence came then, sapping my sudden spurt of anger.

"What you get used to after a while, Torey, is that this is just the way it is. There's no use fighting it."

"I can't accept that," I said.

"I can. I've had to."

> *Dear Mom,*
> *What's Jimmie doing now? He's probably taller than me these days. I was figuring it out and he'd be at least fourteen. I can't remember exactly any more if he was two years younger than me, or was it even less? Was it like eighteen months? I keep thinking about that, trying to remember. It's weird, knowing you've forgotten about your own brother.*

Jane Timmons had wanted me to take up the issue of Sheila's asocial behavior with her, and it was an issue that no doubt wanted exploring, but not that afternoon. For these few hours at least, I wanted Sheila to feel she had control, so we tended to go as she led.

Gloom hung over her that afternoon, as it had on so many others. She lay back on her bed and stared up at the ceiling. I suggested perhaps we could go for a walk, but Sheila vetoed that. She wasn't allowed off the grounds and she could see no point in making a circuit of the barbed-wire fence.

"What would you *like* to do?" I asked at last, when the silence had grown so heavy it threatened to squash me.

"Nothing, really."

There was a quiet pause. She was still lying on the bed, but she brought one hand up to her forehead.

"Well . . ." She paused again, her fingers probing along her hairline. "Remember back when I was in your class?"

"Yes."

"Remember how you always did my hair? I used to love that so much, the way you used to brush it and put it in styles." She glanced over. "Do you . . . I mean, if I gave you . . . Well, it sounds stupid, but would you fix my hair for me?"

"Yeah, I suppose."

Sheila rose up from the bed and went to the dresser to get her hairbrush. Pausing in front of the small mirror, she gave her hair a few yanks with it and grimaced at her image. "If we got scissors, could you cut it for me?"

"Oh, I don't know about that," I said. "I'm not much of a hairdresser."

She held out the brush to me. "I want to cut off these ends. Please, Torey? I'm fed up like I am."

* * *

Gently, I started to work the brush, then the comb, through her hair. It was quite a mess, what with all the bleaching and dying done over the years. Borrowing scissors from Jane's desk, I endeavored to do what Sheila asked of me. I trimmed away the last of the permanent and tried to do in as much of the dyed area as well. This brought her hair almost up to her shoulders in a not very professional blunt cut. Then I just brushed.

Sheila clearly enjoyed my activities very much and it occurred to me as I worked that, given her isolation at the ranch, it had probably been a fair length of time since anyone had touched her. This thought surprised me, but the more I considered it, the more I realized it was most likely true. Indeed, the thought crossed my mind that Sheila had probably spent most of her young life with little positive physical contact.

"Do you have a boyfriend?" I asked.

"Me? Here? No way."

"Have you ever had a boyfriend?"

She didn't respond right away. She had her back to me, because I was still brushing her hair, so I couldn't see her expression, but there was a sense of hesitancy. "No," she finally said.

"Do you want one?" I asked. "Do you like boys?"

"Do you mean, am I a lez?" she asked, pulling away from me and turning. She made a face. "Just because I don't have a boyfriend, you don't have to think that of me." She jerked right back from me. "You're probably thinking now that's why I wanted you to brush my hair. Shit. Give it here. Gimme my brush back."

"Whoa, that's not what I said. And so what, anyhow? I wouldn't care. If I didn't care about Jeff and his preferences, I wouldn't care about you and yours. That's a personal thing, Sheila. I was just asking."

"Yeah, why? What business is it of yours, if I've got boyfriends or not? I don't go asking you about what you're up to, do I?" she responded tetchily.

"Okay, okay. Sorry," I said.

"Hmmph," Sheila snorted and climbed back onto her bed. "Jane put you up to it, didn't she? Jane is so nosy."

"Okay. Sorry."

Silence. Sheila stared at the hairbrush in her hand. Bringing it up, she brushed through her hair on one side, feeling the ends I'd cut. The silence lingered, growing sad as it lengthened. I thought for a moment she was going to cry.

"No, I don't have a boyfriend," she said softly. "And no, I've never had one. I like boys. I liked Jeff. I thought he was a real dude and . . ." A pause. "But all it ever comes down to is fucking, Torey. And I've seen too many dicks already."

"It can be a little more than that, Sheil."

"I can't have children. Did you know that? After what my uncle did that time. You remember? It was when I was in your class. I can't have babies. So, what other reason would there be?" she asked.

Uncertain what to say, I just sat.

"What I'd like is someone just to cuddle me. Know what I mean? Someone who'd put his arms around me without expecting anything more in return, but I don't think I'll get that. So, I've just decided I'll have nothing at all."

✳   ✳   ✳

Dear Mom,

I read in the papers this week where they found someone who'd got murdered 25 years ago and no one had ever known she was missing. Everyone just said she went away and nobody ever bothered looking for her. They thought she didn't want to come back. I get so worried that something like this has happened to you. I want to find you. I want to talk to you and know you're okay. I want to make sure that isn't why you never came back.

When I came the following Saturday, I brought Sheila hair-care items I'd picked up at the drugstore. They were nothing much: a jar of deep conditioner, some styling mousse and a blue headband to keep her half-grown-out bangs out of her eyes. She greeted these gifts with delight.

"Wow! This is great!" She ripped apart the bag rather than opening it and lifted up the headband, shoving it into her hair. "I always wanted to wear one of these. Because I had bangs, it never made sense for me to have one, so I never got one. But this is great. Why'd you do it?"

I shrugged. "Thought you'd like it."

"Yeah, I do. Thanks."

A minute or two passed while Sheila inspected the items more carefully. She unscrewed the lid to the conditioner, fingered it, put the lid back on and then read the directions. "They're probably never going to let me use this stuff here. They make you turn in everything. I reckon they think you're going to smoke it or something. God knows."

I sat down on Angel's bed. She had at least two dozen small stuffed toys lined up against the pillow and my weight on the bed dislodged several. I leaned over and tried to rearrange them.

"I found out when my dad's getting parole. On October twenty-eighth," Sheila said.

"What do you think of that?"

She shrugged. Turning the mousse container over, she sprayed some out onto her hand, lifted it up and smelled it, then squished the foam between her two palms.

"Where's he going? Will he have a job?" I asked.

"He's going back to Broadview. He's got friends in Broadview. See, that's where he grew up. That's where Grandma used to live when she was alive." She rubbed the mousse into her hair.

This was the first I'd heard Sheila mention any other family members. I knew there were others, including her father's brother, Jerry, who had so viciously molested Sheila when she was six. However, Sheila rarely ever spoke of anyone outside her very immediate family.

"Well, that's good news anyway," I said. "It means you can leave here."

Curling her lip, Sheila conveyed a feeling of disgruntled uncertainty. "I dunno. I'm not sure I want to go back with my dad. I mean, it's been about a million times now that he's said he's going to stop taking the stuff and he doesn't do it. I doubt he will this time either and I'm so fed up with getting stuck in these shitholes."

I didn't say anything.

She looked over briefly. "Know what I'm thinking of doing? Going to find my mom. Seeing if I can live with her."

"How would you do that?"

"Well, don't tell anybody"—Sheila glanced around furtively, as if expecting to be overheard—"but I've been saving up my money, 'cause my dad sends me some every once in a while. And last time when I was in town, I went in the library and I got the address of a newspaper in California. I sent them some money to take out an ad. An ad saying who I was and that I was looking for my mother."

"California's a pretty big place. One newspaper won't cover much of it."

"Well, yeah, I know. But as I get more money, I'll take out more ads," Sheila said. "She'll see one of them, I'm sure."

I regarded her. "And then what?"

"Well, I can talk to her then, can't I? And maybe I can go live with her."

"Sheil, I don't think . . ."

She grimaced at me. "You're going to say fuck it, aren't you? I knew you would."

"No, I'm not. I'm just saying go kind of slow on this."

"I know what I'm doing," she replied. "She's probably going to be really grateful I've tried to find her. You hear about this all the time with kids who've been adopted and how their real parents are always so glad when they contact them."

"*Almost* always."

"And she'll be settled and my brother will be there and . . ."

"Don't get your hopes up too high, Sheil."

Her shoulders dropped in an expression of exasperation. "I shouldn't have told you. I *knew* I shouldn't have told you. You *are* going to say fuck it."

"I'm not, Sheila. I'm just saying—"

"I do know, Torey, but it's not going to be like you think. Shit, I don't want to stay with my father. And I sure as hell don't want to stay here. I want to be with *her*. She probably will be grateful I've gone to the trouble to find her. That was a long time ago. It might even have been an accident. I might just have fallen out of the car. Maybe she didn't notice until it was too late. She's probably going to be happy to know I'm okay."

twenty-nine

Dear Mom,
I want to live with you. I'm fed up living with Dad. It's not that any-
thing bad's happened, because nothing bad's happened for a long
time, it's just I get so sick of his ways. Of worrying about him and
worrying about the booze and worrying about the stuff and worry-
ing what's going to happen to our money and worrying about if he's
going to get in trouble again and worrying what's going to happen to
me, if he does. I want to be with you and Jimmie. Please, couldn't it
be that way for a while?

"Can you get me out of here?" Sheila asked when I arrived for my usual Saturday visit. "I'm going nuts in this place."

"You mean find you another group home?" I asked.

"No. God, no. Just get me out. Take me out. I haven't been off the grounds in, like, about three months," she replied. "I want to go to your house. Will you take me?"

"I'm not sure if Jane will let me. You haven't got a very good track record."

"Hah!" she said with delight. "I've got a *very* good track record. I can run faster than any of them." She snickered at the pun.

"Yes, well, I'm afraid that's just what I mean. And Jane won't be conned into giving you another opportunity."

Sheila gave a low, exasperated moan. "I wouldn't run away from *you,* Torey. You know that."

I didn't know that, to be honest. Not that I thought Sheila was ly-ing. Of all the tricks I knew Sheila to be capable of, she had always been remarkably truthful with me. I had no reason to doubt her honesty now; however, she was a born opportunist. Whether or not she could resist the temptation of running away when the chance presented itself, I wouldn't like to judge.

"Come on. Please? Won't you just try?" she pleaded. "I'm so sick of it in here." A brief pause and she brightened. "I could cook for you. Remember? Like I did the last time? You liked that, didn't you? Please?"

"If I do ask, you know what it's going to mean?" I replied.

"What?"

"The point system. You're going to have to earn points."

With a dramatic swing of her arm over her eyes, Sheila fell back on her bed. "Oh, shit, not you too. *God*, Torey."

"You've got to cooperate, Sheila. You could have probably been out of here months ago, if you'd done what you were supposed to."

"God. Played their stupid game? Collected shitty little—what are they? Fucking golf tees or something? You think I'm going to let someone regulate my life with *golf tees*, for God's sake?"

I eyed her. "You will if you want to come home with me."

"Shit, Torey. I thought there was more to you than that." An angry frown on her face, she fell back on the bed again.

The tiger was stirring. Quite abruptly, I realized Sheila was fighting back. Delighted, I egged her on. "We'll get Jane in here. We can set up a point program and as soon as you've completed it, we'll arrange a weekend at my place. How does that sound?"

"Shitty."

"Very well. Have it your way."

Sheila sat up. "I didn't mean *that*. God, you're in a mood today. What's the matter? You on the rag or something?"

I smiled blandly.

She bared her teeth at me in an expression of irritation before crawling to the end of the bed to snag a piece of paper. "Okay, so get Jane then. Let's get this fucking thing out of the way."

*   *   *

Her mind applied to the project, Sheila earned her points swiftly. Jane was stunned, which, I suspect, was just the reaction Sheila was hoping to elicit. Indeed, as her depression lifted and Sheila increasingly became a force to be reckoned with around the group home, Jane appeared a little bit alarmed by what had been awakened.

Two Saturdays later found me in the car with Sheila, tooling back to the city. "God, this is great," Sheila kept saying. "Trees. Look at all these trees. That's what I miss so much out there. It's like a desert there."

Back in my apartment, Sheila went through it room by room. "Geez, it's weird being back here. Know when I was last here? That night with that little boy. Alejo. Geez, like déjà vu. No, no, that wasn't the last night, was it? I came over and cooked for you. That was afterward. God, Torey, it feels like a lifetime ago." She paused and looked back at me. "Remember how I was telling you the other week how I could sort of shut off parts of my life? Make them feel like they happened to someone else?"

I nodded.

"That's what happened here. I didn't mean to. I didn't try to forget this, but now that I'm back, that's how it feels. Like *really* déjà vu. Like I'm visiting some former incarnation, because . . . like I don't think I've ever gone back to a place where everyone else is still carrying on their life, just the way I left them."

Wandering into the kitchen, Sheila caught sight of a group of photographs stuck up on my refrigerator with magnets. Pausing in front of them, she examined them carefully. "Those are pictures from my camping trip," I said. "Look. I caught the largest trout."

"Who's this guy you're with?"

"Hugh. You'll meet him later on, because he's taking us out to dinner tonight."

"So, he's the current fuck, is he?"

"Not quite the way I'd put it," I replied.

"You *do* fuck him, I trust." She was still studying the pictures.

"That's one of those questions, Sheila, that falls into the 'personal' category."

She turned. "We're friends, aren't we?"

"Well, yes . . ."

"So, there's nothing wrong with telling me that, is there? You do fuck him, don't you?"

"Fuck, no. Make love, yes. There's a difference."

She shrugged. "It's all fucking to me."

*   *   *

I had planned to take Sheila out to the shopping mall for the afternoon. Shut away for so many months, she was keen to enjoy the
sights and sounds of crowded places and there weren't many more
crowded than a mall on Saturday afternoon. We ate a quick lunch,
then I popped into the bathroom to brush my teeth before we left.

Still brushing my teeth, I wandered out of the bathroom to hear a
soft tappy sound. Rounding the corner into the living room, I saw
Sheila with the telephone in her hand. "Who are you calling?" I
asked in surprise.

"No one."

This seemed highly unlikely to me and I must have looked it.

Sheila got a silly look on her face. "Sorry. I was playing. Just mess-
ing around. I'm sorry. But, see, you can play tunes with these push-
button phones. And I just wanted to try it . . ."

I still regarded her skeptically.

"Yeah, come here. I'll play 'Twinkle, Twinkle, Little Star' for you."

I was slightly unsettled by the phone incident. Perhaps she was
doing no more than playing with the push buttons and I was being
needlessly wary, but intuition told me otherwise. Throughout the
afternoon I was gnawed by the questions it brought up. Whom had
she been calling? Why? And why didn't she want me to know?

The afternoon was a fairly tense one for me generally. With
Sheila's history of running away, I knew the mall was a chancy place
to take her. I had wanted to give her a happy, carefree time reminiscent of our old times together. Equally, I felt it was important for her
to believe I trusted her, but the hard, cold truth was, I didn't really. I
had been in business with these kids too long to be anything other
than incredulous, and the secret phone call had only served to
sharpen my wariness.

As it turned out, I had nothing to worry about. Sheila was delighted with the trip to the shopping center. She went into each and every
shop, handled most of what she could get her hands on, tried on endless clothes and hats and jewelry and consumed a nightmarish assortment of doughnuts, caramel corn, cookies, pizza slices and ice cream,
all washed down with gallons of Orange Julius. She fell in love with a
funky little number made from what appeared to be someone's ready-
for-the-trash-can jeans. The top was pre-torn and came with its own
supply of safety pins conveniently attached. The skirt barely covered

her bottom. She had already bought a very rude T-shirt with her own money, so I offered to get her the dress. For a glimpse again of her wacky fashion sense, it seemed a reasonable price to pay.

By the time we got home, Hugh was already there. This startled Sheila. She had taken the key to my apartment from me to open the door and clearly had not expected to find someone on the other side. She screamed in surprise and ran back into the hall where I was.

Hugh, the eternal joker, waited until Sheila and I came through the door. Then he took one look at her, threw his arms up and gave an identical startled scream and ran off into the bedroom.

Sheila's jaw dropped. "God, who's he?"

"I'm a burglar. Go away," came a little voice from the bedroom.

"Is this for real?" she asked.

"That's Hugh," I said with enough exasperation in my voice to let him know we'd just about had enough.

Hugh appeared around the corner with a little floral hat I'd worn to a wedding the previous week perched on his head, but his expression funereal. "Yes," he said, bringing his voice way down into a deep double bass, "I'm Torey's friend, Hugh."

Sheila's eyes had widened to the very edges of her face. "And I thought Jeff was bad," she murmured. "God, Torey, where do you find them?"

*   *   *

The evening was delightful. Sheila spent hours in the bathroom getting ready. She kitted herself out in her new clothes, rude T-shirt and all, and then helped herself liberally to my makeup. Afterward Hugh took us out to a Japanese restaurant where the chef, wielding his knife with artistic precision, prepared our meal right at the table. Sheila, who had never used chopsticks, fumbled and laughed and fumbled again, repeatedly dropping food into her lap. In normal circumstances, Sheila was not inclined toward humor. Her dignity, her sense of self were still too fragile to stand up to hearty laughter. However, on this particular evening she was able to see the funny side of her clumsy efforts and, more crucially, able to tolerate and even join in with Hugh's silly remarks. Indeed, Hugh's comments were so absurd that soon all three of us were convulsed with hilarity to the point that Sheila was not the only one unable to work chopsticks.

Afterward we took in a science-fiction movie. Hugh bought us a humongous container of popcorn and then sat between Sheila and me so we could share it. While waiting for the film to begin, the two of them amused themselves throwing popcorn into the air and trying to catch it in their mouths. I was starting to feel just a little uncomfortable with all this merriment, because I could sense we were getting on other people's nerves and I was worried that someone might complain. Yes, we better settle down, Hugh acknowledged. In a rare display of affection, Sheila clutched hold of Hugh's arm and pressed against him in a half-hug.

That evening after Hugh had left, Sheila and I sorted out our sleeping arrangements in my apartment. She was getting the couch in the living room and I pulled the back cushions off to make it roomier.

"Was he high on something?" Sheila asked, as we worked.

"Who? Hugh? No, he's always like that."

"Wow." She paused to straighten the sheet over the cushions. "You're sure he's not high? He doesn't, like, take something and you don't know about it?"

"No. That's just Hugh," I replied. "I think it's one of the things that attracts me to him so much. I love a good laugh."

She nodded. "I guess I never knew people could be like that if they weren't high. Or drunk or something. I didn't know you could make yourself so happy."

*   *   *

Once Sheila was settled on the couch, I got ready for bed myself. I cleaned up, said good night and then disappeared into my bedroom. It was quite late and I was tired, so within moments of turning out the light, I was asleep.

I awoke with a start. The room was dark. Turning to see my bedside clock, I noticed it was only about an hour and a half after I'd gone to bed and I had that hair-raising sensation of no longer being alone in the room. Rolling over in the bed, I raised myself up. "Sheila?" I whispered into the darkness.

For a moment or two there was no response, then she stepped out of the shadows by the door. "I'm sorry. I didn't mean to wake you."

"What are you doing?"

She didn't answer immediately, so I reached to turn on the light.

"Don't!" she pleaded, so I didn't.

I leaned over the side of the bed to see that her blanket from the couch was on the floor. She came forward and lay her pillow down on top of it.

"What are you doing?" I asked again.

"I can't sleep." Her voice was small and childlike. "It's strange out there. I'm not much used to sleeping all on my own. Angel, like, snores and I'm used to her noise. Do you mind if I'm in here?"

"I don't think I snore."

She giggled. "That's all right."

Sheila lay down on the floor and pulled the blanket up over her. Silence descended then. Sleepy, I dozed.

"I liked tonight," Sheila said softly into the darkness. "I like Hugh. You're lucky."

"Yes."

"I had a really good time. That's about the most I can remember laughing in a long, long time," she said.

"Hmmm."

"I hope I get a boyfriend like Hugh someday."

Dozing, I'm not sure I responded.

"Tor?"

I roused myself. "Yes?"

"Do you really fuck him?"

"It seems I've heard this question before," I murmured. "You seem unusually interested in my love life."

"It's just I can't picture you doing it."

I smiled into the darkness.

"Actually," she said, "I'm not sure I want to. It seems so awful to me. I'm not kidding, I'm never going to do it of my own free will."

"You might feel very differently when the right boy comes along."

"No, I don't think so."

A quiet interlude followed, a deep, pensive silence, heightened by the darkness. Then at last her voice, "Tor?"

"Hm?"

"Do you think I'm ever going to get a boyfriend? I mean, if I won't do sex with him, will any boy ever want me?"

"A real boyfriend will love you for much more than sex. And who knows? You *might* feel differently. It's a natural part of loving a man—wanting to touch him, wanting him to touch you."

She didn't respond.

"You've had bad experiences, Sheil. Hideous experiences, that a kid just should never have to go through. You've been fucked up in the real sense of the word and that's tragic. But this isn't fucking, not this natural feeling. It *is* love; it's part of love, and you can tell that, because when it happens, it makes you feel happy."

The conversation drifted away then. I had the sense of a thinking silence again, and then, just silence. Settling back into my covers, I closed my eyes.

"I hope he's like Hugh. Funny like him," she said.

"Yes, I hope so too. Hugh's good." A pause. "Now, I hate to be a party pooper, but it's very late. We'll feel like sheep vomit tomorrow morning if we don't go to sleep."

A chuckle from down on the floor. Then silence.

Then her voice again, soft in the darkness. "You know what this reminded me of, this tonight?"

"What's that?"

"Remember that time with your other boyfriend? What was his name? Chad? Remember when he took you and me out for pizza? This tonight was like then. Fun, like that time was."

"You remember that?" I asked, because I distinctly recalled her saying she hadn't remembered it when she was fourteen.

"Yeah. Sort of. Well, not every little detail, but what I remember was the feeling. Feeling really happy. Being with you and him and feeling so good. I remember thinking, this is what it must feel like, if you got a real mom and dad."

I smiled into the darkness. "Yes, I remember feeling good that night."

"It was that way tonight, kind of, too. You know. Kind of a family feeling. Like . . . well, a belonging feeling."

"Yes."

"It's nice to feel that way. It's nice to think that the people you're with aren't looking for the first opportunity to open a door and shove you out."

thirty

Dear Mom,
I was a lot of trouble in those days. That's probably why you had to do what you did. I think I can understand it, because it was probably the only thing you could do. But I'm a lot better now. Here are my good points:
1) I can cook
2) I can do housework really well
3) I will get a job when I get out of here and earn money
4) I get mostly A's at school and so am on the Honor Roll (well, I was on the Honor Roll at my old school. There isn't one here, but I will be on one, if I go to another school).
5) I will do what you want now, because I'm old enough to know.

October came. Knowing I was her only visitor, I continued to see Sheila on a near weekly basis, and her improvement was remarkable over the early part of the fall. She was keen now to earn points in hopes of a Saturday afternoon spent out away from the ranch and Jane reported much improved cooperation during the week. Sheila still eschewed the company of the other youngsters, but this didn't bother me too much.

With her father's parole coming up at the end of the month, plans were afoot for Sheila's release as well. Jane intended to keep her at the ranch until the middle of November to give Mr. Renstad a chance to get settled. After our last unpleasant parting, I had not talked to Mr. Renstad again and I didn't know if he realized that I was involved with Sheila yet again. As a consequence, all my information came from Jane. She had already told me that Social Services had made his evidencing some sort of stable lifestyle a prerogative of getting Sheila back; however, in October, Jane said that employment in Broadview had been arranged for him through a prison rehabilitation program and all that was left was finding him a place to live.

Sheila took all this news and activity fairly calmly. She'd been through it all on at least three previous occasions, and so maintained an "I'll believe it when I see it" sort of skepticism. And of course, there was another matter.

"Torey! Torey! Come here." She motioned excitedly, when I arrived on the Saturday before Columbus Day. Quickly shutting the door to her room behind me when I came in, she bounced over her bed. "Sit down. I want to show you something."

I sat.

Leaning over her bed, Sheila pulled out the under-bed box where she stored all her treasured possessions. She lifted the cardboard lid and extracted a letter. This she pressed to her chest and grinned at me. "Guess what! Guess what this is." But before I could guess, she thrust it into my hands. "It's from my mother."

I took the letter from her.

"Remember that ad I put in? You know, in the paper? Well, it worked! She saw it and she's written me this whole long letter."

The letter *was* long. There must have been ten or twelve pages written on both sides of the paper in a small, scrawled handwriting. I unfolded it, pressing it flat on my knees, and began to read.

Within the first few paragraphs, my heart sank. There was a strange, desperate note to the writer's prose. She said she had given up a daughter for adoption and then went on for several pages telling a very convoluted story of emotional problems and abusive marriages.

"Sheil, I hate to say this, but . . . I'm not sure this is your mother."

"It *is*. She says the girl was four. *I* was four," Sheila replied. "I mean, how many four-year-old girls could this have happened to?"

"Well, not very many in your exact circumstances, but she doesn't mention the exact circumstances. And besides, she says 'give up for adoption.' What your mother did was not quite what I'd call 'give up for adoption.'"

"Yeah, I know, but she was upset," Sheila countered. "Look how she keeps saying how upset she was. God, it's, like, wrecked her whole life. And I knew that's what it would be like. I knew my mom would be so sorry it happened, and she'd want me back, if she only knew where to find me."

Lifting my head, I regarded Sheila. I had seen that look so often in her eyes. She could have been six again, for all the poignant vulnerability in her expression. So desperately, she wanted this to be true. I reached my hand out to touch her shoulder, but she pulled back.

"She *says* my name is Sheila. She knows that," she insisted.

"Lovey . . ."

"But she *says.*"

"You told her that. Your name was in the advert, wasn't it?"

"But she *says.* Why would somebody lie about something like a name? Why would she want to contact me, if I wasn't her daughter?"

"Because sometimes there are people with very bad problems who can't tell what's real from what isn't real," I replied.

Anger suddenly flared in her eyes. "That's me, huh? That's what you think I am. Crazy. Go ahead, say it, Torey, 'cause that's what you're trying to say."

"That's *not* what I'm trying to say. I'm referring to her, this woman who's written this, not you. I think she wants you to be her daughter. I think she may even believe you are, but you aren't."

"I *am!* That's my mom. I know it is. Read the whole letter. You've just read a few pages. She talks about Jimmie in there. She talks about him and about my having four more brothers too. Younger brothers, 'cause she got married again."

My shoulders dropped. "But you gave Jimmie's name in the advert, Sheila. She's going to know your brother's name is Jimmie before she even wrote the letter, because you *told* her yourself."

Tears came to her eyes. "You're just being spiteful. You don't *want* me to find my mom."

Again, I reached my arms out to her. "Sheila, come on."

Struggling to keep her composure, she turned away from me.

"Sheil, I do want you to find your mom. Nothing would make me happier, simply because I know how happy it would make you; but I don't want you to get hurt even worse than you have been. And I'm so afraid that's what's going to happen here."

"Go away."

"Sheil . . ."

"Go away. Go *on.* I don't want to see you this weekend. Just go away."

*   *   *

No little "Dear Mom" notes came to me during that week, and when I came the following weekend, Sheila said no more about the letter. She wasn't her usual friendly self, so I could tell I had wounded her badly in the disagreement and she was still keeping her distance. I felt it would be unwise to introduce the issue myself, and felt I would get further by simply being warm and supportive and waiting for her to make the next move. We chatted pleasantly enough. Most of the conversation centered around her preparations for leaving the ranch. Sheila was going to be changing from the small, self-contained school room at the ranch to a large Broadview high school, and she was curious about what kind of curriculum would be offered. We discussed the merits of various courses of study and I mentioned the advantages of selecting a curriculum that would enhance her college placement.

This was the first time the subject of Sheila's life after graduation had been raised. She was now a senior and such decisions should have been looming large, but I had thus far never been included in many conversations regarding her academic future. This was partly because school was the one area where Sheila seemed to be managing well on her own, and partly because Sheila's present was so chaotic that it was hard to divert any attention to considering her future. To my shock, Sheila stated that she had no intention whatsoever of going to college after she graduated.

"You're joking."

"No," she replied. "I don't want to go."

"Of course you do," I said.

"No. I'm fed up with school. I just want to be out on my own. Have a place to live where I can be the boss. I'm not going back into school the minute I get out."

This stunned me. With Sheila's IQ, with her interest in ancient history, her facility for learning Latin and reading old texts, I couldn't imagine that she wouldn't be longing for higher education. I tried to explain to her how much different university life was to high school, how easy she would find the lifestyle. She had long since developed the ability to study on her own, as her environment had never been particularly nurturing educationally, and I pointed out how this would set her ahead in the university community, how she was already likely to succeed.

All my words were of no avail. Unlike the week before, Sheila didn't become angry. I don't think she had that much invested in the discussion. This wasn't an important area to her and she wasn't bothered about defending it; however, she remained adamant. When school was finished, she was going to find a job, her own apartment and get on with life. College could wait.

*   *   *

In our office the following Wednesday, Jules and I were enjoying a leisurely chat over coffee when the telephone rang. The phone sat on a chair between our two desks, and consequently we both moved to answer it, but Jules was closer. He picked it up, then grimaced. "Wouldn't you know? If I answer it, it's always for you." He handed it over.

Jane Timmons was on the other end. "We've got a problem here," she said. "Sheila's disappeared."

"Where? When?"

"She had a supervised visit into the city this morning to get clothes and Annie had taken her into MacGregor's department store. I mean, honestly, Torey, we didn't think she was much of a security risk at this point. She's less than three weeks from being released anyway. She went to use the ladies' and Annie was standing right outside, and she just never came out."

"What happened? Is there a window or something?" I asked.

"Yup. But it's on the second floor. God knows how she did it or where she went from there. It's a flat roof, but . . ."

In this brief conversation, Sheila was once more transformed from the pleasant, lively girl I knew into a stranger, familiar with worlds I could hardly imagine.

"The obvious question," Jane continued, "is: she hasn't turned up over there, I assume?"

"No."

"Well . . ."

"Is there anything I can do?" I asked.

"Not really. We've contacted the police. Contacted the prison in Marysville where her father is, although I should like to think she's not going to get that far afield." A pause. "Do you have any ideas where she might turn up? Know any friends or anything?"

The first thing to come to mind, of course, was her mother.

"There was a letter . . ." I started and then briefly explained Sheila's efforts in that direction.

"Yes, we know about all that," Jane said.

"Oh?" This surprised me, because Sheila had given no indication of having shared this with the staff.

"Routine precautions. We go through all the kids' stuff regularly. We'd known she was writing to newspapers down in California, and I'd not given her any hassle about it. I mean, it seemed harmless enough, and God knows, if the kid could turn up another relative who'd take her, that'd be a blessing. Her father's not exactly made of gold, is he?"

"But did you know about this letter?" I asked. "From this woman in northern California?"

"Yeah, I saw it. Holly brought it in last week for me to take a look at," Jane replied. "Sad, wasn't it?"

The offhandedness, both with which Sheila's things were searched and with which her actions were dismissed, annoyed me deeply, making me unwilling to discuss in any detail my feelings on the importance of this material in relation to Sheila's disappearance. I had never especially liked Jane throughout the period I had dealt with her, but now I felt contempt.

That single telephone call was the last I heard on the matter. Jane didn't call me again. I phoned out to the ranch myself on both Thursday and Friday, but Jane was unavailable and the deputy director told me that they had, as yet, had no success in locating Sheila.

*　　*　　*

In the first few days after Sheila ran away, I expected to hear from her, or, like the time with Alejo, I thought she might turn up on my doorstep. I was uneasy, because I feared for her physical safety, but I still felt confident that everything would soon resolve itself. After all, how long could she simply disappear?

Quite a long time, I was to discover. Days turned into a week. One week, two weeks went by. Mr. Renstad was released from prison and moved back to Broadview and Sheila was still missing.

I couldn't believe this. I simply could not believe that the girl could just disappear without a trace, and for the first time I came up against the nightmarish reality of how police and other Social Service agencies dealt with the issue of runaway children. And not for the first time, I was forced to confront how different Sheila's world was from mine.

It was impossible not to worry about her. I could imagine all sorts of things, not the least of them that she had actually found this demented woman in California. Or her mother. In a best-case scenario, I pictured her reunited with her mother and Jimmie, living the kind of life she'd always wanted, and I tried to convince myself that's what had happened and that was why she hadn't contacted me. Unfortunately, several variants of worst-case scenarios kept intruding on my thoughts.

November came and I was having to come to terms with the fact that Sheila had yet again dropped abruptly out of my life. As with all such experiences, time finally started to heal my sense of frustration and even the gnawing worry. One evening, I came across the sheaf of "Dear Mom" letters that I had kept in the front of the filing drawer. Instead of leaving them there, I took them out and put them in a box in the attic with all the other mementos of past children. The next morning, I moved the copy of *One Child* I usually kept on my desk to a place where my eye wouldn't fall on it casually.

✳   ✳   ✳

I was in the midst of a play therapy session with a small, nonverbal four-year-old named Bobby. He was a difficult case, referred to me by one of the other psychiatrists for evaluation, because no one could discern why he didn't talk; and I did not anticipate being disturbed, as everyone knew I was videotaping the session. Nonetheless, just as I was eliciting some excited babbling from Bobby by blowing soap bubbles, my beeper went off. I tried to ignore it, but when I didn't respond, it went off again.

Irritated, I rose and went to the phone on the wall in the therapy room and dialed the front office with one hand, while trying to turn off the video camera with the other. Bemused by my antics, Bobby threw his security blanket over the camera to produce a woolly ending to our taping.

"Well, it's just me who's beeping you," said Rosalie, who worked in the front office. "We've just gotten a fax in for you and I think you ought to come down and have a look at it."

"Right now? I'm in therapy," I said.

"Yeah, Torey, I think you should come right now."

* * *

Bringing Bobby with me, I went down to the office at the front of the building and took the fax from my mail hatch. I read it.

Come away, O human child!
To the waters and the wild
With a faery, hand in hand,
For the world's more full of weeping than you can understand.

The world's not made for some of us, Torey. The little prince found this out. So did Cleopatra and I think I have too. There's nothing here for me. I'm from some other place. I don't belong here. The world's more full of weeping than I can understand.

Thanks for trying. And don't try to fax me back. I'm doing this from a store and I don't want an answer.

Love, Shei   la

"Oh, Jesus," I said, when I'd read it.

"Yeah," Rosalie replied. "When I saw it, I thought you'd better have this quick."

"I've got to get ahold of her." Scanning the paper, I noticed up at the very top in tiny type the fax-sender information. Grabbing the telephone on Rosalie's desk, I rang information. The fax number was identified as coming from northern California, and within moments, I had the telephone number of the store from which Sheila had sent the fax. I phoned immediately.

"Hello, yes, you've just sent a fax to me. It would have been sent by a young girl. Sixteen. Is she still there? This is very important. I must talk to her."

The person who had answered put the telephone on hold and what felt like a hundred years passed, while I waited. Then a click and human sounds followed.

"Hullo?" It was Sheila's voice.

thirty-one

"Sheila? Sheila, it's me. It's Torey."

There was no response. She was still there. I could hear the soft sound of her breathing carrying across the miles between us.

"Sheil? Are you okay?"

"How did you find me?"

"Listen to me. Are you okay?" I asked again. "Where are you? What is this place I'm calling?"

"It's the Copyprint store," she answered. There was a numb quality to her voice. I think I had genuinely startled her by tracing the fax so quickly and she didn't know quite how to respond.

"Are you okay?"

"I don't want to talk to you."

"No, Sheila, don't put the phone down. Please? *Please?*"

"Just leave me alone, okay?" There were tears in her voice. I could hear them in the faint abruptness of her breathing, but she was struggling to keep them subdued.

"No, Sheila. Talk to me. Come on. Stay on the line a bit. Tell me what you've been doing."

Silence.

"What's been happening?"

A sharp intake of air.

"Sheil, don't hang up on me."

"I'm not going to," came the very small voice at the other end.

"Things not been going very well?"

"No."

"What's happened?" I asked. "Can you tell me?"

"I can't talk here. Everybody's listening."

"Well, I want to talk to you. I do. Can you find another phone?

No . . . wait, don't hang up. Wait. Let me think of something."

"I can't find my mom, Torey," she said. "I've been looking for her and looking for her and I can't find her."

"Oh, lovey."

"Oh fuck, I'm going to cry. Oh, no. I don't want to cry here. Oh, no."

"Sheil, I'm going to come and get you."

"Huh?"

"Don't do anything, okay? All right? And I'll come and get you. I'll bring you home. Can you tell me where you are? Where are you staying?"

Tears thickened her voice again. "I'm not staying anywhere. I'm all by myself."

"Okay, well, listen, stay where you are. I've got the fax number. Let me make some arrangements and I'll fax them back to you there. But stay there and wait for me. And *don't do anything*. All right? Promise me?"

She was crying. Whether from anguish or relief, I couldn't tell, but through her tears she promised she'd stay at the Copyprint place until I faxed back.

The next hour was frantic. She was in a relatively small town in northern California, which wasn't served by a commercial airport. In fact, it was a good two hours' drive away from San Francisco, which was the nearest place to have more than one daily flight from my city. And the flight from here to there was two hours. That made four hours from departure the very least I could expect. Then came disaster. We were approaching the Thanksgiving Day weekend; so when I rang the airport to book a seat, I discovered all the economy seats were booked, not only on the next flight out, but also on the one after that. This meant I wouldn't be able to leave until the middle of the following day at the earliest. This was awful. I felt it was critical that I did go get her, rather than rely on her in her unstable state to make her way back here by herself, especially as she had never flown before and was unfamiliar with the general procedures surrounding air travel. I didn't trust how she might react if I tried to call in outside help, such as the police or Social Services, from the California community she was in.

Then, right in the midst of my panic, my beeper went off again. "Curse this thing," I muttered at Jules. Whipping it off, I threw it across the desktop.

Jules regarded it, still beeping, then me. "Don't you think you should answer it?" he asked.

Wearily, I phoned down to Rosalie, who transferred the caller. "Help, help! I'm dying! Save me, Doctor! Quick! An infusion of cabernet sauvignon and T-bone steak!" the caller cried in a weak voice. "Tonight at six?"

"*Hugh!* Honestly. You *know* you're not supposed to do this."

He was totally unrepentant, as he always was, but it sounded so good to hear his voice that I couldn't be angry. I told him the whole horrible story with Sheila and how I felt it was critical that I got to her as soon as possible, but how impossible that was turning out to be.

Hugh listened thoughtfully. "Book a first-class seat out," he replied. "They won't be full."

I snorted. "I can hardly afford economy, much less first class, Hugh. And I certainly couldn't bring her back that way. Even if I can find seats, and I can't. It's even worse coming back. It's the run up to Thanksgiving that's doing it. There's just nothing there."

"I'll pay for it," he said. "I'll get you a ticket. Then maybe you can rent a car. You'll need to rent a car anyway, to get up to her. Then you can just drive home from there. Don't worry. I'll take care of it, okay?"

Stunned by the generosity of his offer, I didn't know quite what to say.

"Well, she's an okay kid," he replied to my silence. "And after all, what's a few bucks in life?"

*   *   *

I told Sheila to meet me in the local McDonald's, as it was about the only place I could think of that would be open late at night, relatively safe for her to wait in and a location I could easily find in a strange town. Hugh financed a first-class ticket to San Francisco for me and I made arrangements to rent a car from there, drive up the coast and pick Sheila up before driving home, a journey of over eight hundred miles.

It never crossed my mind not to do this for Sheila. Always a bit impulsive, I was inclined to get myself into what Hugh termed "grand acts," but I don't think I could have comfortably done otherwise. I always felt a sort of intuitive certainty about my part in a given situation, which, although it made me tend to act first and think later, seldom put me on a course of action that I later regretted. Going personally to get Sheila felt right in this instance, so right, in fact, that I never contemplated any alternatives.

It was ten-fifteen when I pulled under the bright-yellow glow of the McDonald's arches. I could see Sheila through the window, a lone figure hunched over a table. Turning off the ignition, I got out.

She didn't rise when I came through the door, simply lifted her head and watched me. There was a faint smile on her face, an expression of what I took to be relief. Coming to the table, I bent down and hugged her to me. She came willingly, clutching the folds of my wool jacket.

Slipping down on the bench opposite, I regarded her. She was filthy, filthy in the old sense of the word, as she had been when she had first come into my class. Her uncombed hair hung in long greasy strands. The dirt was worn in around her fingernails and up the creases of her skin. Her clothes were rumpled and stained. And just as in the old days, she stank.

"Are you hungry?" I asked.

"Well, I've had some French fries. I thought I better eat something or they'd kick me out."

I myself wasn't hungry. I'd eaten on the plane in a manner quite unlike what I'd been accustomed to and Big Macs were rather an anticlimax, but I went over to the counter and bought one for each of us, along with a large order of fries. I'd had the foresight to bring a thermos flask for coffee to fortify me on the long drive ahead, so I had the girl behind the counter fill that for me, while I got Sheila a milk shake.

Sheila devoured her hamburger and quickly laid into mine, when I said I wasn't hungry for it. Again I was drawn back across the years to see her as she had been, a desperately hungry six-year-old, using both hands to stuff her school lunch into her mouth. There wasn't much more finesse tonight and I guessed she hadn't seen much food in the past few days.

"So, where have you been living?" I asked.

She shrugged. "Wherever I could."

"What kind of money have you got?"

"At the moment? Eighty-five cents. I started out with twenty-three fifty, after I bought my bus ticket, and I've been trying to be careful with it, but . . ." She smiled apologetically.

And so we chatted, while she ate, as if nothing at all had happened. I found out from her that she had used my telephone that Saturday she was over to get bus schedules and prices. She described how she had managed to scrimp out the money she needed from the allowances given the children at the ranch. It was fascinating hearing all this, because it showed such intricate planning, and even I had not suspected anything. What we didn't talk about, however, was why she'd done it and what had come of it. Pulling myself back to observe objectively as we spoke, I looked for the signs of suicidal desperation, which I reckoned were still there.

When she had finished, I glanced at my watch. "Well, I suppose we had better be on our way."

Sheila just sat.

I regarded her.

"I don't want to go back to the ranch, Torey. If you've come all this way to take me back there, you might as well have stayed home, because I'm not going. It's a dead zone there and I'm finished with it."

"No. We'll work something out. Your dad's got a place in Broadview. He's settled . . ."

Sheila still sat.

"Come on, lovey, let's go."

She let out a great, long sigh and let her shoulders drop. Then, wearily, she hoisted herself up from the seat and came with me.

Pulling the car out of the McDonald's, I sped off down the main road and out onto the highway. I love driving, particularly long-distance driving, for the sense of relaxed autonomy it gives me. When I really get going, it's almost a transcendent experience, giving me the feeling of expanding into a state of unhindered freedom.

Having managed to accomplish the most important part of my mission—getting Sheila into the car to come home with me—I was in a superb mood.

Beside me, Sheila sat slumped in her seat. She didn't say anything for several miles. Initially I thought she was going to go to sleep, because it was obvious she was very tired, but she didn't. She just sat, elbow on the car door, hand bracing her cheek, eyes on the road ahead.

The road was absolutely empty. Having chosen the most direct route home, I wasn't on the freeway, but on a minor highway heading due east. At that hour, there was simply no one else driving. In fact, for long stretches there were no lights anywhere, not even from farm buildings.

In the confined space of the car I could perceive Sheila's pain much more clearly than I'd been able to in the plastic cheerfulness of McDonald's. It was almost a physical thing. I would have expected to touch it, had I reached out my hand, and for many miles, I didn't know what would be the best thing to do. Sit in silence? Encourage her to talk? Or maybe just carry on, as if this were all a perfectly ordinary thing to be speeding through the night eight hundred miles from home, and wait for it all to come out in its natural course.

Sheila took down the hand bracing her cheek and folded her arms across her chest. Blowing the hair out of her face, she turned her head and looked over at me. "How come you did this? Came all this way out and got me?"

"Because I love you. Simple as that."

She turned from me, looked out the window at the deep darkness and remained so for a long time. When finally she turned back, I could see tears on her cheeks. They glimmered wanly in the pale green glow of the dashboard lights.

"Want to talk about it?" I asked.

She shook her head. Bringing a hand up, she wiped away the tears, but they came again. And again. She grew visibly upset, a sorrowful anger erupting when she couldn't stanch the tears.

"There are tissues in my handbag," I said and pointed into the backseat.

"I don't want this to happen. I don't *want* to cry."

"It's okay, lovey. I don't mind."

"I *do* mind," she retorted. "I don't *want* to cry. If I let myself start, I'm never going to stop."

"That's been the fear for a long time, hasn't it?"

She nodded and the tears came harder, but she still fought against them. "I'm so fucking angry! I don't want to give in. I don't want to cry. It just makes me weak."

"No, not weak."

"It's not fair! Not right. *You* shouldn't be here. It should have been my mom saying all this to me. Not some teacher." Lifting her head, she looked over at me. "Excuse the term, Torey, but that's all you are. Where are the people who are *supposed* to love me?"

I regarded her.

"Where the fuck *are* they? Where's my mom? Where's my dad, for that matter? Why's it always got to be people like you who do these things for me? Why have my parents never taken care of me? Am I that bad?" And the tears overwhelmed her. Falling into noisy, inelegant sobs, she slumped against the shoulder strap of her seat belt and wept.

I didn't say anything. There come those times when words would seem as if they were a good idea, but in reality they are too paltry for the job.

I remembered another time like this. Drawn back across the years, I was no longer in the nighttime darkness of the car, but in the daytime darkness of the small book closet at school with Sheila, who was weeping in my arms. She'd been a fierce little tiger for so long that they had been the first tears I'd seen her shed, although the school year was almost over. She'd always feared the abyss beneath her tears.

Sheila cried for a very long time. Pulling her legs up and pressing her arms against them, she buried her face and sobbed into the tattered fabric of her jacket. I said nothing, did nothing other than speed us onward through the dark. We were in the mountains by then, the trees coming right down to the road on either side. It had begun to snow, the large, downy flakes falling mesmerizingly before the headlights of the car. The late hour, the darkness, the trees, the snow all combined to create a weird, otherworldly aura. Things no longer felt quite real to me.

At last, the end. She snuffled, hiccuped and struggled to draw

breath, but the crying had ceased. Silence followed, a long, deep silence, so crowded with thoughts as to make them nearly palpable.

"I remember that boy," she said, her voice very, very soft and still
faintly embroidered with the aftermath of her tears, "that boy I took
into the woods."

Watching out through the wipers at the snow, I kept very still.
Sheila had never spoken of the abduction that had brought her into
my class, which had nearly sentenced her to a childhood spent in a
mental institution. Of all the things Sheila had told about over the
years, that incident had never once even been alluded to.

"I used to watch him in his yard. He had a swing and his mom
would take him out and push him in it. I used to watch. He had a
plastic riding car shaped like an elephant. He used to get on it and
his daddy would push him. I used to watch him. And then . . . He
was out there one day by himself and I said, 'You want to come
along?' Or something like that. I don't remember exactly now. But I
undid the latch on the gate to his yard and let him out. And I took
him in the woods.

"I don't think I ever intended to hurt him. I had this piece of rope
with me, but it was just something I had found down by the railroad
tracks. I didn't bring it specially or anything; I just had it. And I
don't remember *wanting* to hurt him, not in the beginning anyway. I
remember walking, taking him into the woods . . . I made him pull
down his pants. I wanted to see his penis. I remember that. I remember thinking, he's just like Jimmie. He *was* just like Jimmie.
And I hated him. Torey, I had some thoughts in my mind then that
. . . I mean, I still remember them just like they were yesterday. I remember *exactly* how I felt looking at that little boy. I just hated him
so bad and I thought . . . You're going to hate *me*, when I say this to
you, but . . . I thought, I want to kill him."

There was a long pause. Sheila lowered her head and regarded
her hands in her lap. "I *was* a wicked little girl. Just like my pa said."

I didn't speak.

Sheila looked over. "Do *you* hate me now?"

"No."

"Why not? I would have. If it hadn't been that boy's lucky day, I
would have killed him."

I had my eyes on the road, but I could see her in my peripheral vision. She continued to regard me. Finally, she looked away. "I'm a murderer."

"He didn't die, Sheila."

"He would have died. It was just luck he didn't." She drew in a long breath. "I can never forget this. I've never told anybody. I haven't dared tell anybody, but it just sits in my mind. Every good thing that ever happens gets eaten up by this thing, sitting there. I think: I am so wicked. No wonder things keep happening to me. I deserve them. I'm so bad even my own mother couldn't stand me."

"Your mother had nothing to do with it. She left you long before you took that little boy. In fact, if I had to venture any explanation, it's that it was the other way around. She didn't leave you because you did such things. You did such things because she left you."

"So why did she leave me then?"

"Most likely, because she had problems of her own. Because she was a very young girl. She was only fourteen when you were born. Did you know that? Fourteen."

No reply.

"So, she would have only been eighteen on that night she left. About a year and a half older than you are now. And she had two kids to worry about and a husband in jail."

Pulling her bottom lip between her teeth, Sheila chewed it.

"I don't think your mother planned to abandon you, any more than you planned to hurt that little boy. I think she was simply overwhelmed. She was pushed to her limits and could cope with not one thing more, not even a small girl acting up in the backseat. And like most of us when we can fight no longer, she ran away."

Sheila made a small, derisive sound. "Well, I sure got her blood, huh? Always running away from my problems."

"Oh, no," I said. "You're not like her. You're much stronger. Much better."

"How can you say that?"

"You might run away when the going gets tough, but the difference is, you come back."

Sheila considered, then slowly nodded. "Yeah, I suppose so."

thirty-two

During the adrenaline phase of this adventure, I'd had visions of driving all the way back home without stopping, but the folly of that idea began to make itself known by about one in the morning. As we came down out of the mountains and started across the wide expanse of Nevada flatlands, I kept an eye out for motels showing signs of life at the front desk so late at night and finally found one on the outskirts of a small town.

Too tired for anything more than a quick wash, I settled into bed soon after we got in the room; but Sheila, who hadn't been in contact with hot water for weeks, judging from the appearance of her, raided my overnight bag for shampoo and conditioner and disappeared into the bathroom for longer than I could keep my eyes open.

The noise of her rummaging through her things when she came out of the bathroom woke me again, and I lay watching her get ready for bed. "I wish I had something clean to wear," she muttered. "Everything's so grotty." Then she slipped into her bed and put the light out.

An ancient radiator beside my bed heaved and sighed in the darkness. I pulled the blankets up close to ward off the November night.

Sheila turned in her bed. "I don't feel sleepy," she murmured. "I keep thinking about all the things we've been talking about tonight."

The radiator belched, wheezed and settled down again.

"And you know? In a way, I feel really angry with my parents. I *was* just a little kid. I feel so cheated. They should have protected me from all of this."

"Yes, I think you're right."

"It's occurring to me now that maybe . . . well . . . maybe I couldn't help how I was. I was an awful little kid; I know I was, but . . . maybe I didn't deserve what my parents did to me."

Good, I was thinking.

*   *   *

Sheila would have quite happily slept around the clock, I think, and no doubt she needed to, because I think it was probably the first real bed she'd had in some time. However, the weather was deteriorating and I wanted to be on my way, so I prized her out at nine-thirty.

Exhaustion was taking its toll with Sheila. Her mood seemed lighter than the night before, but she was by no means chatty. A remark or two would pass between us and then ten or fifteen minutes' silence before the next comment. I amused myself trying to keep the radio tuned.

"I went to see that lady that answered my ad. And, like you probably already guessed, she wasn't my mother. Thank *God.*" A second small smile. "She was just nuts. Like you said."

I grinned over at her. She shrugged.

"What else did you do?" I asked.

"Nothing, really. For a long time I thought, well . . . I mean, I just kept hoping I still might find her. I was in California and she was in California. Someplace. I just kept hoping . . ." Sheila turned her head and looked out the window. "It was pretty awful. I didn't have anyplace to go. I didn't have very much money. I had to sleep rough, mostly. In doorways and stuff. And try to keep away from the weirdos. And I was so fucking cold. And hungry . . ."

"Why didn't you call me?" I asked.

She shrugged. "I dunno. At first I wasn't going to tell you. I hate you when you're right. You don't exactly rub it in, but you sort of . . . emanate it. Besides, I didn't want to go back. I still don't, really."

A pause.

"What do you think I should do now?" Sheila asked. "Go back to my dad?"

"Yes, probably. And if you want to know what I think you should really do, it's knuckle down to your schoolwork, so you can get yourself a scholarship. There's still time, and with your kind of talents, there'll be a lot of universities who'd be eager to accept you. I know what you said about not going to university right after high school, Sheil, but believe me, I think it would be the ideal setting for you. You'd love it. You'd have all the freedom you need, and still it's a protected environment. You can study just what you want and really go. Really let your mind race. I think that'd be so good for you."

She sighed. "Yeah, probably."

*   *   *

After that, Sheila slept. We were within the last hundred and fifty miles and I filled the time trying to figure out the logistics of returning her anywhere. Her father wouldn't be expecting her and I certainly didn't want to let Jane or any of the Social Services get ahold of her at that point. The best idea seemed to take her back to my apartment and then contact her father. The following day was Thanksgiving, so I toyed with the idea of inviting Mr. Renstad over and making a big meal for everyone. Somehow, that seemed appropriate.

Sheila roused as I reached the traffic-light stop-and-go driving of the city. She sat up, stretched and rubbed her face. "God, I'm back," she said, looking out the window. From her tone, I couldn't discern whether she was glad or not. I explained to her my general game plan.

"No," she said.

"No?"

"No. Take me home to my dad." She glanced over at me. "For about the last hour, I've been just laying here with my eyes closed, but I haven't been fully asleep. I've been thinking. Thinking over and over and over what we've been talking about, and I've decided I want to go home."

Surprised, I nodded. "All right."

"Do you remember that summer when I was working with you and Jeff in the summer school?"

"Yes."

"Well, remember that one time I asked you if you thought things were ever going to get better for me, if my life was ever going to be normal? And remember what you said?"

I hesitated, trying to recall.

"I remember it, because I took very close note of it. You said I had to come to terms with things. I had to accept that my mom had left me. Accept that maybe it was just something that had to happen and it wasn't my fault. And then you said I had to forgive and let go."

I nodded.

"Well, I think I've come to the first point. I was just sitting here, thinking it through, and you know, I don't feel like it was my fault anymore. It still hurts me like hell. I still wish it didn't happen, but it did, and I can see now that maybe my mom just had her own problems, that it was just my bad luck to have been part of them."

She pondered a moment. "And maybe that's true for my dad too. Whatever. Anyway, I'm thinking, like, I can't go over it, I can't go under it, I can't go around it. I've been trying all of them. So, I better go through it."

A small silence.

"I think I'm seeing things differently now," she said. "I think I can accept it."

"Good."

Coming up to the junction turnoff for my road, I held the car at the intersection a long moment, but when Sheila didn't say anything further, I stepped on the accelerator and went on through to join the freeway to Broadview.

"You know," Sheila said, "what I've been thinking most about is what you said about letting go. Accepting, forgiving and then letting go. I think I can accept. I think I can even forgive, but I've been wondering and wondering about letting go. Trying to figure out what 'letting go' entails, and all I can think of is that it means living your life forward. Starting to think of the future more than the past."

"Yes, I think that probably puts it very well."

A small, pensive silence. "You know, I don't think I've ever lived my life forward before," she said. "Even when I wasn't remembering things, I was always wanting to go back."

I nodded.

"If my mom was fourteen when I was born," she said, "if my dad was the same butthead he's always been with me, then there probably never was a golden age. It's weird to realize now that most likely there never really was a 'back.'"

* * *

Sheila returned to her father. I didn't make them the all-American Thanksgiving dinner the next day, which would have made for such a storybook ending. In fact, after dropping Sheila off there, I didn't see her again for three weeks.

That journey back from California through the snowy darkness proved to be one of more than physical dimensions, however. Sheila ventured out of other darknesses as well. When we next met in the days just before Christmas, I found quite a different girl. Relaxed and cheerful, she treated me to lunch downtown and spent the entire time relating anecdotes from school.

She wasn't particularly impressed with her new school or her course work, but she was doing well—remarkably well for a girl who had had the disrupted education she'd experienced over the previous year. I was particularly pleased to hear that she had joined the Latin club. More extraordinarily, she very nearly admitted to liking it.

We never spoke of our journey that night, nor of her mother, nor of anything of her past. Instead, we ate croissants, went Christmas shopping together and watched the skaters on the rink in the park. I bought her a copy of Aeschylus's *Oresteia* trilogy, which deals with the family of Agamemnon, as a Christmas gift, knowing that ancient story of matricide and forgiveness would speak profoundly to her. She bought me an Arden edition of *Antony and Cleopatra* and then teasingly included the Cliffs Notes for me.

My own life was taking an unexpected turn over that period. I'd opened the Sunday newspaper a couple of weekends earlier and had seen an advertisement for a midyear vacancy in a special education class for emotionally disturbed children. It was in a small community in an adjacent state. The strange fact was that I hadn't been looking for a new job at the time. I'd thought I was perfectly happy at the Sandry. However, the moment I saw the advert, I'd felt a terrible longing to be back in the classroom again.

I told Sheila that I had applied, although at that point I didn't know whether or not I would get the position. She took my news with the same equanimity that I had taken hers about school and the Latin club. She was bemused by my choice to abandon a well-paying job at a private clinic to return to the classroom. Money was becoming an important issue to Sheila and she had a hard time understanding the rationale behind my actions, but she seemed pleased to think I would be a teacher again.

*   *   *

I did get the job and early January found me almost two hundred miles away from the city in a small town called Pecking. I heard from Sheila occasionally. She never was much of a letter writer, so it wasn't often, and then, as usual, they were seldom letters in the traditional sense. Consequently, I didn't always know what was going on. From what I did hear, she continued to be well settled at her school and with her father. He was making another effort at keeping himself out of trouble. I heard a lot about AA. Sheila joined Alateen, and this was where she met Claire. Claire, who was eighteen and also a senior at Sheila's school, had not come from the same deprived background as Sheila. Indeed, hers was a privileged upbringing of tennis lessons and summer camps. Yet, disguised behind all this was a world of parental drunkenness and abuse. Claire and Sheila found in one another the understanding other peers couldn't give them and their friendship grew.

In March we had a two-day break from school and I came up to the city. Stopping by Sheila's house, I had the opportunity to meet Claire myself. She was a solemn girl with very long black hair and glasses that gave her an owlish look. She had about her that terrible seriousness of adolescence that lends itself naturally to discussions of Sartre or ecology, and Sheila kept agreeing with her when she made dark, profound statements to me. For the first time I saw Sheila as she was, an intelligent, articulate teenager creating her own identity.

*   *   *

I didn't see her again until May, when we met for lunch at a pizzeria in the city. I almost didn't recognize her when I saw her. Her bangs, so long in the process of growing out, had finally reached the length of the rest of her hair and were incorporated in a smooth, blunt cut that swept back from her face and down over her shoulders. She had highlighted it slightly, which brought up the natural blond and drew attention to its glossiness. The punky clothes were gone, but not her natural sense of style. Layered one over the other were two T-shirts, a cotton dress and a denim jacket, teamed with chunky clay jewelry. Her appearance had the modern sophistication of the catwalk.

"Gosh, you're looking good," I said.

"Yeah, thanks." She pulled out the chair across from me and sat down. "I think it's the freedom showing. Six more days of school."

I regarded her. She had been cagey about her plans after graduation. I'd asked her a couple of times in letters, but she had never responded at all, even to tell me which scholarships she was applying for. This left me intrigued and anticipating a surprise. Secretly, I suspected she'd been accepted to a particularly excellent university and was going to use this lunch to tell me.

We chatted amiably, ordered our pizzas, and chatted some more. Sheila told me that Claire had been accepted at Stanford, her first choice.

"And you?" I asked, unable to contain my curiosity any longer. "What are your plans?"

She had been leaning forward, arms folded on the table, as she'd talked with me, and now she lowered her head. There was a smile on her face, but she stayed like that for a long moment. "How am I going to tell you this, Torey?"

I waited.

Finally, she looked up. "I'm not going to college. I got a job three weeks ago working in McDonald's and when I'm done with school, I start full-time."

"McDonald's?" I said in surprise. "Jesus, Sheila, *McDonald's?*"

"Shhhh." She reached a hand across the table and touched my lips. "Don't let the whole place know."

"You're kidding. Yeah? You're pulling my leg."

She shook her head. "No, Torey. I'm not."

"A brain like yours and you're going to be serving hamburgers for a living? Oh, Sheila, you've got to be kidding."

"I like hamburgers."

"But *Sheila* . . ." I protested.

She still had the slight smile on her face. "Look, Mom, I got to do this my way."

"I'm not your mom. No kid of mine would be getting away with this."

"You are my mom. If anybody is, it's been you, 'cause I love you just like one. And I know you love me too." She smiled warmly. "And now, Mom, it's time for you to let me grow up. University later. Maybe. Who knows? But for now, it's going to be hamburgers."

"Oh, Sheila, come on. Not really?"

"Don't criticize. Okay?" she said. "Make it like the old days. Say, 'Sheila, whatever you want to do, that's good. I'm here if you need me. I'm behind you.' Say that to me."

I regarded her. For a long moment I met her eyes, gray-blue in the dim light of the pizzeria. Then a sigh and I grinned. "Very well. You do what you think is right. I trust you."

"Thanks, Mom."

Epilogue

Almost ten years have passed since that afternoon in the pizzeria and Sheila is now older than I was the year I had her in my classroom. She still works in the fast-food industry; however, she doesn't serve hamburgers anymore. Possessed of an unexpectedly astute business mind, she is now manager of her branch and is expected shortly to become one of the youngest franchise holders in her part of the country.

I must admit that, successful as she is, this probably still would not have been what I would have chosen for her, and it is still a little hard for me to come to terms with all that talent being given over to hamburgers. Sheila, when she's in the mood for awful puns, says she relishes her work. She relishes my discomfiture too, I suspect, which is probably the best sign of all. She's her own person now, comfortable with whom she's become. Her decisions, her plans, her self-worth are not dependent on my or anyone else's approval.

Sheila does, of course, still have occasional difficulties. Hers was an enormously deprived and abusive childhood, and it would be unrealistic to expect those experiences not to resurface sporadically. This happens most notably in her interpersonal relationships. She appears to do well in the clearly delineated relationships of the workplace, particularly in managerial situations where there is no question of the personal intruding on the professional. However, she continues to be challenged in her private life and finds it particularly difficult to form close relationships with men. But on the whole, she has developed into a remarkably stable and competent young woman.

Perhaps the best way to end is with the last "Dear Mom" letter I received from Sheila. She'd kept a diary during the middle years of her teens and had copied into it the same "Dear Mom" letters that she'd been sending to me. A few years ago, she came across her old diary and after reading through those letters, she wrote to me telling me about it. Fixed to the back of her letter was this:

Dear Mom,
Things have turned out pretty good for me. I've got a great job and my own apartment and a dog named Mike. I'm sorry, I don't think about you much anymore. I mean to, but I just don't get time. It's too bad you never got to know me. I think you would have liked me. I think you would have been proud.

Love, Sheila